Praise for *Creative Destruction*

Each episode of his "story" is structured to illustrate lessons in leadership. In crisp, clear prose, he takes the reader on a deep dive into the problems and challenges with which he was confronted, mainly involving underperforming or failing businesses.

—**John Collette,**
Retired attorney

Bob McLaughlin and I first worked together when we were assigned to turn around a failing division of Xerox. A couple of years later I recommended him to try to salvage a Xerox venture developing an automatic blood analyzer. These challenges are depicted in the book. Later in our corporate lives he employed my services to turn around a failing telecommunications company. We have remained good friends.

Creative Destruction, From the Marine Corps to the Board Room is an excellent textbook for the development of leadership skills. The key messages for an aspiring leader are to continually develop new skills, to seize the initiative, and to be flexible: Leaders must be ready to change directions to overcome obstacles while pursuing their primary objective.

Time is your most precious asset; minutes are valuable. Act!

—**Dr. Robert J. Potter,** President,
Robert J. Potter Company

Bob McLaughlin was my mentor in the Midwest Division of Xerox. Certain ideas he taught me have affected my entire business career and personal life. Bob's training in decision-making introduced me to operations research. Although I subsequently participated in many different decision-making classes, I have always come back to McLaughlin's method as a checkpoint.

Bob encouraged us to recruit the best people available and train them to be flexible and adapt to ever changing challenges. This is a never-ending process in the pursuit of high performance goals.

Working with McLaughlin was a challenging assignment; his tough-minded management instilled an insistence on attaining difficult goals. However, foremost, he was a teacher who motivated us to learn and grow. Looking back, it was both fun and personally satisfying to work in that environment. Readers will benefit greatly from learning about the details of McLaughlin's experiences and teachings.

—**Richard Green,** President,
National Business Search

Bob McLaughlin is one of the most effective and creative business leaders I have ever worked with, and I have a great respect for and similar perspective to his approaches to business crises and opportunities.

Over the years, Bob mentioned his prior work at Xerox and Fibreboard, but I never heard the full details. I thought

I'd enjoyed many of his best experiences, but this reading illustrated where he honed his skills and filled his tool chest for further Creative Destruction.

I was fascinated to see first-hand how Bob breaks down business tasks into logical building blocks—whether it be hiring for an expanding sales force or analyzing the efficiency of a manufacturing operation—and this book tells it all. McLaughlin's stories illustrate how business can be fun and creative!

—**Tom Lumsden,** Principal,
McLaren Advisory Group, LLC

I had the opportunity to work with Bob when I was a partner at Brobeck, Phleger and Harrison. Bob McLaughlin has powerful leadership presence. When he's the leader, everyone on the team believes "we are going to get this done."

That's because McLaughlin combines keen analytic ability with planning, sales and leadership skills. He can lay out an overarching goal with clear interim objectives in language that employees understand.

Creative Destruction spells out—in interesting story form and with succinct educational principles—how the reader can develop the qualities necessary to become an effective leader.

—**John Larson,** Retired attorney

CREATIVE DESTRUCTION

FROM THE MARINE CORPS TO THE BOARDROOM

Robert McLaughlin

REGENT SQUARE PRESS

Other books by the author

Seek to Grow,
Investing for Growth

The Capture of the U-505,
A Legion of Heroes.

www.captureofu505.com

"FIRE IN THE HOLE"

...is a warning that an explosive detonation
in a confined space is imminent!

This book is dedicated to Kathie, my wife of 65 years, whose love and support was there for me every day of this journey.

She endured my absences in the early days of our marriage when I was blazing new trails across the state of North Carolina.

She displayed a warm and loving reception and provided a beautiful meal when I returned home after dark on those long days with Xerox.

She supported me and inspired me during the time I spent in the wilderness!

She endured my long absences when I was on assignment for The Sutter Group.

Most important to recognize is her role as the Keystone in our Family Arch of Triumph!

In the end, there is nothing but your family
and your story.

Our family, our children and grandchildren, have been
Kathie's and my greatest pleasure!

My purpose in writing this story is to convey the lessons
I have learned about leadership to those who aspire
to become leaders, to convey the qualities required
of an outstanding leader and to provide chronicles
of successful accomplishments in which
I have participated.

This is my story.

Robert McLaughlin
January 2023

CONTENTS

PROLOGUE

Creative Destruction is a teaching document; it is the author's contribution to the experiential teaching of leadership skills. It is a memoir, not a biography, and the author's experiences are not presented in chronological order.

The reader is first introduced to the author's assignment as the CEO of a company operating in the vicinity of bankruptcy, which he turned around and created value for the shareholders.

He then chronicles the 10 exhilarating years he spent with Xerox, a high-growth technology company where he refined his leadership skills, creating three elite marketing organizations and two elite engineering organizations.

The author also experienced excellent training in the Marine Corps, which created the foundation for his leadership skills.

The author formed a management consulting company, The Sutter Group, which assisted executives in turning around financially distressed companies, and chronicles several of those turnarounds to educate the reader.

The author assumed responsibility for some very difficult and challenging business situations. Based on these experiences, he describes how to analyze a situation, identify the opportunities, set the objectives for improved performance, divest the weak performers and return the enterprise to prosperous operations.

THE ATTRIBUTES OF LEADERSHIP

Passion: Passion is required to become an effective leader. Effective leaders also possess a passion for teaching and coaching. You will be raising the performance bar for every organization for which you accept responsibility. It will be your responsibility to teach your associates the necessary skill sets to clear the higher bar.

Trust: This is the paramount attribute required of a leader. Your associates must believe in you. They will be entrusting their futures and livelihoods to you. Therefore, it is imperative that you gain their confidence. It will be necessary to convince your associates that your objectives and your plan to achieve those objectives are in their best interest.

Your superiors, whether your boss, your board of directors or your clients, will be entrusting you with their assets. They must be convinced that you are honest and will report reality. They must be both convinced that you can achieve superior results and be comfortable in providing the financial resources you will require to deliver those results.

Honesty will be your primary virtue!

Courage: You will be taking on some big risks. In order to deliver superior results, you will have to destroy existing thinking and philosophies, reorganize to become more efficient and change business strategies to achieve greater profitability.

I refer to these actions as *Creative Destruction.*

Creative Destruction requires courage. Not everyone will agree with your plan to improve performance. You will be criticized. Reactionaries will place obstacles in your path; they will deny you the necessary resources to implement your plan. You must have the courage to carry on.

Values: Your value system should be superior and distinguish you from others. Your business goal should be to make three blades of grass grow where only one grew before you arrived. The Israelis refer to the concept as "making the desert bloom." The Marine Corps ethos distinguishes the Corps from other military organizations. Your organization should likewise be elite and capable of achieving superior performance.

Aggressiveness: Taking action has to be your default state of being. When faced with a challenge, you will automatically choose to act rather than opt not to take action.

Seize the initiative. Time is a valuable asset; a faster-moving competitor will ultimately defeat you. Be comfortable taking calculated risks. Be flexible and ready to change direction at any time while continuing to pursue your objective.

Resilience: You will inevitably suffer defeats and experience losses during your journey. Develop your resolve to return to the arena, determine the cause of the failure, take corrective action and continue the journey to your objective.

I wish you good fortune on your journey!

FIBREBOARD CORPRATION

I was appointed CEO of Fibreboard in early 1973. I was 39 years of age. The United States GDP had grown six percent in the first nine months of 1972; during this period, Fibreboard was marginally profitable. But the company had major operational problems. The balance sheet was highly leveraged. The ratio of debt to EBITDA (earnings before interest, taxes, depreciation and amortization), a common measurement of a company's ability to finance and repay its debt, was eight, an extraordinarily high ratio.

The debt-to-EBITDA ratio was a financial warning signal similar to the red flag with a black square in the middle that indicates the approach of hurricane-force winds. We had to reduce sail and batten down the hatches; it was going to be a wild ride!

We would be navigating whitewater.

In March 1973, inflation in the U.S. economy began to rise rapidly. This was the result of the massive federal government spending to finance the war in Vietnam. The money supply increased dramatically, and high consumer demand for goods and services resulted in increased prices.

The Federal Reserve Board began to raise the federal funds rate to choke off the inflation, and by August 1973, that rate was increased to 11 percent.

Mortgage rates for the purchase of homes increased. Demand for new homes dropped dramatically and lumber prices plummeted. The forest products division of Fibreboard was hemorrhaging cash.

The decline of the U.S. economy was accelerated by the oil embargo imposed on the U.S. by the Arab oil-producing countries in retaliation for the U.S. supporting Israel during the Yom Kippur war. The price of a barrel of oil in 1972 was $1.80 and would escalate to $11 a barrel in 1974. Soaring gasoline prices accelerated the rate of inflation.

The U.S. entered a recession in early 1973. Some 2.3 million jobs were lost; the rate of unemployment was the highest the nation had experienced since the end of World War II. The recession was accompanied by continued high inflation and the economy was experiencing stagflation.

The economy would not recover from the effects of stagflation until 1975.

The Fibreboard board of directors was composed of five successful CEOs and one COO of prominent public companies. The seventh member of the board was a retired CEO of Fibreboard who had preceded my predecessor.

I was an officer with Xerox Corporation when I was introduced to Fibreboard. I recognized that I was going to need financial analysis capabilities to identify Fibreboard's operational weaknesses, the root causes of those weaknesses and the corrective action steps needed to restore profitability.

I asked Bob Verhey, who had been my financial analyst at Xerox, and two of his associates to come with me to Fibreboard.

I felt the board of directors had a sense that the company's financial situation was deteriorating rapidly, but the Finance department did not have the ability to provide future cash flow projections. Verhey initiated the development of our cash flow projections, our cash availability from our bank lines of credit and the time horizon when we would run out of cash.

The board of directors instructed me to determine if the acquisition of a privately held lumber company that had recently been approved by the shareholders of both companies could be unwound.

DAYS ONE TO SEVEN

Verhey, his two analysts and I met with the senior management. I gave a "Fire in the Hole" introduction, alerting them to expect change, and then asked the CFO, "What actions are you taking to stop the hemorrhaging of cash?"

The CFO had taken no action; he was essentially maintaining the status quo. As I went around the table, the responses from the operational managers were the same—they were conducting business as usual.

I had Verhey provide an analysis of our cash position, available bank credit and a cash flow analysis illustrating that at current weekly uses of cash combined with some one-time cash-out requirements such as quarterly interest payments to our bond holders, we would hit the wall within 45 days, meaning there would be no cash available and we would be forced to declare bankruptcy.

I provided the analysis to the board of directors, who were shocked.

CASH MANAGEMENT

I outlined to management the operating procedures that needed to be implemented immediately to stem the outflow of cash.

Cash management would be controlled by myself, Verhey and the controller. I would authorize all checks to be cut. If I was not available, Verhey had the authority, and if he was not available, the controller had the authority. Checks to reimburse vendors would be cut, signed and distributed on Friday of each week.

Accounts payable were to be extended from the practice of paying in 30 days to 60 days. I instructed the divisional managers to inform their major vendors of our intentions.

Division managers were to assume personal responsibility for the collection of aged accounts receivables. We would continue offering a one-percent discount for payments received within 10 days of invoicing.

I instructed all of the division managers to work down their raw material inventories to a 10-day supply. The lumbermills that were purchasing logs on the open market were to cease all purchasing.

The lumbermills to which we supplied logs from our fee-owned timberlands were to cease all harvesting activity.

Finished-goods inventories were to be reduced to zero. If we did not have an order for finished goods in inventory, the goods, if possible, were to be sold for cents on the dollar.

The production of goods was to be initiated only if we had an order. If we had no orders, the factories were to be temporarily closed until we could generate a sufficient level of demand to justify reopening the factories or mills.

We had five banks providing credit. I asked the CFO to accompany me on visits to each of the banks. My intention was to advise the banks of the cash-management procedures we had put in place and that we would not be making interest payments in the near future. I asked for formal amendments to our financial agreements; Bank of America was the only bank that formally agreed to concessions. The other banks agreed to go along with the delinquencies and monitor the situation.

CURTAILMENT OF CAPITAL EXPENDITURES

Fibreboard had invested in a facility to manufacture calcium silicate, an industrial-insulation material, in Ruston, Louisiana, in 1970. The company had been involved in the manufacture of asbestos insulation but had to close its plants because asbestos caused mesothelioma, a deadly form of cancer. The manufacturing and marketing of calcium silicate was a profitable business and in 1971, the board authorized the investment in a second plant that was under construction in Grand Junction, Colorado. The construction of the facility had been completed, and the company was receiving and installing production equipment.

We instructed management to continue the acceptance of equipment but to discontinue installation. The factory was to be secured. We asked to see the contracts for the purchase of the equipment to determine if we had the ability to negotiate modified terms of payment.

The board had authorized the investment for the construction of a plant to manufacture fiberboard, an engineered, plywood-like product made from woodchips and a binder that were placed under extremely high pressure. The plant was located in Rocklin, California. Woodchips were to be supplied by the company's three lumbermills operating in the area. The plant was scheduled to begin operations in two weeks. The company could not tolerate the negative costs of the startup operation. We ordered the management not to start up the operation.

The board had authorized the previous management to take 15,000 acres of prime timber land in the area of Truckee, California, to develop a ski resort named Northstar. In late 1972, Northstar had hundreds of unsold condominiums and developed lots for the construction of homes. The ski hill was operating and was generating cash during the winter months.

Nevertheless, the Northstar real estate development was hemorrhaging cash paying the interest on the construction loan. We ordered all development construction to cease.

The board had authorized the purchase of a fourth ski lift to be delivered in the spring of 1973. We attempted to cancel the order, but the vendor's position was that the lift had been designed for the elevations of the Northstar ski hill and could not be resold for use by another ski hill operator. We took delivery of the equipment in a warehouse in Truckee. We negotiated a payment contract with the vendor that stretched out the payments for two years.

The Northstar real estate development was being conducted by a subsidiary company of Fibreboard. When the Fibreboard board of directors became aware of our cash situation, they instructed me to terminate the Northstar board of directors. The Fibreboard board of directors became the directors of the Northstar subsidiary.

I recommended to the board that we stop all development activity and begin a search to replace the CEO. The board approved both measures.

THE STOCK ACQUISITION OF A PRIVATE LUMBER COMPANY

The company the Fibreboard shareholders approved for acquisition was located in Grass Valley, California, which owned no fee timberland. The transaction was set to close in 10 business days. Although the closing would not require an outflow of cash, we would be acquiring an enterprise that was losing money and whose debt required cash payments for interest and principal payments. Verhey calculated that the acquisition would accelerate the date we would run out of cash by three days. We had to stop the acquisition.

The board of directors had been approving the acquisition of lumbermills, investments in the expansion of existing businesses and investments in new businesses and real estate development without the adequate cash flow to support this level of activity. These investments had been financed with debt.

Lehman Brothers was the investment banking advisor to the company and had advised the company on the acquisition of the private lumber company located in Grass Valley. The firm advised me that the agreement could not be unwound. It occurred to me that Lehman Brothers would not receive a fee if the transaction was not completed. I lost faith in the firm.

Brobeck, Phelger & Harrison (BP&H) was the general counsel for Fibreboard, and the lawyer representing Fibreboard informed me that the transaction could be aborted if both parties were in agreement. The seller had not negotiated a breakup fee, so there would be no cash cost associated with the termination of the agreement.

The BP&H counsel and I met with the owner of the Grass Valley lumber company and his attorney. The value of Fibreboard stock was declining daily and had now declined 35 percent in value since the acquisition price had been agreed upon. I suspected that the seller might want to get out of the deal. I explained the financial condition of our company and pointed out that if we were to hit the wall and file for protection under the bankruptcy code, his Fibreboard stock would most likely be worthless. I suggested that we abort the transaction and survive to put it back together at a later date. He agreed; we dodged a bullet.

The retired former CEO of Fibreboard, who was the sponsor of the real estate development at Northstar, expressed his displeasure with our cessation of construction at the resort. I explained to him that we had to take every step possible to reduce the outflow of cash and avoid hitting the wall. His proposal to continue development was not supported by other directors.

Verhey and his analysts had been evaluating the cash flow of each manufacturing plant, plywood plant and lumbermill. The lumbermills and plywood plants that were purchasing timber on the open market were hemorrhaging cash. The cost of the timber plus the added value required to produce a two-by-four or a sheet of plywood was greater than the market price of the units.

I ordered the Oregon lumbermill acquisitions, the lumbermill acquisitions in Tennessee and Louisiana and the California plywood factory, all of which had no fee timber to supply their operations, to cease operations.

The vice president of the forest products division strongly objected to my initiative. He had obviously contacted some of the directors who called me and expressed their displeasure that I had not consulted or advised the board that I was taking this action.

I explained to the board members that our cash situation dictated that time was of the essence in implementing actions to conserve cash and that I was taking these actions to ensure the survival of the enterprise. I had to act. I apologized for not informing them of my intentions.

The implementation of our programs to stop the hemorrhaging of cash required time. Many of the managers were not accustomed to responding quickly to orders. Some delayed informing our suppliers that we were going to be slow in payment of our obligations. In many instances, I had to meet with crucial suppliers. Verhey was good at this; the controller also played a key role. The CFO was not effective.

We gradually reduced the hemorrhaging and were extending the time available to us before we would hit the wall.

Metropolitan Life held 100 percent of the company's bonds and was the company's largest creditor. I flew to New York and met with Robert Schwartz, the chief investment officer, and Dan Clarke, our account manager. I informed them of the steps we had implemented to stop the hemorrhaging of cash and advised them of my initial thinking for the sale of assets to pay down debt. I informed them that my goal was to reduce the debt-to-EBITDA ratio from the current ratio of 8:4. They applauded the steps that I had taken to date and encouraged me to develop the plan to sell assets.

CHANGES TO THE MANAGEMENT CULTURE

Verhey, working with management, created performance variables for each of our divisions and each manufacturing plant, lumber and plywood mill within the divisions. We conducted operations reviews for each division each month. We identified unfavorable performance and required the development of corrective action plans to be submitted and reviewed within two weeks.

Management had not been subjected to this type of performance measurement or demands for the creation of plans to improve performance.

In an early review, we uncovered a debilitating management practice involving the transfer pricing of kraft paper from the mill to the corrugated box plants. The company operated the only paper mill in California, located in Antioch. The mill represented the largest single operating asset, excluding the fee timberland, owned by the company. The mill was composed of a linerboard machine, a medium-board machine and a solid-bleach sulfate paper machine.

The linerboard and medium-board were transferred to container box plants where a machine combined two linerboards separated by medium board to create corrugated-board, which was then used to manufacture corrugated boxes.

Fibreboard was transferring paper to the box plants at an artificially-created price plus freight that resulted in the landed cost of paper being identical for each container plant.

The delivered cost for the paper shipped to the container plant in Honolulu, 2,400 miles from the mill, was the same as the delivered cost to the Antioch box plant, which was one mile from the mill.

This practice generated a distorted financial return on the assets employed; it understated the return on the paperboard mill and overstated the profitability of the Honolulu box plant.

When we changed the transfer price to market plus freight, the Honolulu plant became unprofitable and cash flow negative. We were now dealing with reality.

When I brought the practice to the attention of the board, the retired former CEO of the company criticized me for making the policy change, stating, "The policy made the financial performance of each of the box plants fair for each of the managers when comparing their performance."

I responded that the practice might have been fair for the managers, but it was not fair for the shareholders. I did not have to defend my decision; the other directors endorsed the change.

ACTIONS TO IMPROVE THE PRODUCT MIX OF THE PAPER DIVISION

We initiated a sales commission plan in the paper division similar to the plan I had introduced to the West Coast operations of PPG Industries in 1962. All of the salespeople were salaried; they were order takers, not salespeople. We put them on a program that included a salary plus commissions.

Fibreboard had a packaging design department that was underutilized. The department had the capability, in the case of the container operations, to design a container to ensure the protection of a valuable product during shipment. In the case of our folding carton operations, the department had the capability to enhance the appearance of a customer's product on the grocery shelf, which increased the customer's revenue.

We were not utilizing the resources of the department to improve revenues and profits.

Eighty-five percent of the production of the San Jose container plant was sold to canneries. Tomatoes were packaged in a can and did not require a box of superior strength to protect the product during shipment.

In 1973, Silicon Valley as we know it today—the home of companies manufacturing computers, iPhones and electronic devices—did not exist. There were many companies, however, that were producing electronic equipment of high value that required protection during shipping.

The technical specification regarding the strength of a container was referred to as the burst strength. The selling price for a high burst-strength container resulted in a greater profit margin. In addition, high-value products required interior reinforcement to hold the product securely in place during shipment. The reinforcement pieces were high profit-margin items.

We used the industrial classification manuals for each state in which we were doing business to identify companies producing high-value products requiring superior packing to protect the product during shipment.

The salespeople were assigned budgets to penetrate specific accounts in their territories that produced high-value products. We taught them how to use our packing design department to design superior packaging, which resulted in fewer returns of damaged goods and a lower packaging cost than their current method of packaging. We were now selling economic benefits rather than merely taking orders.

In 1973, the U.S. economy fell into a recession. The recession would last into 1975. The container division would generate profits throughout the recession.

By the end of 1973, the product mix of the San Jose container plant had made a complete turnaround from 85 percent of its production going to canneries and 15 percent to other categories to 85 percent of the production going to manufacturers of high-value products and less than 10 percent of the production going to canneries!

In a board meeting, the retired former CEO of Fibreboard informed the board that he had received a telephone call from the CEO of Del Monte Foods complaining that Fibreboard would no longer sell boxes to their canneries. He then turned to me and instructed me to accept orders from Del Monte, stating, "Del Monte has been a loyal customer for 20 years."

I did not have to defend our marketing strategy; board members suggested that his instruction to me to change my strategy was not a good idea. I'd had enough of his obstruction to the changes we were making to improve the profitability of the company. I met with two talented directors who were supportive of the strategies I was proposing and asked them if they thought the director could be persuaded to resign. He resigned the following week.

THE PROPOSED SALE OF ASSETS TO REDUCE DEBT

Within 30 days, we developed a strategy for the sale of assets, which included:

+ The recent acquisitions of lumbermills in Oregon, Tennessee and Louisiana, which had no fee-owned timberland to support the mills.

+ The plywood mill in California, which had no fee-owned timberland to support the operation.

+ The Honolulu container plant, a small operation with a 10-percent market share that was losing money. We had more profitable market opportunities for the use of the liner and medium board on the mainland.

♦ The Northstar real estate development.

♦ The Australian subsidiary, which was a small operation, marginally profitable and a user of cash.

Lehman Brothers' representatives attended the board meeting and advised the board not to authorize the sale of the lumbermills and the plywood plant. Their rational was that the recession would eventually end and these entities would return to prosperous operations. When they concluded their remarks, I excused them from the meeting.

Verhey created model profit and loss and cash flow statements for each operating entity that showed that even if the assets we were recommending to be sold returned to prosperous operations, the cash flow required to service the interest and principal payments on the existing debt would result in insufficient cash being available to finance maintenance capital expenditures in the existing businesses and working capital to finance increased revenues.

In addition, our current liabilities were significant. The bottom line was that we had to reduce debt.

The board endorsed our objectives of reducing the EBITDA-to-debt ratio from 8 to 4 and reducing the debt-to-equity ratio from the current ratio of 150 percent to 50 percent.

The board approved the sale of the list of assets we had proposed for sale. The achievement of our financial objectives would require additional asset sales, but these asset sales represented the first steps in a long journey to return the company to prosperous operations.

I felt the members of the board were embarrassed that they had allowed the company to get into such a poor financial condition, and each time the press reported on action steps we had taken to conserve cash, such as discontinuing the dividend, mill and plant closures, their embarrassment increased.

My knowledge of corporate finance was the result of my education provided by Xerox while attending a Harvard Business School six-week session conducted exclusively for Xerox executives at Exeter Academy. Colyer Crum was the professor of finance who taught our classes on corporate finance. He emphasized that there were limits to the amount of debt the cash flow of a company could support. He identified the debt-to-equity ratio and the EBITDA-to-debt ratio as two critical ratios to monitor.

:::::::::

Several months into my presidency, I telephoned Crum seeking his advice. He informed me that he had been following Fibreboard's financial performance since I became CEO. He advised me to put the company into bankruptcy, stating that I would be free to reorganize the company under the protection of the Justice Department.

When I attended the class at Exeter Academy, I was aware that Crum was serving as a trustee of the Pennsylvania Railroad, which was in bankruptcy. He was very familiar with the benefits of reorganizing a company while under the protection of a bankruptcy court.

I responded to Colyer stating that I was confident we could turn around the financial performance of the company and return it to a state of prosperous operation. I insisted that bankruptcy was not an option on my watch.

I expressed to the board my disappointment with the responsiveness and advice I was receiving from Lehman Brothers as our financial advisor. No board member suggested that I recruit a new advisor; no one suggested I come before the board if I wanted to change advisors. The board was silent on this issue.

Two Individuals were Accumulating Fibreboard Stock

In addition to the challenge of turning around Fibreboard's financial performance, we were faced with the challenge that two individuals were accumulating Fibreboard stock.

Leon Simkins was the President of Simkins Industries, a highly successful recycled paperboard and folding carton manufacturer located on the East Coast. Simkins had accumulated eight percent of Fibreboard's stock, and his objectives, as he related them to me, were to bring about changes in the board of directors, gain control of the company, spin off the Fibreboard recycled paperboard mills and folding carton plants to Simkins Industries and then sell the remaining assets.

Stephen Roman, a Canadian businessman, had accumulated five percent of Fibreboard's stock. Roman immigrated to Canada at age 19 from Slovakia. He was described as a rugged, outspoken mining engineer who did not hesitate to use profanity to get his point of view across to listeners.

Roman was a speculator who, in 1953, purchased the outstanding shares of a penny-stock Canadian mining company that had abandoned its mines because of flooding. He raised the capital to restore operations and developed the company, Denison Mines, into the largest producer of uranium in the free world. Stephen Roman was a rich man.

I received a telephone call from a San Francisco attorney who informed me that he represented Mr. Roman, who was in San Francisco, and that he would like to meet with me.

I had replaced the large rectangular desk in my office with a small elliptical desk, and I had a sufficient number of chairs available in the office so that I could sit with visitors. I believed that my position behind a huge, rectangular desk inhibited the exchange of good ideas.

I sat next to Roman during the meeting. He was very blunt in conversation; he had invested in the company several years ago and had now suffered severe losses. He had been accumulating shares at depressed prices in order to accumulate five percent of the outstanding shares and therefore be in a position to demand a board seat. He stated that he had no intention of taking control of the company; his goal was to restore the profitability of the company, eliminate his losses and walk away with a profit.

I outlined the actions we had taken to stop the hemorrhaging of cash, the changes we had initiated in management practices to improve profitability and the recent authority the board had granted to me to sell assets and pay down debt.

He pounded the arm of his chair and declared, "This is good; I applaud your efforts. I can help you. I want representation on your board."

He brought up the subject of Leon Simkins, who he described as a corporate raider. He informed me that Simkins had approached him to form an alliance to take control of the company. Roman stated that he would not ally himself with Simkins. He informed me that he could be helpful in purchasing Simkins' position in the company's securities.

After the meeting, I assured Roman that I would recommend to the board to extend an invitation for him to join the board. He responded as though he never heard what I said. "I demand a seat on the board. I own five percent of the stock of the company, and collectively, the present board does not own one percent!"

His attorney intervened. "Steve, Mr. McLaughlin has said he will recommend that you be given a seat on the board. I think we have accomplished what we came to achieve. Why don't we depart and let Mr. McLaughlin get back to work."

His attorney presented me with his card and asked that I call him when the arrangements could be made and that he would assist with any paperwork that had to be completed for the Securities and Exchange Commission.

I talked with our BP&H general counsel inquiring about the steps to be taken before recommending to the board that they extend an invitation to Steve Roman. He said he would look into the matter and get back to me.

:::::::::

It was several days later that he asked for an appointment. He came into my office, placed his felt hat on my desk, sat down, and before I could come around my desk and take a seat beside him, announced, "You cannot do this!"

The conversation went something like this:

"I cannot do what?"

"You cannot bring Steve Roman onto this board!"

"You are not advising me of any laws we would be breaking if we extended him an invitation. You are not alerting me to losses the company may suffer as a result of Roman being a member of the board. You are stating, 'Don't do it—a command!'"

"That is correct."

"Have you informed the board of my intention to recommend inviting Roman to join the board and, if so, did the board instruct you to deliver this message to me?"

His response was yes! I was angry. I spoke to him of my displeasure with his action. I looked to him for advice on how to get things done within the law. I would expect him to advise me if he thought the board might object to my recommendation; however, his informing the board of my intention was, in my mind, a betrayal of trust.

I asked him why the board objected to my suggestion and got a lot of meaningless dialogue. I pressured him for an answer to my question. I finally got my answer: "Steve Roman is not our kind of people."

What came out in our subsequent conversation was that the directors did not desire to be associated with a rough-talking Slavic miner and stock speculator.

I grew up in a steel mill town on the Monongahela River near Pittsburgh. My high school class was composed of students of Polish, Hungarian, Italian and German descent. In my senior year, the president of the class was a black man. I never developed prejudices concerning someone's ethnic background.

I felt that it would be beneficial to the corporation to have a friendly five-percent holder of our securities on the board. Also, I had committed to Steve Roman that I would recommend to the board that he be extended an offer to join the board. I felt I was compelled to introduce the idea to the board while realizing the board would decide to extend the offer.

I went into the board meeting and announced that I had a meeting with Steve Roman, an owner of five percent of the company's stock, and that he would like to have a seat on the board. I recommended we extend an invitation to Mr. Roman. I offered to answer any questions about my meeting with Mr. Roman and emphasized that I wanted the board to hear any objections that any director had to my recommendation. I answered the questions regarding Roman's intentions and objections. I emphasized to the board that I felt Mr. Roman could be helpful in blocking Mr. Simkins' efforts to gain control of the board.

::::::::

The board voted unanimously to extend an invitation to Mr. Roman.

Mr. Roman nominated the chief financial officer of Denison Mines to take his seat on the board. The CFO was of great help to me supporting the financial strategies I was recommending to the board. Steve Roman never attended a board meeting even as a guest.

My relationship with BP&H was ruptured. I felt it was going to be difficult to rely on the general counsel for advice going forward; however, I took no action to replace the general counsel.

Kathie and I had been introduced socially to John and Pam Larson. John was a corporate attorney with BP&H and had just returned from Washington, D.C., where he had served as an Assistant Secretary in the Department of Commerce. John and Pam were building a new home in Ross, California, which was close to our home.

He was a young man, younger than I, competent and aggressive. He had a reputation for making deals happen under terms that were beneficial to his clients.

Shortly after the Roman event, I received a call from the BP&H general counsel requesting a meeting. He arrived with John Larson. He informed me that the firm had decided it would be in everyone's best interest to make a change in their representation of the company. If it was acceptable to me, the firm wanted to have Larson serve as our general counsel

I assumed the change had been introduced to the board members and received approval before our meeting. It was a very smart move on the part of the firm; John and I worked very well together and would become very close friends.

I was dissatisfied with the advice and the responsiveness I was receiving from Lehman Brothers; we were hemorrhaging cash and had to act and act fast. Lehman was not keeping up with the pace of the decision-making required to save Fibreboard. I felt we were a low-priority client.

I made inquiries to four prominent investment banking firms to determine if they would represent Fibreboard. I was turned away by each firm as they felt the financial situation was so bad and the prospect of recovery so low that they were not going to be associated with a failure.

I had the good fortune to meet with two young, aggressive partners at Morgan Stanley who enthusiastically responded to my strategy. They convinced their engagement committee, which had to approve all new relationships, that Fibreboard could be turned around and that the relationship would be beneficial to Morgan Stanley.

When I informed the board that I was terminating Lehman Brothers and engaging Morgan Stanley, several directors expressed their displeasure that I had not sought out the board's advice before engaging a replacement.

I made a major mistake in not communicating with the board; however, no board member had offered me advice when I complained about the performance of Lehman, and no one had suggested that if I wanted to make a change, I should first consult with the board. No boundaries had been established on my authority.

A board member whose company had a strong relationship with Lehman Brothers resigned from the board.

I now had competent and aggressive legal and financial advisors. The asset sale strategy was going to be successful!

In order to survive, we had to stop Leon Simkins, who was accumulating Fibreboard stock. Morgan Stanley recommended that we retain Joseph Flom, a partner in the New York law firm of Skadden, Arps, Slate, Meagher & Flom. Flom was a highly competent lawyer who specialized in developing strategies to take control of companies but who could also be employed to defend a company from being acquired.

Flom developed a strategy to defend the company and set about to determine if Simkins had violated any security laws in his purchase of the Fibreboard stock or failed to make the proper filings with the Securities and Exchange Commission.

It was John Larson who recommended the action that would eventually stop Simkins. John introduced me to an associate at the SEC with whom he had worked during his assignment in the Commerce Department.

I had a breakfast meeting with the associate in the SEC executive dining room. I outlined the steps we were taking to save the company and therefore save jobs in a bad economic climate. I expressed that the monies we were expending to defend the company could be used to preserve jobs, and Simkin's strategy, if successful, was going to destroy jobs.

He agreed with me and asked if I knew the name of the bank that was providing financing to Simkins. Flom's firm had identified the bank that was providing his funding. I passed this information on to the SEC associate, who responded, "I'll see what I can do for you."

Simkins did not purchase additional shares of Fibreboard stock. I did not know why he stopped accumulating the stock. He eventually sold his position to Steve Roman. Thirteen percent of the outstanding Fibreboard shares were now in friendly hands.

SALE OF CORPORATE ASSETS

An axiom for the profitable operation of lumbermills was that it was uneconomical to haul harvested logs more than 50 miles to a mill. Management was disciplined to purchase timber within a working circle whose radius was no more than 50 miles from the location of the mill.

If there were multiple competitive mills whose working circles intersected with our working circle, there was going to be fierce competition in bidding on timber sales. In the case of our Oregon mills, there were multiple competitive intersections within our working circles.

We established the selling prices for the mills by first estimating the cost reduction in bidding for future timber sales if the buyer closed our mill. We inflated the costs over the next 20 years and then discounted the inflated costs to determine the present value of the investment the buyer could pay for the mill and achieve a 20-percent internal rate of return (IRR) on their investment.

This method of determining a selling price for which buyers could make a superior return on their investment resulted in high selling prices for the mills. If potential buyers did not understand the discounted cash flow (DCF) method of determining an IRR on an investment, we educated the buyers and their financial advisors if they employed an advisor.

We were able to obtain high selling prices for the mills, which resulted in significant cash to pay down debt.

The mills in Tennessee and Louisiana did not have competitors within their working circles. We were able to find bidders for the operations and achieve sale prices above the original costs of acquisition.

We financed the cost of a consultant to assist the general manager and employees of the Honolulu container plant to purchase the operation under an employee stock option plan (ESOP), which enabled them to obtain long-term, government-guaranteed financing at below-market interest rates.

I met with the presidents of Vail Associates and the Aspen Ski Company in an attempt to sell Northstar. Neither was interested. I then hired a highly talented IBM marketing manager who was tired of corporate and city life and wanted to live in the mountains to assume the presidency of Northstar.

I was criticized by a director for the hire in that the candidate did not have real estate development experience. I responded that we were not going to be investing in further real estate development. We required the skills of a competent marketing executive to sell the hundreds of unsold condominiums and building lots that were hemorrhaging cash.

Bank of America was the sole construction lender for the project. The economy was experiencing severe inflation, and the Federal Reserve Board had increased the federal funds rate to 8.7 percent to fight the rampant inflation. Mortgage rates for the second-home market were in excess of 10 percent. The market for Northstar condos and developed home lots was dead.

Bank of America recognized it had to take a write-off of the construction loan. The bank did not want to foreclose on the project. The president of Northstar, working with the bank, came up with a creative plan in which the bank would offer below-market financing to buyers of the condos and building lots. The logic was that the bank would prefer to make multiple small loans to creditworthy individuals rather than one huge construction loan to a failing company.

Northstar discounted the selling prices of the condos and building lots.

The president of Northstar justified the expenditure of significant advertising dollars in the San Francisco market announcing the "Great Land Sale"; the inventories of condos and developed lots were sold out in 10 months. Bank of America recovered the principal of the construction loan and the unpaid interest.

The operation of the ski hill in the winter generated sufficient cash to render the operation to be cash flow neutral for the year. We were not able to find a buyer for the project and never installed the new chairlift that was in storage in Truckee.

I made several trips to Australia. I recruited a new general manager for the subsidiary who improved the profitability of the operation and then offered to buy the company. We received a good price for the assets.

We were unable to find a buyer for the plywood plant in California. We reopened the plant in 1975 when the recession ended, the economy had improved and we were able to make a profit operating the mill.

PRODUCTION COSTS

A low-cost producer of goods or services can dominate a market. A high-cost producer of goods or services will struggle to survive.

Fibreboard's paper division belonged to the Fiber Box Association, which represented companies involved in the production of container board and corrugated boxes and the Paperboard Packaging Council, which represented companies involved in the production of recycled paperboard, solid bleached sulphate paper and folding cartons.

Both associations provided production cost comparisons to their members who provided their production costs in a format that had been agreed upon by the membership to an independent accounting firm. That firm then ranked the cost performance of each company in deciles (1 to 10). The lowest-cost producers were ranked in the first decile and the highest-cost producers in the tenth decile.

The reports did not identify the companies in each of the deciles; they did report the average production cost of the companies ranked in each decile. The report also identified the decile ranking of the reporting company.

Fibreboard's production costs ranked in the tenth decile in the surveys of both associations. Fibreboard's paper mills, container plants and folding carton plants had among the highest production cost operations in the universe of reporting companies. Typically, our production costs were 15 to 20 percent higher than the best-performing competitors.

The low-cost producers set the market price and dominated the market. Verhey's analysts were able to model the low-cost producers' P&L statements assuming the SG&A expenses were identical for both the competitive companies and Fibreboard, which illustrated that the profit before taxes (PBT) of the low-cost producer was 150 percent greater than Fibreboard's.

The low-cost producer was not going to raise prices for finished goods to a point where the high-cost producer could generate a satisfactory profit.

The substantial PBT the low-cost producer generated enabled them to generate extraordinary free cash flow (FCF) which, in turn, enabled them to invest in new, highly productive replacement equipment. This enabled them to reduce their costs even further. The amount of FCF enabled them to invest in new mills, factories and equipment to expand their market share and eventually drive the high-cost producers out of business.

Verhey's analysts had early on conducted financial analyses of the dominant public companies in the container and folding carton industries, e.g. Weyerhaeuser, Potlatch, Boise Cascade and International Paper, all of whom owned substantial acreages of fee timber. The one company that dominated the container and folding carton markets, though it owned only limited acreage of timber, was the Container Corporation of America, (CCA).

CCA executives were officers of both the Fiber Box Association and the Paperboard Packaging Council. I became active in both associations and was asked to speak at meetings on the subject of management. I developed a friendship with the executive vice president of the folding carton division of CCA. He invited me to tour the company's bleached paper mill in Wisconsin, a recycled paper mill and a folding carton plant in Chicago.

On entering the recycled paperboard mill, I immediately noticed the smooth, high-pitched humming sound produced by the paper machine operating at high speed. Fibreboard's dated, timeworn and slower machines produced an irregular thumping sound when operating.

The plant was well-lit. The floors were painted, and traffic lanes for equipment movement were differentiated from lanes for pedestrian traffic. The work environment was far superior to any Fibreboard mill.

At the conclusion of the tour, I asked my host if the company would share with us the financial statements and production numbers for the plants I had visited. I expected the answer to be no, but I felt there was no harm in asking. To my surprise, the answer was yes. The statements arrived by mail the next week. What was their motivation? After reviewing the information, I concluded that our performance in comparison to the results CCA was able to achieve was meant to persuade us to exit the business.

We were able to use the information to identify segments of our manufacturing processes that could be improved with minor capital investments and better management. We did not have sufficient cash flow to replace old, unproductive equipment.

THE ROOT CAUSE OF FIBREBOARD'S POOR PERFORMANCE

I asked the corporate secretary to provide me with a brief history of Fibreboard's origins and history. Fibreboard had been a subsidiary of the Crown Zellerbach Corporation (CZ), a San Francisco-based forest products and paper production company. Fibreboard's primary products were industrial insulation materials and floor tiling made from asbestos.

In 1956, CZ became the subject of a U.S. Department of Justice antitrust lawsuit claiming the company was involved in the restraint of trade. The Department of Justice prevailed in its lawsuit, and to satisfy the government's claims against the company, CZ was forced to divest itself of assets.

CZ was aware of the mounting claims being made against its Fibreboard subsidiary for mesothelioma cancer deaths that resulted from exposure to asbestos insulation produced by the company. Although Fibreboard had discontinued the production of asbestos-containing products, the company would not be able to escape the liabilities for the deaths and human suffering caused by exposure to its products.

CZ transferred valuable timberland assets and lumbermills to Fibreboard, which I assumed would turn the company into a viable entity. CZ completed its obligation to divest assets through the transfer of slow, dated, timeworn and narrow paper machines, the folding carton plants and the corrugated container plants to Fibreboard. It spun the entity off to the shareholders of CZ.

Fibreboard, the stand-alone corporation, had been condemned to an early death at the time of its origin!

I also asked the corporate secretary to provide me with the minutes for the board meetings that were convened in 1971 and 1972. What I was looking for was an indication of how the corporation intended to finance the numerous acquisitions and capital investments that were made in those years. Corporate secretaries are inclined to keep brief minutes of board meeting proceedings, but the minutes revealed that management had made a presentation supporting an acquisition or investment and that the board had approved the action and nothing more.

What became conspicuous to me in reading the minutes was that there had been a high rate of absenteeism among the directors. In particular, some directors missed half of the board meetings in 1971 and 1972.

The International Shareholders Services (ISS) organization was founded in 1999. It reviews corporate proxy statements and makes voting recommendations to shareholders, monitors board member attendance and recommends voting against the election of any director who attends fewer than 75 percent of the previous year's meetings. If the ISS had been active in 1971, it would have censured several Fibreboard directors.

ORGANIZATION CHANGES

It took several meetings and extended discussions to gain the board's approval to terminate the CFO because he was a long-term employee of 20 years and had been with Fibreboard when it was a subsidiary of CZ. Fortunately, we were in a financial position at the time to provide a good severance package plus he qualified for his full retirement benefits.

On my urging, the board elected Bob Verhey as vice president and CFO. The five banks were elated by his appointment. MetLife, our bond holder, had not had as much exposure to Bob as the banks did, but they also applauded the change.

At 31, Bob Verhey became the youngest CFO of an NYSE company at the time.

The vice president of the forest products division was appointed to that position after the Oregon mills had been acquired by my predecessor. He was a competent manager, but he resided in Oregon, and I wanted him to relocate to San Francisco. He was reluctant to relocate; he found another job to his liking in Oregon and resigned. I employed an executive recruiting firm to find a replacement.

The vice president of the folding carton division failed to adapt to the raised performance bar and resisted the performance measurement techniques we employed. We had to terminate his employment.

The executive recruiter identified David Ecklund, a middle manager with CCA, as a replacement candidate. I was impressed with David's management philosophies and his CCA performance. I extended an offer for employment and informed him of my relationship with the senior management of CCA. We discussed what he thought the reaction of the CCA management might be. We agreed that David would inform his manager of his decision to leave CCA and see what the reaction would be.

When David was onboard, I called my friend at CCA and apologized for raiding his personnel.

His reply was a great surprise to me:

"David is a highly qualified manager; the assignment he will be undertaking at Fibreboard will be challenging... He will be receiving excellent training working directly for you. If things do not work out, David will be welcome to return to CCA... He will have gained invaluable management experience."

David's management skills transcended the skills of his contemporary operating managers at Fibreboard. He and Verhey became my most trusted lieutenants.

We introduced computer-generated performance reporting on critical performance variables similar to reports we had used at Xerox, We sponsored the adage that if we do not measure it, we cannot improve it!

We raised the performance bar and invested in training programs to provide managers with the necessary skills to clear the raised performance bar; however, several division managers resisted the changes and were reluctant and slow to implement change. There were times when Verhey and I had to intervene and implement the change.

THE RETURN TO PROFITABILITY AND POSITIVE CASH FLOW

In mid-1974, we were making modest profits and generating positive cash flow to the extent that we were able to begin installing the equipment in the new calcium silicate manufacturing plant in Grand Junction, Colorado.

We were able to start up the Fibreboard plant in Rocklin in late 1974.

We did not achieve the goal I had set for the reduction in debt. The balance sheet was still overleveraged; the ratio of debt to equity exceeded our goal of 50 percent, and the debt-to-EBITA ratio was beyond our goal of four.

David Ecklund had made major improvements in the profitability of the folding carton division, but I made the decision that we would never have adequate cash flow to finance the ongoing capital requirements of three businesses—forest products with the fee timberland, the four lumbermills in California and the new fiberboard plant in Rocklin; the paper business with the mill in Antioch and the four corrugated container plants in California and one in Arizona, the folding carton business with four recycled paperboard machines and two folding carton plants and the Industrial division; and the new calcium silicate plants in Louisiana and Colorado.

CCA was a financial success because it focused on one business—making paper and then converting it into containers and folding cartons.

The folding carton division was the least profitable of all the Fibreboard divisions. Verhey, Ecklund and I created a compelling financial proposal to justify the sale of the folding carton division and the application of the proceeds to pay down debt.

When we proposed the sale to the board, however, we encountered four members who were adamant in their objections to the sale.

I felt that we failed to communicate the consequences of our highly leveraged balance and the investment funds required to sustain and grow the several profitable businesses with which we were involved.

Our cash flow was inadequate to properly fund all of Fibreboard's businesses.

We proposed the divestiture because it would strengthen our balance sheet and improve our cash flow, which we considered to be a victory. But I felt that some board members were viewing the action to be a defeat as though we were destroying the corporation.

Instead, we were proposing *creative destruction*—the divestiture of poor-performing assets that would result in improved cash flow which, in turn, would enable the corporation to fund the remaining profitable businesses to prosper and grow.

We had suffered a setback, and I had to come up with a plan to achieve board consensus to sell the folding carton assets. I referred to my adage, "You cannot learn anything about improving your business standing at the base of the flagpole at corporate headquarters." And I extended it to improving our corporate governance:

Directors will gain a greater appreciation of the challenges and opportunities facing management if they depart the boardroom and visit the corporation's operating facilities.

I informed the board that we would conduct the next board meeting at the recycled paperboard mill and folding carton plant in Stockton, California.

The board members were able to observe the operation of aged, narrow and slow paper machines that required significant annual capital maintenance expenses to operate.

After the factory tour, we met in a conference room and again reviewed our operating costs versus the operating cost indexes of the low-cost producers in our industry plus the production statistics and operating costs of CCA's modern paperboard machines.

We presented new information provided by paper machine equipment vendors with pictures, operating specifications, estimated production costs and the investment cost for a state-of-the-art recycled paper machine.

We illustrated that if we were able to invest in one state-of-the-art paper machine, we could produce 120 percent of the tonnage produced by the two existing machines at Stockton and at a lower cost per ton. We would become a low-cost producer of paperboard. The same investment opportunity was available to replace the two paperboard machines in Los Angeles.

The investment required to purchase and install two state-of-the-art paper machines was estimated at $500 million. Fibreboard's balance sheet and cash flow could not support that level of investment.

The board approved the sale of the folding carton division.

I would employ the concept of visiting companies' factories and offices to educate board members throughout my career as a CEO, and when I became a director of a corporation, I encouraged the chairman of the board to schedule board meetings at the company's operating facilities in order to enhance the directors' understanding of the challenges and opportunities facing management.

When we made the decision to sell the folding carton division, David Ecklund stepped up and offered to form an ESOP and buy the division.

After the closing, it took him more than a year to develop and implement a creative strategy for success. He sold the two paper mills to a Japanese trading company that invested in new state-of-the-art paperboard machines and sold the paperboard in Asian markets.

David then consolidated the two folding carton plants into a new plant in northern California and invested the proceeds of the sale in modern carton-making equipment. He focused the majority of his sales on one product line—Chinese takeout food pails. His company became the dominant low-cost producer of Chinese takeout food pails in the western United States. He made himself and his employees wealthy.

RETURN TO PROSPEROUS OPERATIONS

By late 1974, we had sold one-third of the corporation's assets. The balance sheet had been deleveraged. We had achieved our goals of a debt-to-equity ratio of 50 percent and a debt-to-

EBITDA ratio of four. The recession was moderating, and Fibreboard was achieving modest profitability and positive cash flow.

We were able to remove the wage freeze we had imposed in 1973 and grant salary and wage increases. During the recession, we had been able to maintain excellent relations with the unions that represented our hourly workers.

We were able to restore our accounts payable payments to our vendors to normal terms. The five commercial banks were extremely pleased with our new debt levels. MetLife was extremely pleased that we had not defaulted on our bonds.

The recession officially ended in early 1975. The Federal Reserve Board had increased the Federal Funds Rate to 16 percent during the first quarter of 1975 and then dramatically reduced the rate in April to 5.25 percent; mortgage rates declined, the housing market recovered, the price of lumber soared and our forest products division generated superior profits and cash flow.

The national GDP improved dramatically in 1975; industrial production improved, the container division's profitability improved substantially and the Industrial Insulation division generated superior profits.

Between 1973, the beginning of the recession, and the termination of the recession in 1975, the Standard and Poor Stock Index had declined 48 percent.

Fibreboard's stock price actually improved during the recession because the market price decline in 1972 was so severe when the company was operating in the vicinity of bankruptcy that we were able to sell assets and improve our cash flow.

Fibreboard's stock price reached a new high in 1975. Steve Roman sold his stock at an acceptable profit, and his CFO resigned from the board.

We had returned the company to prosperous operations. Management had set the goals and objectives to achieve a strong balance sheet and had driven the stakes in the ground for the improved performance of each of the operating divisions.

Management developed the strategic vision for maximizing shareholder value.

THE DEATH LIST

On September 5, 1975, Lynette "Squeaky" Fromme, a member of the Manson Family commune and cult who lived an unconventional lifestyle that included the habitual use of hallucinogenic drugs, attempted to assassinate President Gerald Ford in Sacramento, California.

During her trial, the prosecution described the cult's motive for the attempted assassination of President Ford as an act meant to deliver a wakeup call to all government and corporate leaders who were refusing to halt environmental pollution.

In December 1975, my administrative assistant informed me that an FBI agent was in the reception lobby asking to see me. I was confident that he wanted to inform me that we had violated some federal law and that the Justice Department was filing a lawsuit against the company. I suggested to my assistant that she introduce the agent to our corporate secretary. She returned and informed me that the agent said he had to speak with me personally. I asked the corporate secretary to join us.

The agent informed me that the prosecuting attorney in the Fromme trial had introduced into evidence a death list of people responsible for environmental pollution who were to be assassinated by the cult.

The presiding judge at the trial ordered the FBI to inform each person on the death list of the existence of the list and to suggest they take whatever precautions they thought necessary to protect their safety. The roll of intended victims was a distinguished list of CEOs of major lumber and paper corporations in the United States.

The Fibreboard board of directors acted swiftly to authorize the retention of a security consultant who recommended the hiring of security personnel to act as sentries at our homes during the night. They would escort the children to and from school and perform as sentries during school recesses. The potential kidnapping of our children was of great concern to Kathie and me, and the danger was reinforced by the consultant.

The consultant arranged for the installation of an alarm system to secure our home, and the system was monitored by both the security firm and the Ross Police Department whose station was three-quarters of a mile from our home.

We did not experience a threatening incident, and after six months, the employment of the security personnel was discontinued.

I am unaware that there were any attempted assassinations or kidnappings of family members of any of the individuals on the death list.

1976

Fibreboard's balance sheet was in good order. All of the operations were profitable and generating positive cash flow. However, two off-balance-sheet liabilities were endangering the survival of the corporation.

The collapse of the equity and bond markets during the recession from 1973 to 1975 devastated the value of Fibreboard's pension fund assets. In 1976, we found ourselves with a significant unfunded pension liability. If we were unable to restore the value of the fund to properly satisfy our future pension liabilities, we could be forced to declare bankruptcy.

The unfunded liability was a ticking time bomb that could destroy the company.

The second off-balance-sheet liability threatening the company was the mounting claims for asbestos-related deaths. The company had product liability insurance, but we had no idea of the ultimate dollar value the claims would amount to or at what point the insurers would run out of money, deny further payments and choose to declare bankruptcy. In addition, the legal fees paid out to defend the increasing number of lawsuits were becoming significant.

Several companies that had produced asbestos-containing products in the past filed for bankruptcy in 1976.

We also had an environmental operational issue to deal with. The company had made the required technology investments to reduce emissions in its pulp mill that supported the production of liner board and medium board in the Antioch paper mill to meet the air pollution standards set by the California Environmental Protection Agency, (CEPA).

We were compliant, but our concern was that the agency might raise the emission standards beyond the ability of future technology to achieve the new standards, forcing us to abandon the mill. My observation was that the CEPA was more inclined to close the mill than they were to tolerate its continued operation.

In my visits to competitive paper mills in the South, the operators reported that local environmental agencies regarded the emissions from the pulp mills as the smell of money in the form of payrolls and were inclined to set reasonable emission standards for operation. The CEPA was not inclined to be cooperative to preserve jobs.

Working with Morgan Stanley (MS), we set about to determine if Fibreboard was a viable corporation. Could the company thrive and grow in the capital-intensive, highly competitive paper industry?

We first completed the study to determine the investment and the cost of capital to enable the company to become a low-cost producer of linerboard and medium board to support the container plants. The cost for two state-of-the-art paper machines was $600 million.

We developed pro forma P&L statements for the future operation of the division, which after the investment would be a low-cost producer of linerboard and medium board and have additional production that would enable the company to expand its market share.

If we were to maintain our standard of a 50 percent debt-to-equity ratio, the investment, simply stated, would be financed with $400 million of new equity and $200 million of new debt.

The future profits and cash flow the division would contribute to the corporation were not sufficient to justify an equity offering at a small discount to the existing Fibreboard stock price. MS believed that we could not raise $400 million of new equity.

MS then completed a sum-of-the-parts analysis. It valued each division of the company as a stand-alone entity, totaled the values of the entities, subtracted the debt and divided the balance by the number of outstanding shares to calculate the value of the combined parts of the company versus the market value of the company as reflected in the current market capitalization.

The analysis showed that the sum-of-the-parts valuation was higher than the market capitalization.

The company's timberlands were the crown jewel of the assets representing some 67 percent of the company's total value. The lumbermills represented 13 percent of the total value, which when combined with the timberlands, the forest products division, represented an estimated 80 percent of the company's total value.

The paper division represented 15 percent of the company's value. It was not viable as a stand-alone business if the paper mill at Antioch was at risk of being shut down by the CEPA.

The industrial division, a small and profitable entity, represented about four percent of the company's value.

The Northstar real estate development represented one percent of the company's value. The land was valuable, but the market for second homes had not recovered, and it was not known if a buyer for the property could be found.

MS concluded that the company could be liquidated piecemeal for a greater value to the shareholders than the current market value, but they recommended selling the company in a stock purchase agreement to an entity that would pay a premium to acquire the company's timberlands, lumbermills and plywood mills, and under such an agreement would assume the off-balance-sheet liabilities for the asbestos-related claims and the unfunded pension liability.

I decided not to deliver all of this information to the board in one meeting. I wanted them to have time to digest the information we would be providing and to allow time for the directors to develop questions to which we could respond in a future meeting. I suggested to the board that we meet monthly during the next three months to address the continuing strategy for the company.

In the first meeting, we introduced the high-risk problems the company was facing, which included the mounting claims for asbestos-related deaths. BP&H was defending the company and provided a comprehensive outlook for future claims, the outlook for the involvement of the Federal and State governments to create legislation to protect the claimants and the positioning of the insurance companies to limit their payments. BP&H also addressed the conditions under which the company would have to consider bankruptcy.

We informed the board of the investment required to achieve the position of low-cost producer in the paper division, and MS presented the obstacles to raising new equity.

We reviewed the unfunded pension fund liability. BP&H reviewed the potential for bankruptcy if the company was unable to improve the asset value of the fund and be able to meet its required distributions. Actuaries from the pension fund management firm presented estimates of future contributions that would be required under various assumptions of future market performance. The estimated required cash contributions over the next several years were significant.

We requested that the board members submit any questions they might have and indicated that we would be prepared to respond to their questions at the next meeting.

We provided the board with a preview of the information that would be presented at the next board meeting, which included the sum-of-the-parts study and the recommended stock purchase plan for their consideration. We requested that they submit their requests for information they deemed to be vital to their decision-making and to request any additional strategies they wanted to be considered before the next meeting.

We provided a board package containing all of the information to be presented at the meeting two weeks before the meeting to allow time for an adequate review by the directors.

At the second meeting, MS made a presentation entitled "Maximizing Shareholder Value and The Risks of Going Forward." They presented their sum-of-the-parts analysis, which showed the liquidation value of the company was greater than the current market capitalization but excluded the risks of the off-balance-sheet liabilities for the asbestos claims and the unfunded pension fund.

The liquidation option revealed it would not be possible to obtain the computed value for the paper division as we expected an integrated buyer would have sufficient paper production to supply the acquired container plants and therefore would have no need for the Antioch paper mill. A nonintegrated buyer would not want to take on the risk that the CEPA could force the closure of the Antioch mill.

MS pointed out that the sale of the paper division would require a significant write-down of the value of the Antioch facility.

The MS partners pointed out that if the company was able to complete a successful liquidation of all of the company's assets, the asbestos claimants and the Federal and State governments would most likely obtain a court order restricting the distribution of the proceeds until the value of a trust fund could be established to satisfy present and future asbestos-related claims. No one knew what the valuation of the fund would be, but it was recognized that the liquidation option would not maximize the return to Fibreboard shareholders. BP&H litigation attorneys reinforced the logic and the conclusion.

MS concluded that the only viable option available for the board of directors was to find a buyer for the corporation that would pay a premium for the timberlands and assume the risks of the asbestos claims, the liability of the unfunded pension fund assets and the risk of the possible closure of the Antioch mill.

MS presented a list of 10 domestic and 2 international forest product and paper companies whose balance sheets and free cash flow could support the cash purchase of the Fibreboard stock at a value to meet or exceed our proposed sale price.

I suggested to the board that they may want to think about the recommendations and return in a month to make their decision. They requested an opportunity to meet in an executive session. When we were all asked to rejoin the meeting, the board announced that they agreed with the recommendation and authorized me to enter into an agreement with MS to find a buyer for the company.

MS put together an offering memorandum describing the operations of the company and the financial performance of each entity. John Larson produced confidentiality and non-disclosure agreements for execution by potential buyers that protected the company.

MS engaged with three potential buyers that had the financial capability to purchase the company and expressed an interest in reaching an agreement to purchase the company within a range of values that would be satisfactory to the company.

It took 90 days for the buyers to complete their due diligence, and we agreed to enter into the negotiation of an exclusive definitive agreement with the Louisiana-Pacific Corporation (LPC) based on the superior price they were willing to pay to acquire the company.

It was clear to the MS partners, John Larson and myself that the LPC management coveted the acquisition of Fibreboard's timberlands.

LPC made extensive inquiries regarding the pension fund assets. They met with the CEPA and gained an appreciation for the risk of a forced closure of the Antioch mill.

They made extensive inquiries to BP&H, requesting their records on the number of claims that had been made against the company and BP&H's legal defense strategies that were being employed to defend the company. In my deposition taken by the LPC attorneys, when asked what I thought the cost of settlement of the claims might be, I responded honestly, to the best of my knowledge, that the number might go as high as $70 million.

Several years after the sale of the company, the insurance companies, representing Fibreboard paid $2 billion into a trust fund for the benefit of claimants. Nationally, 65 trust funds were created, and the total contributions to those funds by insurance companies and corporations amounted to $30 billion.

The penalties for the production and marketing of asbestos-related products were costly, but Fibreboard had survived for 23 years before the account became due.

John Larson, Morgan Stanley, Bob Verhey and I negotiated an all-cash purchase of the outstanding shares of Fibreboard for a premium over the current market price. John negotiated a definitive agreement that protected the Fibreboard shareholders and was a win-win agreement for Fibreboard and Louisiana-Pacific.

The next steps were to obtain the approval of the two boards of directors and then gain the approval of both companies' shareholders.

The advice the corporation received from Morgan Stanley and BP&H had been excellent.

The day before the board meeting to approve the sale of the company to LPC, two board members asked to meet with me in my office. They notified me that the board did not intend to approve the sale of the company to LPC the next day. Furthermore, the board was dissatisfied with my leadership and would offer me the opportunity to resign, and if I did not resign, the board would terminate my services.

It was now the eleventh hour and fifty-ninth minute of a three-year journey to maximize shareholder value, and they were calling a halt to the quest.

My sport analogy: The football team was playing for the national championship, and with one minute to play and leading by 14 points, the owners of the team called for a timeout, fired the coach and announced their intent to forfeit the game for the national championship!

I had been working long hours each day for three years. I had maintained my physical stamina, but at this point, I became emotionally drained.

I reviewed the situation with Kathie that evening; we agreed that I should resign and negotiate an advantageous termination agreement.

I met with the board in an executive session the next morning. I asked if the board had hired a financial advisor who provided an opinion that the sale of the company was not in the best interest of the shareholders, or did the advisor believe the agreed-upon purchase price was inadequate?

There was no reply to my question. If the board had independently hired an advisor, they were not about to reveal it to me.

One or more of the directors may have asked their investment advisor to review the offering memorandum and offer an informal opinion. I had trouble believing that one director could convince the other four original directors that the sale of the company at a premium relative to the market value was a bad deal in light of the off-balance-sheet liabilities the company had incurred.

I asked the board if they were aware that if Fibreboard called off the sale or was unable to gain stockholder approval for the sale, Fibreboard was obligated to pay a large break-up fee to LPC. Members of the board acknowledged their awareness of the fee.

I was suspicious that something else was in play here. I suspected that the board was not going to allow me as CEO to cross the finish line victoriously.

I negotiated that my severance pay and vested retirement benefits were to be paid to me in lump sums in the form of cashier's checks and the vestment date of all stock options granted to me would accelerate to today's date. The cashier's checks and stock certificates were to be delivered to me the next day by messenger.

I was asked to have the corporate secretary join the meeting. He would draw up the agreement, and I would then be recalled to review and sign it.

The Morgan Stanley partners with whom I had worked for two years and their associates were using my office to make phone calls and to be productive while waiting to be called into the meeting. When I related to the two partners what had transpired in the executive session and that the directors did not intend to approve the sale, they were shocked and immediately phoned their senior partners in New York.

I packed my personal things in a box, I was recalled to the board meeting, I reviewed and signed the agreement, and when I returned to my office, the MS partners were still on the speakerphone with their senior partners.

They interrupted their call to say goodbye and expressed what a pleasure it had been to work with me. Then they added, "This isn't over! We will be in touch."

John Larson explained to me that he was an advisor to the corporation and could not inform me as to what was transpiring with the board. I understood his position. Bob Verhey was in the same position.

I assumed that the board would not be able to justify Fibreboard going forward as a viable corporation with the off-balance-sheet liabilities for asbestos-related deaths and the unfunded pension liability to which it was exposed.

Some days later, I assume after receiving excellent legal advice from John Larson and Morgan Stanley, the Fibreboard board of directors approved the sale of the company to the Louisiana-Pacific Corporation. The shareholders of Fibreboard overwhelmingly approved the sale. The purchase was approved by the LPC shareholders.

Fibreboard ceased to exist as a corporate entity.

The Fibreboard directors were talented, successful businessmen. I had obviously pissed them off. I realized I had to improve my communication skills.

Bearings

✦ *Work for a superior, or in the case of working for a board of directors, as a CEO, who shares your value system. Conduct due diligence on the value system of your potential boss or the individual directors of the board if you are being considered for the position of CEO.*

✦ *Conduct due diligence on the financial performance of the company you are considering working for and compare the target company's performance with the performance of competitive companies. If the performance of your target company is inferior, find out the cause of the inferior performance. Visit the company's plants or offices of operation. Talk with employees. Determine if it is a good company to work for.*

✦ *You, the leader, will be required to create the vision for the state of affairs you want to achieve for the entity. You will have to drive the stakes in the ground for the company and individual performance. Few boards of directors will perform this role. Develop your plan to enhance shareholder value, and request buy-in and approval from the board.*

✦ *Employ excellent financial and legal advisors who share your value principles. Do not tolerate mediocre performance from an advisor you inherit when taking on the responsibility for an organization.*

✦ *No matter what career path you choose to follow, you should acquire financial acumen either through direct experience in finance or through education. Adopt the highest standards of financial performance. Survival in any business is all about making sound investments, generating a positive cash flow and profits and maintaining a strong balance sheet.*

✦ *Avoid personally educating or lecturing board members on financial performance variables. Have your financial advisor conduct the education; the board members will more readily accept the advice coming from a consultant than if they receive it from someone whom they consider to be a subordinate.*

✦ *It is essential to your success to know your cost of production of goods or provision of services. Determine your competitors' costs. Invest to achieve low-cost producer or provider status.*

✦ *Focus your company's strategy on the production and marketing of a few goods or services that you can finance to achieve low-cost producer status and grow the business to dominate a market. The primary cause of corporate failure is when a company becomes involved in more businesses than it can properly finance. A properly financed competitor, focusing on a single product, that has achieved low-cost producer status will eventually drive you out of business.*

✦ *Act and act decisively to solve the problems in a distressed situation. Halfway measures that partially solve a problem are useless in achieving success.*

✦ *Courage will be your sustaining attribute. People usually reject change. Your superiors and your boards of directors are not exceptions to this generalization; they will object to your strategies that require change, they will object to the speed with which you are implementing change, they will take issue with the* state of affairs you intend to achieve and some will place obstacles in your path to slow you down and deny you the resources required to achieve your objectives.

◆ Some wacko may go as far as marking you for assassination! Be courageous!

◆ The road to recovery as a prosperous enterprise is a long journey. Maintain your physical stamina. Exercise regularly—run, ride a bike, walk and work out. Get an annual physical checkup. Adopt a healthy diet, and get eight hours of sleep each night.

◆ Continue to sharpen your saw. The Navy Seals have an adage: "Your last easy day was yesterday!" You will need new skills to overcome the increased challenges of each new day.

◆ Concerning trustworthiness, Trust Avenue is a two-way street! If you find yourself in a situation in which your superior is not trustworthy, run—do not walk— to the nearest exit!

THE WILDERNESS

For the first time in my career, I was unemployed.

I had assumed responsibility for Fibreboard, a failing company operating in the vicinity of bankruptcy, and stopped the hemorrhaging of cash, which bought time to improve the operations and avoid bankruptcy.

I managed the company through the longest recession since the Great Depression. We sold assets and strengthened the balance sheet, we improved the profitability of all of the remaining businesses, and we generated positive cash flow.

The company was encumbered with two off-balance-sheet liabilities that had the potential to force the company into bankruptcy. Fibreboard was not a viable going concern.

Working with competent advisors, we created an exit strategy that maximized the return to Fibreboard shareholders.

Three years as the CEO of Fibreboard provided me with invaluable experience. I achieved numerous successes, which strengthened my self-confidence.

In the months and years following the sale of the company to Louisiana-Pacific, I met a number of former Fibreboard shareholders and bondholders, all of whom were happy about the outcome.

I was a director of the San Francisco Chamber of Commerce during the three years I was CEO of Fibreboard. Walter Shorenstein, a highly successful real estate developer, was the chairman of the board of the Chamber. I attended the scheduled board meeting the day after my resignation as CEO of Fibreboard. My resignation made the headline of the business section of the San Francisco Chronicle that day.

After the meeting, Shorenstein approached me and asked if I would accompany him as he returned to his office; he mentioned that he wanted to talk with me about joining his company.

Walter's financial partner in his commercial office development business was the MassMutual Life Insurance Company. Walter had developed a good working relationship with IBM, and his strategy for many of his office developments around the United States was to enlist IBM as the anchor tenant and name the building for IBM. With IBM as the anchor tenant, the building would be, say, 25 percent leased before construction began, assuring a successful leasing program. MassMutual was confident the project would be successful.

Walter wanted me to join his organization as president. He was interested to know if I had departed Xerox on good terms. He explained the relationship he had with IBM and was intent on developing a similar arrangement with Xerox. We agreed to talk further.

The following week, I received a phone call from Jim O'Neil, the president of Xerox's Copy and Duplicator Division (CDD), where I was vice president of field engineering before my departure to Fibreboard.

Jim informed me that he would like to send an emissary to meet with me in San Francisco to explore opportunities that would prompt me to return to Xerox. It was typical of Jim's leadership style not to be directly involved. If I had been in his position, I would have invited the candidate to fly to Rochester,

New York, for a direct, face-to-face meeting to explore the opportunity.

The emissary he sent was the program manager, who was now a vice president. I had recommended that O'Neil terminate him four years earlier. Nonetheless, the meeting went well. The financial return on a free lunch is infinite!

I had a difficult relationship with O'Neil when I returned to CDD after spending three years salvaging expansion businesses engaged in highly technical markets outside the mainstream business of Xerox.

I was not going to be a subordinate to Jim O'Neil a second time. Kathie and I had no desire to return to Rochester. I politely responded to Jim, thanking him for the opportunity but explaining that we were determined to remain in San Francisco. If David Kearns, the president and CEO of Xerox, had made the call and the opportunity was in Stamford, Connecticut, my response might have been different.

When I informed Walter Shorenstein of the inquiry from Xerox—coupled with the news that my good friend, Tom Trolle, who had been the Controller at Xerox, had now been appointed as the vice president of corporate real estate—Walter presented a formal offer of employment, which included incentive compensation of a small percentage interest in each of five shopping centers he owned in California. The ownership would vest on the fifth anniversary of my employment. He also offered a small percentage interest in any future office building development in which Xerox would be the anchor tenant.

I initiated my due diligence on Walter and his company. Walter was highly thought of by his clients, and I received high praise for him from the chief investment officer of MassMutual. One interviewee alerted me that there were several former presidents of the Shorenstein Company who were walking wounded on the streets of San Francisco.

I politely turned down the opportunity. I would have entered a new business, real estate development, and learned a new set of skills. It might have been the biggest mistake of my career.

Walter and I remained friends for years. He owned a yacht that he used to entertain clients on San Francisco Bay. I would arrange for a guest card for Walter to dock his boat at the St. Francis Yacht Club and have dinner in a private dining room overlooking the bay. Walter's daughter owned a prestigious theater in San Francisco, and I was able to obtain center-row tickets for sold-out performances.

Walter was a major financial donor to the Democratic Party, and he was particularly helpful to me when I was the CEO of Spreckels Sugar. When I had a problem with the Department of Agriculture, Walter introduced me to Senator Dianne Feinstein, who at that time was Chairwoman of the Senate Agriculture Committee.

While at Fibreboard, I joined the American Association of Manufacturers to learn about modern manufacturing techniques. During a meeting in Boston, I had the opportunity to have lunch with the general manager of the Johnson Controls manufacturing plant in Livermore, California, which manufactured seating for the Toyota auto manufacturing plant located in Fremont, California. He invited me to visit his plant.

My visit to the plant began with an orientation conducted by the GM and three of his management associates. The plant employed the concepts of the Toyota Production System (TPS). The manufacturing process was broken down into cells, and each cell was manned by a team of workers who were all cross-trained to perform the work of any of the team members. The team, with the help of the factory personnel department, interviewed and selected new team members. Any associate had the authority to stop the production line if they observed a quality deficiency in the product by pulling a chain to stop the production line.

When the production line was stopped, a musical tune unique to that particular cell was broadcast over the plant's public address system. The plant management and QA personnel mounted bicycles and rode to the location of the music. The QA personnel then recognized the problem and worked their way upstream to locate its source. Once the problem was corrected, the production line was restarted.

Toyota maintained strong alliances with its suppliers. First, if you desired to be a supplier to Toyota, your factory had to be located within 25 miles of the Toyota factory. The supplier had to identify three alternate shipping routes to the Toyota plant on which the trucks would be rerouted in case of traffic delays.

TPS disciplined suppliers to produce only what products were needed when they were needed. Toyota provided the Johnson Controls plant with daily production requirements organized by time of day for the type and color of the seating that would be required for the type and color of the vehicle coming down the Toyota production line.

Seating was loaded into trailers for delivery to Toyota on a first-in/last-used basis. There was no space in the Toyota plant for seating inventory. The seating was unloaded from the trailer and onto a conveyer that went directly to the production station where the seats were installed. The style and color of the seats had to match the type and color of the vehicle.

Johnson Controls was required to maintain an inventory of all types and colors of Toyota seating to be used in emergency situations such as a trailer truck being stuck in a traffic jam or an emergency in the Johnson Controls plant that required the production line to be stopped.

At the conclusion of my orientation and factory tour, I used the restroom located in the associates' locker room. There was a shift change at that time, and the locker room was filled with associates changing their clothes. As I was drying my hands, a few associates approached me and inquired why I was visiting their plant. I responded, and they asked me if I had any questions they could answer for me. I was impressed! It was their plant; they had pride of ownership. They were happy, productive workers. I learned a great deal about modern production techniques on that visit.

During my visit, I learned that whenever Toyota introduced a new product, they would invite a team of Johnson Controls associates, which included cell team members, QA personnel, engineers, and accountants, to visit Toyota suppliers in Japan who had been manufacturing the product for months to observe how to efficiently produce the product.

I was also made aware that Johnson Controls sent new employees to Tokyo to be educated in TPS at Toyota University.

After leaving Fibreboard, I had time available to sharpen my saw! I went to my friend at Johnson Controls and asked if he could somehow employ me on a phantom payroll and include me in the next available Toyota University enrollment. I would reimburse Johnson Controls for any expense the company incurred and pay for my travel expenses.

I spent 10 days at Toyota University learning TPS. It was an extraordinary learning experience, which I valued as being on par with the financial education I received attending the Harvard Business School sponsored by Xerox at Exeter Academy. I would employ these new skills frequently in the ensuing years.

Four of the best takeaways I adopted from that education included the concept of kaizen, the economics of the experience curve, the real cost of carrying inventory, and the benefits of establishing alliances with vendors.

Kaizen is a Japanese word that encompasses a concept. It involves empowering the team that produces a product to continuously make small changes to reduce the cost or the time to produce the product. Management provides engineers and accountants to support the team's efforts to achieve these efficiencies.

The kaizen concept is based on the continuous flow of the production process. Process mapping is employed to follow the flow of work through each step in the process. The time in each step is measured; delays and waste are identified and eliminated. The product is never allowed to be out of the team's sight. It cannot be transferred to another department for completion. The transfer of a partially completed product is regarded as the commitment of the product to a black hole.

The team is responsible for the completion of all work, and the product never leaves the team's worksite until it is transferred to shipping for delivery to the customer.

Kaizen employs the sub-concept of gemba: The team is empowered to recognize defects in the product, to stop production, and to engage in the solving of the problem.

Kaizen involves transparency. Production goals are set by the team and management posts production results by product line in prominent locations throughout the plant. The successes of team cost-reduction programs are posted throughout the plant for all associates to review. Team competition develops as a result of the sharing of this information.

Profit sharing is an integral part of kaizen.

Kaizen encourages the development of strong alliances with vendors and customers.

The economics of the experience curve is a proven concept. With every doubling of production volume in the early life of a product, the labor cost to produce the unit will decline by 20 percent. Therefore, if the labor cost is, say, 30 percent of the unit manufacturing cost (UMC), the overall cost to produce the product will decline by 6 percent.

We were shown 10 case studies of UMC for various products that supported the concept. Toyota expected and contracted for a four-percent reduction in price for every doubling of the order volume for a product in the early years of production.

Vendors to Toyota had to employ the concepts of kaizen to continuously reduce costs.

We were introduced to the real cost of carrying inventory; traditional wisdom in the late 1970s in the United States was that the cost of carrying inventory was equated to the cost of capital. We were taught at Toyota University that the real cost of carrying inventory was 20 to 25 percent annually, which included the cost of the warehouse in which the inventory was stored, the cost of shrinkage and obsolescence, the cost to audit the value of the inventory quarterly and the opportunity cost lost due to the inability to use the funds committed to inventory to finance more productive investments.

Once the real cost of carrying inventory was recognized, the creation and funding of inventory were to be eliminated.

Raw materials and parts inventories were to be eliminated by working in alliances with vendors. Toyota did not expect vendors to carry the burden of carrying inventory. Each week, Toyota shared with their vendors their estimated needs for product for the next 30 days. Toyota expected their vendors to produce and deliver the product just in time (JIT) for use.

Following the principles of kaizen that a product was to be produced only when needed to fill an order and on completion was to be shipped directly to the customer JIT for the customer's use, there was no need for a finished goods inventory (FGI).

The concept contributes significantly to the liquidity of any manufacturing organization.

My search for a CEO position was producing few offers of employment. I was considering changing my mind about not relocating our residence and expanding my search nationwide.

Three events would occur that would lead to a complete reorientation of my business career. The first event was my engagement with the AMPEX Corporation in an advisory role, which resulted in a recommendation from the president to consider a role of a management consultant.

The second event was my employment as an interim CEO to salvage a startup venture, AWD. The success of this turnaround resulted in an introduction to Tom Lumsden, the San Francisco manager of Price Waterhouse's advisory services for financially distressed corporations. Tom and I formed an alliance in which we would turn around financially distressed companies for 25 years.

AMPEX

Dick Elkus was a good friend and CEO of AMPEX, which manufactured reel-to-reel, audio and video tape and recording equipment, which was sold to the motion picture and television industries. AMPEX products were the gold standard in the industry and dominated the global market.

In 1975, Sony Corporation of Japan developed a videotape recording device (VTR) housed in a cassette for the recording of TV programs at home. The motion picture industry was able to record motion pictures on the cassettes, which could be sold or rented to consumers for home viewing. Sony was manufacturing the VTRs in Japan and exporting the product to the United States.

Dick Elkus explained to me that his management team had created a business plan to enter the VTR market; management thought this would be a natural product extension of their reel-to-reel, audio and video recording products. He wanted me to review the business plan, point out weaknesses in the plan and suggest strategies to strengthen it. He provided me with a copy of the business plan. We signed a simple letter of agreement arranging for my compensation.

The AMPEX management's strategy was to limit the investment in the venture to result in their achieving a 20-percent market share in the U.S. market in five years. They identified this as a low-risk strategy for entering a highly profitable market.

My observation was that low-market-share competitors cannot compete against dominant-market share producers who, as a result of their dominance, are the low-cost producers and will eventually drive a high-cost producer out of the market.

On the day I was to meet with management to present my review of their business plan, a front-page article in The Wall Street Journal announced that Sony Corporation was investing $500 million to build a VTR production plant in Arizona. The announcement was a very fortuitous event for AMPEX.

The announcement presented me with a novel opportunity to convince the AMPEX management that their strategy for entering the market was flawed.

I challenged the team to develop a model of the Sony manufacturing facility. I put it to them this way: "If your board of directors gave you $500 million to invest, what would you build?" Our objective was to determine Sony's unit manufacturing cost (UMC).

This model would take several weeks to develop, and I spent many hours coaching the team when they ran into challenges as to how to estimate certain costs. Engineers have a tendency to develop four-decimal-point accuracy. I introduced them to the idea that they did not need that degree of accuracy in developing elements of the model.

We gathered all of the available public financial information on Sony Corporation, particularly on their VTR product line. We determined that Sony was achieving a 36-percent gross profit margin on the VTR product line.

I spent a lot of time at the whiteboard explaining the concept of index modeling to the team. We developed three indexed business plans, which are illustrated below in Table A.

First, we created an indexed analysis of AMPEX's original business plan. Next, we created an indexed business plan of what we estimated to be Sony's plan. Finally, we created an indexed and revised business plan for AMPEX that would be required to compete with Sony, which, because of their low-cost-producer status, would set the market price for VTR units.

TABLE A

	AMPEX Original Plan	Sony Created Plan	AMPEX Plan to Compete on Price
Selling Price	166	125	125
COGS	100	80	100
GP	66	45	25
GPM %	40%	36%	20%
SG&A	41	31	41
SG&A %	25%	25%	33%
PBT	25	14	(16)
PBT %	15%	11%	(13)

Observations:
AMPEX Original Plan:
1) We were 100 percent certain of AMPEX's UMC.
2) AMPEX had set its selling price to achieve a 40-percent GPM.
3) AMPEX estimated its SG&A cost to be 25 percent of revenues.
4) AMPEX expected to achieve a PBT ratio of 15 percent.

Sony-Created Plan:
1) We were highly confident that Sony's UMC was going to be 80 percent of AMPEX's cost.
2) We assumed that Sony would be satisfied with a 36-percent GPM and therefore would set the selling price at an index of 125.
3) Sony's SGA costs were typically 25 percent of revenues, and this was the cost-to-revenue ratio AMPEX had used in its business plan.

4) The bottom line was that Sony could achieve an 11-percent PBT using its business model.

AMPEX Plan to Compete on Price:
1) In order to compete on price, AMPEX would have to reduce its assumption on selling price by 25 percent.
2) Reducing the selling price reduced the GPM from 40 percent to 20 percent, a 50-percent reduction that was devastating to the business plan.
3) We assumed AMPEX would expend the same absolute dollars to sell the number of units of product in the original plan, so we used the index cost of 41 in the modified plan.
4) The conclusion was that the plan to compete on price with Sony would result in an operating loss of 13 cents on every dollar of sales!

Several of those in AMPEX management challenged the rationale of the index modeling. I encouraged them to develop the Sony plan using absolute dollars based on the intelligence the team had developed. The outcome to compete with Sony on price was identical to that of the index model we had developed.

I reported privately to Dick Elkus that the original plan, labeled as low-risk because it involved investing to achieve only a 20-percent market share, was an extremely high-risk plan that was going to result in a significant write-off at some time in the future.

I urged him to consider matching Sony's investment in plant and equipment and going head to head with them in gaining market share with the objective of achieving a minimum market share of 50 percent.

He responded that AMPEX did not have the financial capability to invest $500 million in the VTR market and also satisfy the investment required to support their fast-growing core business selling reel-to-reel recording tape and equipment to the TV and movie industries.

AMPEX abandoned the idea to enter the VTR market.

Dick Elkus offered me a vice president position at AMPEX and pointed out that I would be a candidate for the CEO position upon his retirement.

I politely declined the offer, but Dick advised me to become a consultant to management as he felt I had a unique way of strategizing a business plan. I began to give thought to this option. Dick and I would remain close friends until his death.

AWD

My closest friend, Doug Moorhouse, was the CEO of Woodward-Clyde Consultants, a global engineering design firm. Our friendship had developed as a result of being competitors involved in racing Cal-34 sailboats on San Francisco Bay. We were fierce competitors on the water. Doug berthed his boat on the same dock where I berthed mine, and after a race, I would invite him and as many of his crew who wished to join us to come aboard and have a beer.

Doug and I shared a common value system, and we both set high performance standards for our corporations and the performance of our boats. We had a great deal of respect for each other on land.

Woodward-Clyde had entered into a joint venture with Dow Chemical and the Guy F. Atkinson Company (GFA), which was involved in heavy civil engineering construction projects such as dams, tunnels and the development of airports.

AWD was formed with the idea of participating in the remediation of large polluted sites. The three partners believed this was a high-risk business and desired to create a legal corporate shield between the parent companies and the work to be performed.

The business development concept was that the AWD engineers would respond to requests for proposals (RFPs) by generating a work plan to remediate a polluted site and submitting a proposal. If AWD obtained the contract, they would employ the parent companies to perform the work.

Doug informed me that the AWD had been in business for one year but had not been successful in obtaining a major contract. The board of directors had removed the CEO, and Doug asked that I come in as an interim CEO until they could recruit a permanent CEO who was an experienced construction manager in the environmental remediation field.

I met with the board of directors. I gave a *Fire in the Hole* speech; I made it clear to the directors that I would not perform as a caretaker. I would act; I would introduce change.

The board accepted my assignment; I negotiated a nine-month contract. If AWD recruited the permanent CEO in fewer than nine months, I would still be compensated for the nine months. I also committed to full-time work for the first two months of the contract; after that, my commitment would be for 15 days each month. I had to make time available to pursue a permanent placement for myself. We entered into a simple letter agreement for my employment.

The AWD board informed me that they had been told the company had perfected contracts for $50 million of work, which would be generating revenue within 90 days. They requested that I verify the existence of these contracts and report back to the board as soon as possible.

AWD had established three offices, located in San Francisco, Houston and Newark. The GM of the San Francisco office was an Atkinson manager, and the GMs for the Newark and Houston offices were WCC managers. The vice president of marketing was a Dow employee.

AWD was burning cash at a monthly rate of approximately $2 million. The launch of a new business utilizing three offices of fully staffed engineering personnel was absurd. The launch should have started with one office that could bid on projects anywhere in the U.S. As revenue contracts were secured, the number of offices could be expanded.

In my first meeting with management, I asked the question, "How many executed contracts do we have in which work, generating revenue, will be initiated in the next 90 days?" The answer from the three office GMs was, "Zero!" The vice president of marketing was silent on the matter.

On further investigation, I discovered that the former CEO and the vice president of marketing had been lying to the board regarding the backlog of executed contracts. I reported this to the board members, who were shocked. I asked that the vice president of marketing be removed. The situation was identical to an experience I had with Xerox when I discovered a branch manager had been forging customer orders.

My plan was for the three office GMs and me to conduct the marketing. The Environmental Protection Agency (EPA) Superfund Sites were well-known, and it was a simple task to be qualified to be on the request-for-quote (RFQ) roster.

The Dow board members handled the removal of the marketing vice president; he was returned to the corporate offices in Midland, Michigan.

I spent time with executives of GFA, WCC and Dow learning their core capabilities and the minimum size of projects they were interested in undertaking.

I was able to develop a business model for projects involving GFA and WCC in which the requirement for GFA capabilities would generate $50 million of revenue and WCC involvement would generate $10 million of revenue for a total project revenue of $60 million.

Dow's contribution to the partnership was the exclusive use of their patented process for the cleanup of polluted groundwater; the process was named Aqua Detox. The chemical process was housed in a five-story tower at a typical installed cost of $5 million. The ancillary infrastructure to support the installation, i.e., roads, fencing, storage tanks, piping, shops and laboratories, totaled an additional $3 million.

We concluded that we needed to identify groundwater remediation projects of substantial size, requiring the use of eight Aqua Detox towers and generating contracts of $60 million each. We were able to identify 10 aquifers in the United States that the EPA had identified for remediation and that met our minimum revenue requirement.

The Aqua Detox process was four times the installed cost of a conventional groundwater cleanup system, but Aqua Detox could clean up the polluted water in a large aquifer in 20 months versus 240 months of operation for a conventional system.

We obtained a contract to clean up the Los Angeles Basin Aquifer, installing eight Aqua Detox towers at a contract price of $70 million. I will address how we were able to achieve this success later in the chapter.

I inquired as to what projects we were developing proposals for. The Newark office identified a LUST (leaking underground storage tank) project involving the removal of 1,000 underground storage tanks from gasoline stations in south Florida.

I asked numerous questions and then issued instructions to stop work on the proposal. I explained that there was no way we could win this assignment and make money. I went on to suggest that the contract would be awarded to McLaughlin & Jones, a fictitious partnership, both of whom were residents of south Florida. Jones had a Ph.D. in chemistry and McLaughlin owned a backhoe and a dump truck. The partnership had very little overhead to cover and would be the low-cost bidder. We were not going to expend our engineering resources developing proposals for small contracts that could be fulfilled by small companies with limited resources.

To illustrate to management the need for large revenue and profit contracts, I went to the whiteboard and drew a cross section of a dam. I showed the height of the dam in dollars: $20 million, our annual fixed costs. The area downstream of the dam I labeled "The Land of Profitability."

Then, I illustrated that it would take thousands of small projects, each generating small droplets of profits, to fill the reservoir before it would spill over the dam into the Land of Profitability.

I then illustrated a large volume of water entering the reservoir, representing the profits available from winning large revenue and profit projects. A picture is worth a thousand words!

I concluded by reminding them that our parent companies had the capabilities and the experience to successfully perform these large contracts, and only five other companies in the United States had the resources to compete for them. We would have limited competition!

We developed our marketing plan to identify EPA Superfund sites and aquifer cleanup sites that would be awarded in the next 90 days and be capable of generating minimum revenues of $50 million to $80 million within 120 days.

Management estimated that it would take four months to secure four contracts meeting the criteria.

I advised the board of directors of the marketing plan we had developed, which they applauded. I advised them that implementing the plan would require $10 million of fresh capital to achieve a state of positive cash flow. I had talked with our banks, which were willing to provide $3 million of new debt. Therefore, each partner would have to come up with $2.5 million of new capital.

I also offered an alternative. I pointed out that it had been a mistake to open three fully staffed offices when the company was launched. I suggested closing the Newark and Houston offices and increasing the engineering staff in San Francisco. The board inquired as to when we would be in a financial position to reopen the Newark and Houston offices. I estimated we could reopen the Newark office in nine months and the Houston office in 15 months if all went well.

The board instructed me to keep all of the offices open and to secure the bank financing. They committed the partners to meet the call for fresh capital. Dow was the richest of the three partners and had a significantly larger free cash flow than the other two. The Dow executives sponsored the idea of keeping the offices open and retaining the staff.

It was common practice in the engineering/construction business when bidding on a project to add 15 percent to the total estimated cost; this provided a profit and covered the cost of administering the project. Companies engaged in this industry were operating on razor-thin profit margins. There was little margin available for making an error in execution. I regarded the engineering/construction business as a highly competitive, high risk-business!

The AWD project managers were pricing Aqua Detox projects in this same manner, adding 15 percent to the project cost. I introduced the concept that Aqua Detox was a patented process that was not available to competitors and was 70 percent lower in cost than the conventional method of cleaning up large quantities of underground water. I initiated the practice of pricing the Aqua Detox portion of the cost, a patented, black box solution, at a 40-percent markup.

The installed cost of an AquaDetox tower represented 60 percent of the total project cost; the ancillary costs to support the operation represented the remaining 40 percent. If we priced the Aqua Detox solution at a 40-percent margin and the ancillary work at a 15-percent margin, the project profit margin increased to 30 percent—double the profit margin of 15 percent using the industry's conventional method of pricing.

AQUA DETOX PROJECT PRICING WEIGHTED AVERAGE PROFIT

	Percent of Total Cost	Profit Margin	Weighted Profit
Aqua Detox Cost	60%	40%	24%
Ancillary Cost	40%	15%	6%
Project Profit			30%

I also introduced the concept of engineering the conventional method of remediating groundwater and then comparing the two options side by side in the proposal. I had to educate the engineers about using the discounted cash flow (DCF) method of comparing the two investments while discounting the future operating costs to present value.

The Aqua Detox method could complete the remediation of a large aquifer in 20 months versus 240 months for the conventional method of cleanup. We first inflated the costs for both methods using the estimated future cost of labor, materials and maintenance capital for each month of operation. We then discounted the inflated cost back to a present value using the DCF method. The present value of the Aqua Detox investment was typically 70 percent lower than the conventional method.

It was also common practice in the engineering/construction business to submit RFQs by mail. The client would review the proposals, submit questions to the contractor if there was a need for clarification and announce the winner.

I took the position that we would not submit an Aqua Detox proposal by mail; we would insist on a face-to-face meeting with the client. Furthermore, we would insist that the client include finance people in the meeting. We were not going to take the chance of presenting our proposal to engineers who were not familiar with the DCF concept or how to compare the value of two investment options.

The AWD project managers expressed hesitancy about their ability to insist on face-to-face meetings with clients. I felt we had to sell the client on the benefits of the face-to-face meeting before the submission date for the proposal.

We arranged for a meeting with the Los Angeles County officials responsible for the remediation of the Los Angeles Basin Aquifer. We informed them of the patented Dow process, which was capable of cleaning up the aquifer in 20 months versus 240 months using the conventional method. Although the initial investment for Aqua Detox was greater, the cost of operating the conventional method over 240 months discounted to present value was significantly greater than the Aqua Detox method.

The officials agreed to the face-to-face meeting and the inclusion of financial people in the meeting. We were successful in acquiring our first Aqua Detox contract for $70 million.

I initiated two action steps to improve the strength of our proposals. The first step was to change the orientation of the GMs and project managers. Instead of proposing AWD, they would write a proposal on behalf of the parent companies.

We emphasized the experience of the parent companies who were going to be performing the work. In the case of GFA, we emphasized successful contracts they had performed, identifying the number in millions of cubic yards of material they had excavated, the number in thousands of cubic feet of concrete they had poured, etc. We stressed the experience of the project manager who would be managing the project and the experience of the engineers in designing the scope of work (SOW) to be performed.

The second innovative step was the employment of three retired engineering/construction managers to review our proposals, identify weaknesses and recommend changes to strengthen the proposals. I likened the activity to the red team playing the blue team in a practice session before submitting the proposal on game day. It was similar to the role Dick Elkus had asked me to play at AMPEX.

AWD purchased its legal advice from GFA. The general counsel of GFA was brilliant, aggressive and a great teacher. He taught me how to increase the profitability of a contract once we had won the bid and were performing the work.

If a client introduced a change in the SOW or a change in the specification of the work to be performed through the introduction of an engineering change notice (ECN), AWD was not obligated to detail the costs to perform the work. He encouraged us to include a profit margin of 40 percent in submitting the cost to perform the revised SOW.

The GFA general counsel also alerted me to the fact that some of the required skill sets to perform the work in a contract might not be available within the parent organizations. He taught me how to negotiate an exclusive agreement with a firm providing those skills, preferably local to the job site, which would be bound to perform the services exclusively to AWD. AWD had the authority to modify the pricing of their services in the event we felt their profit margin was excessive and their pricing might jeopardize winning the bid.

I personally adopted the two concepts and would successfully employ them in my future career as a consultant.

I met many of our competitors at association meetings. The most interesting was an environmental remediation company that on occasion used its own funds to purchase a contaminated site, remediated the site and then sold the site at a significant profit. For the purposes of this book, I will refer to the name of the company as Brown to Green Corporation (BTGC). I would use their services several times in my later career.

By the fifth month of operations under my leadership, AWD was winning multiple bids and generating cash; we were on our way to becoming cash-flow positive.

TOM LUMSDEN OF PRICE WATERHOUSE

AWD's corporate office was located in the GFA corporate offices in South San Francisco. There was a knock on my door, and the gentleman who entered my office identified himself as the Price Waterhouse (PW) senior audit partner on the GFA account.

He said he had been informed of the successes we were achieving at AWD; he further stated that PW had a department that assisted in the turnarounds of financially distressed businesses. The partner in charge of the practice in the San Francisco office was Tom Lumsden; the PW audit partner expressed that he would like to arrange a lunch and introduce the two of us to each other.

The luncheon with Lumsden was a career-changing event; he was a mover and shaker oriented to initiating change and influencing events. He was one of the smartest people I met in my business career. We shared many performance values. We hit it off! Our business relationship would develop into a lifelong friendship.

The AWD board hired the permanent CEO in the seventh month of my employment. The AWD management had developed into a force during those seven months. The board of directors paid me for the two months remaining on my contract and included a nice bonus for my services.

I had made no progress in my search for a CEO assignment. I was still operating in the wilderness.

Several weeks went by before Tom Lumsden called and requested we have lunch, at which time he introduced me to US Leisure, a privately held San Francisco corporation that had recently filed for bankruptcy. Lumsden's concept was for us to form a partnership in which he would be the trustee of the corporation and appoint me as the COO to manage the operations during the bankruptcy reorganization. This was going to be an authentic assignment in *creative destruction*!

We would be required to present our credentials to the law firm representing the debtor and the two law firms representing the two creditor committees that had forced the company into bankruptcy. We then needed to win the "beauty contest" among the competitors who would be vying for the assignment.

If we won the beauty contest, the bankruptcy court would need to approve our contracts. The submission of our contracts would be supported by the three law firms.

I was totally unfamiliar with the operation of a company under the protection of the bankruptcy court; I perceived the involvement in a bankruptcy case to be a high-risk assignment and chose to create a corporation in which to provide my services and protect my personal net worth.

Before familiarizing you, the reader, with the formation of The Sutter Group and the successful assignments of providing executive talent to turn around financially distressed companies, I will introduce you to my successful experiences with the Xerox Corporation.

I joined Xerox in 1962; the company was known as Haloid Xerox and generated $100 million in revenue that year. In the following years, Xerox experienced years of revenue growth exceeding 100 percent per year. The opportunities for advancement were significant, and the corporate growth brought about opportunities for placement in new, advanced technical fields. I spent 10 exhilarating years with Xerox. It was a great learning experience!

✸ Bearings

♦ *If you find yourself surviving in the wilderness, maintain a list of objectives, the states of affairs, you desire to achieve. These objectives will be your way points on which to set your compass bearings for finding your way out of the wilderness.*

✦ *Opportunities will materialize from sources you never thought possible. If you have a reputation for competence, people who share your values will seek you out!*

✦ *Never abandon your criteria for working only for people you can trust!*

XEROX CORPORATION

My first management position was with PPG Industries. I was given the responsibility of the Pacific Coast Region for the sale of industrial finishes. The operation was unprofitable.

I transformed the operation into a revenue-generating enterprise and achieved profitability in the ninth month.

I had a meeting with my superior, the vice president of marketing for industrial finishes, and inquired what my reward would be for this accomplishment. He responded that I could expect a $75-a-month increase in salary at the beginning of the New Year. I expressed my disappointment and updated my resume.

I subscribed to *Sales Management* magazine. I read the November 1962 issue, which included an article on the Haloid Xerox Corporation, a small photographic paper manufacturer located in Rochester, New York.

The company had survived manufacturing photographic paper while operating in the shadow of Eastman Kodak, the dominant global marketer of photographic film, paper, cameras and photographic production equipment.

Joe Wilson was a young, brilliant CEO, a Harvard Business School graduate who had taken over the leadership of the company from his father. Joe was exploring markets for opportunities to diversify the company. He learned that the Battelle Memorial Institute in Columbus, Ohio, was selling a patented process for copying images named xerography, which was a blend of the Greek words *xeros* meaning dry and *graphos* meaning writing.

The concept of xerography had been developed by Chester Carlson, a physicist and patent attorney, in his kitchen in Queens, New York, in 1938. He was looking for an easier way to make copies. Carlson failed in his efforts to sell his invention to corporations over the course of several years and finally sold the invention to the Battelle Memorial Institute in 1944. Battelle agreed to invest money to commercialize the invention, and Carlson retained the rights to participate in future revenues.

In 1947, the Haloid Photographic Company bought the rights for xerography from Battelle. The story, as told in Rochester, is that the top executives and many employees took out second mortgages on their homes and invested in a secondary offering of Haloid stock, which provided the money to purchase the patents.

The first xerographic product was a manually-operated device named the Haloid Standard. A second, automated machine was introduced two years later that made copies from microfilm. It was named the Copyflow.

In 1962, Haloid Xerox introduced the 914 office copier, which generated a dry copy of a document in less than a minute. The 914 was as large as a desk, the cost to manufacture the machine was high and the selling price required to generate a profit would have drastically limited the size of the market. The corporation made the strategic decision to lease the 914 rather than sell it. It was a brilliant marketing concept. Sales Management estimated that the company's revenues for 1962 would exceed $100 million.

The *Sales Management* article went on to say the company was opening new sales offices and needed sales managers who could drive growth as it expanded the sales force.

I found a listing for a regional office of Haloid Xerox in Redondo Beach; it was a five-minute drive from our home in Palos Verdes Estates. On Monday, I called the office and introduced myself to the regional manager; he agreed to see me that day.

:::::::::

My meeting with Roy La Hue, the western regional manager for Xerox, went very well. He examined my resume and noted that I had served as an officer in the Marine Corps. He informed me that he was a retired Marine "bird colonel." Bingo!

He went on to say that Xerox needed managers who had experience in managing large organizations with high performance standards and that retired Marine officers met those standards. He had hired a retired Marine major to be the technical manager of the San Francisco branch and Joe Trumpeter, a retired lieutenant colonel, as the technical manager in the Los Angeles branch.

La Hue offered me a job as the regional technical manager on his staff. He explained that the staff position would enable me to become familiar with the company, its products and its customers and that he would place me in a sales management position as soon as one opened up as a result of expansion or as a replacement.

Before he extended a formal offer, however, he wanted me to interview Ray Hay, the Los Angeles branch manager.

He also informed me that Xerox required that new management candidates be interviewed by RH&R International, an industrial psychology firm that evaluated candidates to determine whether they had the orientation and skills to manage high growth.

La Hue asked me if I objected to being interviewed by a psychologist. I responded that I had no objection. I did not reveal that I had been introduced to RH&R during my time with PPG Industries and that I had read their playbook.

I knew every question the psychologist was going to ask. I prepared "mini-stories" of my management experiences to answer his questions that would highlight my skills in managing high growth and demonstrate that I was highly motivated to succeed and that my orientation was to take action. In baseball terms, I hit every pitch he threw at me out of the park!

The interview with Ray Hay went well. He was seven years my senior, and he'd had a successful marketing career with National Cash Register before joining Xerox a year earlier. He was arrogant; he let you know he was good. He would become a mentor to me, but it would be a difficult relationship.

I joined Xerox in December 1962. The company closed out the year with revenues of $100 million. It was a small-cap company with high growth potential.

I was hired as the regional technical service manager, but La Hue informed the regional branch managers that I would be performing as the regional operations manager advising the branches on methods to improve both sales and technical performance.

Hay, the Los Angeles branch manager, and the San Francisco branch manager were recent hires; they were competent and required little attention.

The managers of San Diego, Portland, Seattle, Denver and Salt Lake City were long-term Haloid employees and were uncomfortable managing entities that were expected to grow revenues at 100 percent or more each year. La Hue asked me to focus my efforts on those branches.

I was impressed with the amount of data Xerox generated. The company segmented sales and technical performance into critical variables and then measured these variables against regional and national performance. Poor performance was easy to recognize. This was a prime example of the management concept *calculi segmentation*, which I adopted when I was in the Marine Corps.

The use of computers became widespread in American business beginning in 1954. In 1962, Xerox was very proficient in the use of computers to measure performance. In comparison, PPG Industries, which was eight times the size of Xerox in revenues, limited its computer usage to reporting financial results and accounting.

I realized I had to gain experience in the use of computers. I had to "sharpen my saw" in order to grow. I attended night school at UCLA studying computer science and operations research.

::::::::

The long-term Haloid branch managers had a hard time adapting to the high performance standards of a company that was growing so fast. All of the Haloid branch managers would be replaced over the next 18 months.

In June 1963, a district sales manager allocation was granted to the Los Angeles branch. La Hue asked that I fill that position working for Hay. He felt the position would provide more direct customer experience and be beneficial to my orientation.

In December 1963, Hay was promoted to Vice President of Marketing, and La Hue appointed me to be the Los Angeles branch manager.

LOS ANGELES BRANCH MANAGER

Marketing headquarters in Rochester assigned an annual budget for machine installations and revenues for each product line: the 914 office copier, the largest revenue generator; the Standard Xerox, a manually-operated machine used to make masters for offset lithographic machines; Copyflow, an automated xerographic machine used to produce copies from microfilm, principally used by county recorder offices; and photographic paper. The region assigned a budget to each branch within the region.

Headquarters strictly controlled the hiring of sales personnel, service technicians and managers. In December of each year, a branch manager would receive allocations to hire additional personnel the following year.

As the year progressed and Manufacturing was capable of delivering more 914 office copiers, branches received an increased revenue budget for the product line; it would be effective in three weeks. The branches were also given allocations for the hiring of additional sales and technical personnel to produce additional revenue and maintain the machines. These upward budget revisions would be delivered randomly throughout the year until the end of the third quarter. The performance bar was continually being raised.

Hay, my predecessor, had a passion for teaching. He conducted a management development program for the branch that included the district managers and candidates for management positions. On my arrival, I participated too. Hay did all of the teaching. He asked me to develop and present a session on recruiting skills.

When I became the Los Angeles branch manager, I continued the management development program, but I made one modification to improve the program. I purchased books on various management subjects such as planning, control, personnel administration and training. I issued the books to individual candidates and instructed them to develop lesson plans and present the subject to the class. I presented the class on recruiting skills.

It was a great learning experience for the candidates and allowed me to assess whether the candidate had a passion for teaching.

Joe Trumpeter developed similar training programs for technical service managers.

We placed advertisements in the Los Angeles Times announcing that we were hiring sales personnel and would be conducting walk-in interview sessions in a downtown hotel.

The ad listed a series of performance obstacles that a potential candidate had to clear. We wanted it to be the first screen to discourage candidates who were unqualified from attending the session.

The theme of the ads read: "...if you can leap tall buildings in a single bound...we can provide an opportunity to earn extraordinary compensation!"

We rented a small ballroom in a downtown hotel. We staffed the reception area with secretaries and customer trainers who asked for each candidate's resume and issued an application form.

The district sales managers, the management candidates and I conducted short interviews asking several open-ended questions. The applicants' responses gave us a good idea of their selling skills. We described our products, the potential markets and our highly rewarding compensation plan. We informed each applicant that we would get back to them within a week.

When we returned to the branch office, each of the interviewers would present the top candidates they had interviewed. The district managers and I conducted a further screen and invited the most highly qualified applicants to come in for interviews the next week. Time was of the essence; we had to fill the allocations for the opening of the new year and knew for certain we would be getting upward revisions in our 914 revenue budget early in 1964.

I made it a point to send a positive rejection letter to each candidate we turned down, thanking them for their interest. I wanted to maintain an image of a good employer in the community.

We were required to send employment packages for each new hire to the regional office and receive approval before extending an offer of employment.

The regional office was overwhelmed with applications. In addition to sales personnel, we were hiring three technical service personnel for every new sales hire.

So, I began hiring people without the regional office's approval. Our completed employment packages were arriving at the regional office before they had issued the approval to hire the candidate. Later, I was able to convince La Hue that my branch was capable of hiring highly qualified personnel, so Region's approval was unnecessary.

Once we filled our allocations for sales and technical hires, we would encourage the remaining qualified candidates to stay with their present employer. We would be receiving additional allocations for hiring and were confident we could offer them employment within four weeks. We referred to this group as our "reserve company."

We never stopped the walk-in recruiting sessions in the downtown hotel.

Whenever we were able to identify candidates with skills superior to those in the reserve company, those individuals were given a higher priority for hiring.

Whenever we received an upward revision in our 914 revenue budget, due to take effect in three weeks, we could have our new sales hires onboard in a week, trained in two weeks and in a territory producing revenue in week three.

Every organization has an undisclosed billet on its organizational chart. That billet is for the organization's drummer. I wanted every person—sales, technical, administrative and even customers who entered the branch—to sense the muffled sound of the drummer beating out the cadence. I wanted everyone to sense the energy we were generating. We were taking action, moving forward, achieving our goals and clearing the raised performance bar! The leader of an organization also performs the role of drummer.

We started the year with four district sales managers, 40 sales personnel and 150 technicians. We ended the year with 10 district sales managers and 110 sales personnel. The thinking of senior management was that each district sales manager could effectively manage and coach 10 sales personnel.

We finished the year with more than 300 service technicians and 30 service managers. All of the managers had been developed and promoted from within.

We finished the year at 120 percent over an ever-increasing revenue budget. I attributed our success to the fact that we never put a tarp over our recruiting machine; we placed regular ads in the newspaper and invested money in the hotel walk-in recruiting sessions continuously throughout the year.

The time and money we devoted to the development of sales and technical managers was also a major contributor to our success.

My fellow branch managers in the Western region were unable to achieve this level of financial performance.

Our district managers had designated new territories before receiving the allocations to hire additional sales and technical personnel. The managers had selected those applicants they wanted on their team from the sales and technical reserve companies. When we received the allocations for additional hires, we immediately contacted the applicants, made the offer of employment and had them onboard quickly.

When the upward-revised 914 revenue budget and new-hire allocations came out, I received calls from my contemporaries complaining about the increased revenue budget and stating it would be impossible to recruit the new hires in time to generate the increased revenue.

I listened to their bitching over a speakerphone and at the same time, my administrative manager was handing me completed hiring packages for my signature. The employment packages for our new allocations were hand-delivered to the regional office that afternoon.

Branch managers and district sales managers were required to achieve 100 percent of the revenue budgets for each product line in order to qualify for a performance bonus. Once this goal was achieved, the greater overall revenue accomplishment achieved versus their original budget qualified them for an ever-increasing bonus. It was a highly motivating compensation program.

I reviewed the personnel files of the 40 salespeople who were on board when I assumed responsibility for the branch. I was interested in determining the skill sets of our personnel.

I recognized the photo paper budget was going to be difficult to achieve. If I distributed the budget equally to each salesperson, I knew I would come up short because they could make higher commissions selling the 914. They would ignore the photo paper budget requirement. In addition, they did not have the technical knowledge to sell the product.

I discovered that we had a salesman onboard who, before joining HX, had been an independent businessman working as a "kidsnapper," a photographer who photographed grade school and high school class pictures, received orders from the school and had local photo shops produce the pictures. Every photo shop in Los Angeles County had been his supplier and owed him big time.

I persuaded him to assume responsibility for the entire branch's photographic paper budget, and I expanded his territory to include existing 914 customers. The commissions generated by the copy volume of these additional machines compensated him for the time he spent selling photographic paper. He achieved the branch budget for photo paper in just three months. Always take an inventory of the skill sets of the people in your organization.

The unit placement budgets for Standard Xerox and Copyflow machines were few. I assigned the budget for Copyflow machines to salesmen who already had responsibility for county recorder offices. I informed their district sales managers that I wanted the purchases completed before the end of the first quarter. I gave similar assignments for the Standard Xerox machines; we met our goal before the end of the first quarter. We could then focus 100 percent of our attention on generating 914 revenue.

The senior marketing management at headquarters were all Harvard Business School graduates who had successful marketing careers before joining HX.

They were excellent managers, setting ambitious goals and continually raising the performance bar. They provided quality leadership, creating generous compensation programs for commissioned sales personnel and generous bonus rewards for sales management who could excel. I thrived in this corporate environment.

Jack Rutledge, Executive Vice President of Marketing and the driving force behind Xerox's marketing effort, visited the branch. Roy La Hue did not accompany him. He spent three hours with me asking questions and taking notes.

He was particularly interested in our financial performance. I attributed our success to our recruiting program and outlined how we were able to attract large numbers of potential candidates through our lunch-hour, walk-in recruiting sessions, which made it easy for employed candidates to engage with us.

I described how we developed our managers' recruiting skills, which enabled us to quickly identify candidates with superior selling skills.

He was particularly impressed with the concept of maintaining a "reserve company" and the pace at which we were able to fill allocations for new hires throughout the year.

The transition from PPG Industries to Haloid Xerox was like stepping out of a coffin and being strapped onto the side of a high-trajectory rocket!

In November 1964, Roy La Hue was promoted to vice president of sales. The regional managers would report directly to him. His replacement, who had no Xerox marketing experience, had been hired by corporate staff. I was disappointed that I had not been given the assignment.

I had a meeting with La Hue and asked if I had been considered as his replacement. He responded that he had recommended me for the position but that "they, meaning headquarters, thought you needed more experience."

La Hue promoted Joe Trumpeter to the position of director of national service. It was a great promotion for Joe. I promoted one of his service managers to replace him within the branch.

La Hue's replacement was ill-suited for the job. Several people in senior management who interviewed him made serious mistakes, and the RH&R International psychologist who evaluated him had failed. He was not a manager for change!

I basically ignored him.

In December, La Hue informed me that the company intended to open a branch in Detroit that would be dedicated to serving the automotive industry, responsible for the Big Three automotive accounts and large, original equipment manufacturers. He asked if I had a candidate in my management development program who would be qualified to assume this role. I recommended Don Smith, and La Hue gave him the assignment.

In February 1965, Roy La Hue called me and offered me the Midwest regional manager position in Detroit. The incumbent, a former IBM manager, was being transferred to a newly formed division within the company, the Information Systems Division, as vice president of marketing.

 *Bearings*

♦ *Time is a precious asset; use it effectively. If you do not put it to good use, you lose it. You can never recover it. Train and motivate your organization to act, and use every minute of every day producing results.*

♦ *If your organization can move faster than your parent organization, you are free to ignore standing orders. You can violate rules, and as long as you are generating extraordinary results, you will not be reprimanded.*

♦ *Set high performance standards for the recruitment of personnel. Train your subordinates to develop superior interviewing skills in order to recognize the best-qualified candidates. To achieve extraordinary results, you will need to employ people with extraordinary skills. Your people will be your most precious assets.*

♦ *Seek out opportunities to improve your skills. Anticipate what skills will be required for the next level of responsibility you aspire to achieve and find an education source that can provide you with those skill sets. Discover books written on the subject. Sharpen your saw!*

♦ *Take inventory of your organization's skill sets. Deploy your personnel resources to maximize your results.*

Midwest Regional Manager

The Midwest Region headquartered in Detroit was created as an outgrowth of Xerox's original Midwest region, which had been headquartered in Chicago to reduce the regional manager's span of control. The Chicago region was renamed the Great Lakes region.

The Midwest Region was composed of seven branch offices: Detroit Metro, Detroit Automotive, Cleveland, Akron, Columbus, Cincinnati and Indianapolis.

My predecessor, who was in the position for three months before being appointed as vice president of marketing in the Information Systems Division (ISD), had recruited a highly talented regional staff.

Bob Koza, Administration, was recruited from General Motors; Ron Dunbar, Personnel, was recruited from Ford; Bill Bradley, Technical Service, had been a successful Xerox branch manager of technical service and Bill Winiger, Training and Development, was recruited from General Motors. All of these men would be promoted to Xerox headquarters positions and would be highly successful in post-Xerox careers.

My highest priority was to assess the capabilities of the branch managers. I relied heavily on the advice of the regional staff. My predecessor provided me with his assessment, and I had the RH&R evaluations.

I outlined my thinking on performance standards to the regional staff and particularly emphasized the quality standards for personnel recruitment and development.

The staff accepted the challenge and were in agreement that the performance bar would have to be raised. Except for the Detroit Metro and Detroit Automotive branches, we would have to maintain tight controls on the other branches and approve all new hires.

We implemented two actions to assist in accelerating the hiring process and controlling the recruitment standards.

Dunbar arranged to hire part-time administrative help with experience in personnel recruitment. They would scan and highlight application forms and resumes for key words and phrases implying success, high levels of motivation, etc. The candidates who passed this screen were given high priority for review by the staff. Those candidates who failed the screen were eventually reviewed by the staff and usually rejected for employment.

Hiring temporary employees enabled us to handle the surge in employment packages that accompanied each increase in our 914-unit placement and revenue budgets. Bob Koza created methods for paying these temporary hires. We were violating Xerox policy as well as state and federal labor laws, but we got the job done.

Dunbar revamped our letter of employment for sales and technical personnel making it conditional upon the successful completion of the candidates' training.

I authorized the regional trainers and the regional staff to terminate any trainee, sales or service, who they observed in training to be incapable of meeting our standards of performance.

Winiger enhanced the recruiting skills program I created for the Los Angeles Branch and developed a superb training program for the development of branch, district sales and technical service managers.

We introduced the concept of walk-in recruiting sessions and stipulated the branches would not discontinue their recruiting efforts. The Indianapolis and Detroit Metro Branches had responsibility for entire states, and we encouraged them to advertise and conduct walk-in recruiting sessions in outlying cities such as Ann Arbor and Grand Rapids in Michigan and Fort Wayne and South Bend in Indiana.

In three months, the branches had improved their recruiting capabilities to the extent that we were able to abandon the tight controls on hiring.

Winiger developed an enhanced sales training program. He incorporated many of the ideas I had adopted from The Benefit Company training I had been exposed to at PPG Industries.

I established the primary mission of the region to be the recruitment, training and development of a cadre of people capable of producing extraordinary financial results.

Roy La Hue called me to say that the Great Lakes regional manager was being promoted to a position in headquarters. He recommended the Detroit Metro manager, who he had managed before the spin-off, be his replacement. La Hue wanted to know if I thought he was qualified for the position. I agreed that he was.

La Hue informed me that he would be sending me a replacement manager for Detroit Metro who was a long-time Haloid employee he thought could manage a Xerox branch. I referred to this action as a "cram down." I was unable to promote from within, nor was I given the opportunity to interview and approve the candidate.

The candidate was the poster child for career advancement within Xerox. He had been a Haloid Xerox employee for 10 years. He was initially employed by Haloid as a factory janitor; he ascended through the manufacturing ranks and was promoted into an administrative job in Haloid marketing. Someone at headquarters thought he was now capable of managing a Xerox branch.

MY FIRST INVOLVEMENT WITH AN
UNTRUSTWORTHY MANAGER

The region allocated its assignment of 914 copiers to each branch. Our intention was to provide equipment to the branches with the highest backlog of orders. The 914 was as large as a desk. Distribution shipped the equipment to a warehouse/-drayage firm in each branch city. The branch coordinated the delivery of the machine to the customer with the drayage company and then scheduled a technical service representative to install the machine.

Several months had gone by since the placement of the long-time Haloid employee as the Detroit Metro branch manager.

Bill Winiger informed me that the district sales managers from the Detroit Metro branch who were enrolled in our management development program had complained to him about the poor leadership qualities of the new manager. I had not placed him in a management development class; he was sent to me as a qualified Xerox branch manager. After hearing Winiger's report I realized I should have monitored his performance more closely.

Bob Koza informed me that we had a problem with the Detroit Metro branch. The local warehouse vendor in Detroit was complaining to him that the branch was not providing delivery instructions for the machines in inventory. Something was wrong.

Bob Koza, Bill Bradley and I made a visit to the branch. Bradley met with the tech service manager to determine why the 914s were not being installed. Koza and I met with the branch manager and the administrative manager to get answers to the same question. The branch had submitted signed customer orders to the region, but the branch was not installing the machines. The answers Koza and I were receiving were double-talk.

Bradley discovered the cause of the problem. He interrupted our meeting and asked Bob and me to step out. He informed us that the tech service manager had told him that at least a third of the orders submitted to Region were phony! We confronted the branch manager, who confirmed that he and the administrative manager had created and forged customer signatures on the orders. The customers were legitimate, but the orders had never been executed by a responsible manager.

I reported the situation to La Hue. He instructed me not to terminate the manager; because he was a long-time Haloid employee, his fate would be determined by Joe Wilson, the CEO of Xerox. I was instructed to relieve him of his responsibility and inform him that someone from headquarters would be in touch with him. He disappeared. I assumed he was given an attractive severance package.

Trustworthiness is a paramount attribute of a competent leader.

I promoted Jim McNabb, a district sales manager from the branch, who was in our management development program, to become the branch manager.

Detroit Metro had once been one of our best-performing branches. But we learned that the branch manager had created an oppressive atmosphere; he threatened the district managers with termination if they did not meet their unit sales goals. Morale plummeted. Sales production fell off, and the branch manager created phony orders to protect himself.

I labeled him a thief. He had robbed the region and the company of revenue. The machines sitting in the warehouse could have been allocated to another branch, installed and generated revenue. Far more important was that he was destroying the morale of our most precious assets—our people.

I had experienced incompetence in managers, but this was my first encounter with a thief. As I progressed in my career, I would encounter many more thieves.

THE RISE AND FALL OF MANAGEMENT

Ray Hay had apparently pissed someone off at headquarters, as he was relieved of his vice presidency and assigned to be the Mid-Atlantic Region manager, which was an outgrowth of the Atlantic Region. Ray was resilient, and if he chose to remain with the company, I was confident he would make a comeback. We were now peers.

We kept in touch by phone and exchanged ideas. The regional managers met quarterly in Rochester. We would plan to have dinner together once during the meeting. We shared common values.

We were also avid competitors. Hay gave me a lot of heat that my region was accomplishing only 88 percent of our regional revenue budget. I smiled and replied, "True!" and then pointed out that we were 175 percent over last year's revenues! We had been sandbagged by someone on La Hue's staff when the 1966 budgets had been allocated to the regions. Hay's region was over budget but nowhere near generating revenues of 175 percent over the previous year.

During the regional meetings, La Hue would single out Hay and me to provide success stories on how we were able to achieve our recruitment goals and sales production successes. There was not universal acceptance of our ideas among our peers.

I observed that those who chose not to adopt our ideas did not have the self-confidence to raise the performance bar for fear of failure, and they did not have a passion for teaching their associates how to clear the raised bar, which would have ensured their success.

La Hue called some months later and informed me he intended to remove the Western regional manager. He asked if I could recommend any of my branch managers to fill the position. My first reaction was to wonder how La Hue had tolerated his performance for so long. I had felt he was ill-suited for the job when he was first appointed as La Hue's replacement. My observation of him during our regional managers' meetings was that he was incapable of meeting the Xerox standards of performance.

I recommended Jim McNabb, the manager of Detroit Metro. He had restored the morale of the organization, raised the performance bar and was achieving record levels of sales production. He exhibited superior leadership skills. La Hue interviewed Jim and installed him as the regional manager.

We replaced McNabb with a district manager who was in our management development program. We expanded the branch offices in the region to include Dayton, Louisville and Ann Arbor and filled the manager positions with candidates from our management development program.

The most notable member of that group was Dick Green, the Dayton branch manager. He was a salesman in the Cincinnati branch when Bill Winiger discovered him. He responded positively to the region's ethos and was quickly promoted to the position of district sales manager and then branch manager of Dayton. He would become a member of the headquarters' marketing team. Post-Xerox, he formed his own investment company and then founded Xerox-X, a Xerox alumni organization. Dick was an achiever.

Our region had provided two branch managers for other regions.

The outstanding success of our management development program was the result of the creative capabilities and dedication of Bill Winiger, Ron Dunbar, Bill Bradley and Bob Koza.

In the fall of 1966, Ray Hay returned to Rochester as vice president of marketing, and he asked me to join his staff as director of product marketing.

❋ _Bearings_

+ _Honesty is an essential attribute of a successful leader._

+ _If you need help, ask for it. Asking for help is not a sign of weakness. It is a sign of strength._

✦ *Develop the skills to mobilize your organization to effectively achieve your goals. Organize your resources, your people, to produce results in an allotted time frame. Remember that time, a precious asset, if unused, is lost.*

✦ *Be flexible; organize your resources to overcome an immediate challenge. You can return the organization to its original state when you have overcome the challenge.*

✦ *Assign ancillary duties to your managers to assist your organization in achieving the organization's goals e.g. budget planning, territory creation, recruiting and training. Delegate! These assignments are most likely not included in their job descriptions, but if they are talented, they will respond and handle the extra duties with ease.*

DIRECTOR OF MARKETING

The organization consisted of a manager and a team of analysts. The number of analysts on the team depended on the revenue the product line was generating. The active product lines at the time included the 914, the 2400 (a high-speed product designed to replace lithograph machines), the Copy-flow and the Standard Xerox.

Our responsibilities included:

✦ Forecasting for annual unit placements and revenue generation.

✦ Budgeting for each region for the active product lines, including interim increases in regional budgets as the year progressed and as Manufacturing was able to produce more units. I realized that it was Ray Hay's organization that had sandbagged the Midwest region in the allocation of the 1966 budget.

✦ Working closely with La Hue and Finance in developing these plans.

✦ Developing the hiring requirements for sales and technical personnel to fulfill the revenue forecast. We worked closely with La Hue's organization to develop this plan.

✦ Pricing for the monthly rental of the equipment and the charges for copies generated beyond the monthly minimum. Again, we worked closely with La Hue and the Finance organization.

✦ Generating the manufacturing build schedule for each product line. Our demand schedule for product had to be balanced with Manufacturing's ability to produce units, which was often constrained by their ability to obtain parts from their suppliers and their ability to recruit and train new workers. Manufacturing's constraints would cause us to modify our forecasts, budgeting and sales compensation plans if they could not immediately meet our production demands.

+ Designing the sales compensation plans for each product line, we were aware that we could direct and control a salesperson's efforts through their wallets. We were able to direct effort to a product line in which inventories were building up by increasing the commissions on the product. We worked closely with La Hue and Finance in this effort.

+ Preparing for the launch of a new product line, the 813, which was a desktop copier. We prepared for a controlled rollout, first limiting the introduction to key cities within the Eastern region and then expanding to additional regions as Manufacturing was capable of producing more units and Joe Trumpeter's organization could recruit and train additional technical service personnel. During the launch, I spent a great deal of time in the field with the product manager talking with branch managers, salespeople, tech service personnel and customers. We needed real-time intelligence to modify our forecasts, pricing and compensation planning.

+ Suggesting advertising programs, which had to be approved by corporate advertising staff. The corporation tightly controlled the image to be generated by the advertising and the budget. Joe Wilson, the CEO, personally approved all advertising.

I also had direct responsibility for the manufacturing of Haloid photographic paper. On my first visit to the factory, I got a tour of the production line. We entered the factory through a series of doors, always ensuring the entry door was closed. The coating and packaging operations were conducted in complete darkness. We were issued a pair of what must have been the earliest version of night-vision goggles. The control rooms for applying photosensitive materials to the paper were lit with red light bulbs. The paper moved from the coating application stations into ovens for curing. The finished product was coiled into large rolls and transferred to the slitting, cutting and packaging department. All of the activities were conducted in the dark.

We met in a conference room following the tour. I had a keen interest in training, so my first question was, "How do you conduct training for new employees? Do you have a mock-up of the production line, the control stations and the packaging sections in some other area of the plant so you can train people in lighted areas?"

The plant manager silently solicited comments from his managers by a gesture or by just making eye contact. No one responded. The plant manager responded, "Bob, we have not hired any new personnel in twenty years." This told me a lot about the business.

I also realized that all of the managers in the room had to be millionaires. They each had invested in the secondary offering of Haloid stock in 1947, which raised the funds to buy the rights for xerography from Battelle Memorial Institute.

I conducted a securitization study of the Haloid operation. No one from senior management requested the study, and if they had, they probably would have asked Finance to complete the work. Hay did not suggest I complete the study. The operation was my responsibility, and I initiated the action to conduct the evaluation.

Financially, the operation was a user of cash. There was no growth opportunity for the business, and the return on the investment to purchase new equipment to make the business cash-flow positive was unable to meet the corporate standards for an internal rate of return (IRR) of 40 percent on new investments.

The most compelling reason for the business closure was the distraction of the field management and sales force from their primary mission of generating revenue from our xerographic products, which were 10 times more profitable than Haloid photographic paper.

I made the point that all of the Haloid personnel could be absorbed into manufacturing and administrative positions in the Xerox operations in Rochester. It turned out that many of the people were so wealthy they opted for early retirement.

Hay's initial response to the report was, "Do you realize what you are proposing? Haloid is the mother of xerography; it is the Wilson family's company!"

After much persuasion on my part, Hay finally agreed that the operation should be closed. Jack Rutledge had an initial reaction similar to Hay's; he finally agreed with the logic of our study and sponsored the recommendation. We made the presentation to Joe Wilson. He agreed with our recommendation and after the presentation asked me to come to his office. He thanked me for the report and complimented me on the quality of the financial analysis. He commented that it was the right thing to do.

My financial analysis skills were on par with the skill sets of the Harvard MBA graduates in Finance and senior management as I was a graduate of the Elmer C. Larsen School of Business at PPG Industries.

I conducted similar securitization studies on the Copyflow and Standard Xerox product lines and recommended they be discontinued.

I recommended that the managers of these product lines working for me take jobs in field operations to obtain direct sales experience. We absorbed the analysts into our active product line teams.

Our relationship with the Information Systems Division (ISD)

Jack Rutledge established the marketing concept that Xerox would show one face to the customer. He did not permit ISD to create its own sales organization. ISD had to rely on La Hue's copier/duplicator sales organization to market its products.

I was the interface with the vice president of marketing of ISD, who I had replaced as the Midwest region manager. He would provide us with unit placement budgets and suggested commission plans for the placement of their units.

The dilemma we faced was this: If we allocated additional sales personnel to the field organization, how could we ensure the sales organization was going to devote sufficient time to the sale of ISD products?

In addition, ISD was recommending large commissions for the installation of their communications and computer-oriented equipment. We were concerned that the attractiveness of the plan would divert efforts for the placement of our copier/ duplicator products.

I spent time in the field with the ISD vice president of marketing visiting branches to get a feel for management's intentions as to how they intended to manage their personnel to attain the ISD goals. The smart branch managers were going to assign specialists to sell the products, but this strategy was contrary to Rutledge's concept of "one face" to the customer.

The salient observation I came away with during the field visits was the difference in the sales cycle required for ISD products versus the cycle for copier/duplicator products.

The rental agreement for a copier/duplicator product spanned 30 days; there was no large financial commitment on the part of the customer. The sales cycle for a copier/duplicator product could be approved by a local manager in perhaps 30 minutes.

On the contrary, the lease agreement for ISD products was for one year and had to be approved by the Information Technology (IT) department manager. The sales cycle could take 30 days or longer!

I was convinced that a copier/duplicator salesperson could earn far more money each month selling multiple copier/duplicator products than he could make selling one high-commission ISD product.

Rutledge, La Hue, Hay, the vice president of ISD marketing and I had several meetings to discuss our intended strategy. Rutledge prevailed with his concept of one face to the customer. He instructed La Hue not to allow the field organization to use specialists to sell the ISD products. He instructed Hay to implement the generous placement commissions ISD was recommending.

I was convinced the strategy would not work. The field organization would not devote the time required to sell the ISD products and as a result, ISD would fail to meet its revenue goals.

SHARPENING MY SAW

Xerox sponsored continuing education to enhance the skills of its executives. During my tenure as manager of product marketing, I participated in three outstanding training sessions.

IBM COMPUTER CONCEPTS FOR EXECUTIVES

The firm was using IBM computers, so IBM offered a week-long class entitled "Computer Concepts for Executives" for its customers. I was selected to attend the class. The objective of the training was to familiarize executives with the capabilities of computers and the technical language of computer science so they could communicate effectively with IT personnel.

The class was conducted in the Time-Life building in Manhattan. It started with the introduction of the binary numbering system; we were not expected to become computer programmers but were introduced to writing computer code in COBOL and FORTRAN languages.

For graduation, each student was given an assignment to write code to solve a simple problem. My assignment was to determine the distance from the base of the Leaning Tower of Pisa at which a tennis ball would come to rest after being dropped from the low side of the top of the tower.

I was provided with the height of the tower, the velocity of the tennis ball when it struck the ground, the coefficient of expansion of a tennis ball at various velocities, the angle of the slope of the concrete path at the base of the tower and the distance from the base of the tower at which the path leveled out.

I wrote the program. The input device for a computer in 1968 was a key-punched card. I took the program to the computer room in the basement of the Time-Life building where a keypunch operator keyed the punch cards. The program calculated the correct answer, and I was free to depart for my hotel. Those who failed to solve their problem returned to the classroom to rewrite their program with the help of an instructor until they got it right.

It was a great learning experience.

THE HARVARD BUSINESS SCHOOL EXECUTIVE DEVELOPMENT COURSE

Xerox engaged the Harvard Business School to develop a six-week program exclusively for Xerox executives to be conducted by HBS professors during their summer vacation. The program was conducted at the Phillips Exeter Academy. Participants resided at Exeter for three weeks, returned home for one week and then returned to Exeter for the final three weeks of instruction.

The emphasis of the schooling was on finance and human resources, which I called the care and feeding of our people. Joe Wilson, the CEO of Xerox, valued its human resources as the company's most precious assets.

Colyer Crum was the lead Harvard professor who conducted the classes on finance in the session I attended. He was brilliant and an outstanding teacher. We established a strong relationship and would stay in touch for many years.

The finance education was broken down into two sections: operational financial analysis and corporate finance. I was proficient in operational financial analysis due to the training and experience I'd received working for Dr. Larsen at PPG Industries.

The corporate finance training focused on balance sheets and cash flow financial statements at the corporate level. The focus was on how to raise equity, how to value equity, the use of debt and the correct balance of debt and equity to finance corporate growth. The course also covered the methods to evaluate the return on investments using internal rates of return (IRR) and discounted cash-flow (DCF) analysis. I had used both of these techniques while at PPG Industries.

We were taught the importance of the cash flow statement in determining the financial health of a corporation and in particular the importance of EBITDA—earnings before interest, taxes, depreciation and amortization.

Xerox rented its equipment and retained the ownership, so the cost of the equipment was capitalized and not expensed. The cost did not appear on the profit and loss statement. The manufacturing cost appeared on the balance sheet as an asset and was depreciated over the equipment's expected life. The depreciation was a non-cash expense, which reduced taxes and added significantly to the company's cash flow—and could be used to finance future growth.

Crum alerted us not to be overwhelmed by large numbers, millions and billions of dollars, in comparing the financial statements of two companies. He encouraged us to merely knock off three or six digits at the end of the numbers so that the arithmetic of the comparisons was easier.

He also encouraged us to avoid using four-digit accuracy when suggesting actions to correct poor performance. Peter Drucker made this same point in his book, The Practice of Management. Drucker said you do not need a scalpel to remove organizational fat caused by poor management. The fat can be removed with an ax!

Crum taught the class to use index modeling rather than large, actual numbers when comparing the financial performance of two companies or to illustrate the changes in financial performance we intended to bring about through the implementation of a new strategy.

A simple illustration appears below:

	Company A	Company B
Net Sales	100	100
Cost of Goods Sold (COGS)	80	60
Gross Profit Margin (GPM)	20	40
Selling, General Admin Expenses (SG&A)	15	10
Profit before Taxes (PBT)	5	30

The illustration shows emphatically that Company B is six times more profitable than Company A, and if you are going to make improvements in the performance of Company A, the model shows that the COGS in Company A is 33 percent higher than Company B, and the SG&A is 50 percent higher.

The use of index modeling made the illustration and communication of the differences in the performance of two entities simpler and easier to understand.

I would use index modeling throughout my business career.
The Xerox Management Development Program was one of the best education programs I would be exposed to in my business career.

A ONE-DAY SEMINAR

Xerox sponsored a one-day seminar on the subject of listening. I returned home exhausted. Effective listening requires the expenditure of a great deal of energy. I retained the acquired skills throughout my business career.

 Bearings

◆ *Sharpen your saw! Lumberjacks felling trees prior to the introduction of the power saw in the late 1940s used two-man, eight-foot-long crosscut saws. They would stop work mid-morning and mid-afternoon to sharpen their saws. The sharpening of the saws made them more efficient at their work. The work was easier. Lumberjacks referred to the dull blade of a crosscut saw as a "misery whip."*

◆ *Education will keep your saw sharpened. Never abandon your quest for education. Your work will be easier, and advancement will come more rapidly when you keep your saw sharpened. Do not allow your saw to become a "misery whip."*

◆ *Think about your future. What skills will you need for the next higher level of responsibility? Attend night school to acquire those skills. Read books about the skill sets you want to acquire that were written by people who preceded you down this road.*

✦ *Choose an employer that invests in the development of its people; sign on with organizations that will send you to seminars to improve your skills. The ultimate prize would be to be associated with an organization that would pay for an advanced degree. When interviewing, ask whether the employer offers continuing education opportunities.*

✦ *If your employer will not provide you with an opportunity to sharpen your saw but you feel there is an opportunity for future growth with the company, arrange for time off, not vacation time, and pay for the education yourself. Ask to be paid your salary during the time you are sharpening your saw.*

✦ *If your employer will not give you the time off, update your resume and begin the search for a growth opportunity with an employer who values human talent!*

MAJOR ORGANIZATIONAL CHANGES

Joe Wilson, the president and CEO, chose to become chairman of the board. The board appointed Peter McCullough, who had been the president and chief operating officer (COO) of the company, as president and CEO. No one was immediately named to be the new COO.

The first action that Peter took was to move the corporate headquarters to Stamford, Connecticut. All of the corporate departments were relocated to Stamford. The Copier/Duplicator Division (CDD) and Information Systems Division (ISD) remained in Rochester.

Peter's second major action was to announce that Xerox was merging with CIT Group, a bank holding company. The announcement was made while I was attending the Harvard Executive Development Program at Exeter. Colyer Crum led the class in an analysis of the purchase price and other financial measurements to determine the benefits to Xerox and CIT Group shareholders. He then created a simple index model on the blackboard, first showing the Xerox balance sheet and then the CIT Group balance sheet. He then created a balance sheet for the combined companies.

He turned to the class and, pointing to the combined balance sheet, asked, "What is it?"

I volunteered, "It's a bank."

Crum, who was six-foot-four and weighed perhaps 220 pounds turned and with the flat of his hand, slammed the blackboard where the combined balance sheet was displayed so hard that our classroom chairs jumped a sixteenth of an inch off the floor!

He exclaimed, "It's a bank! And that is why you cannot buy a ticket on American Airlines from New York City to Rochester—because every investment manager of every pension fund, insurance company and investment house that had

Xerox stock in its portfolio is traveling to Rochester to inform Peter McCullough that they are not paying 40 times earnings for a bank!"

There was so much opposition from the investment community to combining the companies, the merger had to be unwound. It was a serious defeat for Peter and the Xerox board of directors.

When the merger was announced, the price of Xerox stock had fallen dramatically, but it rallied after the merger was called off.

The index model illustrating the balance sheet of the combined companies was a highly effective communication tool. The fact that a merger could be called off was an important lesson for me. I would use the modeling technique to illustrate that a proposed merger was not in the best interest of the company and gain acceptance from my board to call off the merger when I became the CEO of an NYSE company.

Time went by, and Peter McCullough announced his appointment of Archie McCardell as President and COO. McCardell had been the CFO of the Ford Motor Company of Europe. His appointment came as a shock to the Xerox organization as the company had prided itself on being able to develop and promote executives from within the company. Several senior executives who felt they were qualified to be COO chose to retire or move on.

THE FRIDAY NIGHT MASSACRE

It was late in 1967 on a Friday evening after business hours when an announcement was made that the president and all of the senior officers of the Information Systems Division had been terminated. Ray Hay was named as the new president of ISD reporting to McCardell.

Hay called me on Saturday morning and asked me to join him at ISD. He informed me that I would be replacing three vice presidents: the VPs of Marketing, New Product Planning and Program Management. None of the replacement managers were named as a corporate vice president. We were all named as directors.

I was not familiar with the role of Program Management, so I would have to educate myself on the role and functioning of the position.

This would be my first management role in salvaging a business operation.

Hay's team assembled on Monday morning. Bob Potter, a brilliant engineering manager who headed up product engineering development at CDD, was responsible for Engineering; David Powell headed up Manufacturing, and Leon Berg assumed the role of CFO. ISD was hemorrhaging cash at the rate of $10 million a year. Hay informed us that we had one year to make ISD a viable business.

We learned that the products being developed were not meeting performance specifications, Engineering development mileposts were not being met and the development costs were significantly over budget.

Unit manufacturing costs (UMC) were beyond the targeted costs in the business plan; Engineering and Manufacturing had failed in their design efforts to meet the UMC goals.

Several products had been launched with severe reliability problems that resulted in frequent emergency maintenance and high technical service costs. These products would have to be recalled.

Revenue budgets for products released for marketing were not being achieved. I was not surprised; the concept of one face to the customer was not supporting the ISD revenue objectives.

Hay and I were in agreement that for ISD to be successful, we had to have a dedicated sales organization. He instructed me to develop a marketing plan.

We knew that the ISD communications and computer-related products had to be approved for lease by the corporate

IT departments of major corporations. Therefore, the product launch could be focused in those cities with high concentrations of corporate headquarters. We focused our efforts on New York City, which I felt could support two salespeople, Pittsburgh, which in 1966 had the second-most corporate headquarters in the U.S., Chicago, Houston, Dallas, Atlanta, Los Angeles and San Francisco.

Washington, D. C. would be the best location to support U.S. Government placements.

The marketing plan included a mere 10 dedicated sales personnel.

The product launches would be geographically focused and tightly controlled. We intended to expand the geographic coverage once we were achieving our initial placement and revenue goals.

We developed a generous compensation plan that would attract CDD sales personnel to join the ISD organization.

Hay and I met with Archie McCardell, Jack Rutledge and Roy La Hue. McCardell approved the plan, but Jack Rutledge was not happy that his concept of one face to the customer was being discarded. La Hue committed to providing us access to interview and recruit anyone in his organization. Corporate Human Resources provided us with the names of sales personnel who had experience with IBM and other computer manufacturers.

We would rely on CDD to train technical service personnel and service our products.

La Hue granted me permission to interview Harvey Leopold, my recommended replacement as the Los Angeles branch manager when I was promoted to Midwest Regional Manager to assume the leadership of the ISD sales organization.

We were able to attract the top CDD government sales representative to join ISD. This was a big win. He was familiar with the purchasing protocols of the General Service Administration (GSA). He was very effective and was trusted by GSA personnel.

The role of Program Management as defined in the Xerox job description was to ensure that Engineering, Manufacturing, Marketing and Finance had attained their performance goals as outlined in the business plan, which would ensure the product launch would result in a profitable performance and meet the Xerox performance goal of a 40-percent IRR.

::::::::

I needed to educate myself on the role of Program Management. I searched for literature in local bookstores, but the best source of books was the CDD Research and Development librarian whose primary role was to search the globe identifying technical books and papers being published about technological developments. She was able to obtain several excellent books on program management for me.

I told Hay I was going to disappear for a few days. Kathie arranged for a babysitter for the children, and we departed for a resort in Florida on a Wednesday. I read the books, took notes and developed several ideas regarding the management and control of new product development. We returned to Rochester on Sunday. I paid for the trip.

::::::::

ISD Engineering had three products under development and was evaluating the feasibility of reengineering the microfiche printer that had been recalled due to poor reliability.

The three products under development were an electronic mobile printer for the law enforcement and military markets, an electronic computer printer that was faster than the current market printer and a facsimile machine that Xerox had purchased the patents for from the Motorola Corporation.

As we evaluated each of the ISD products under development It was unclear as to what stage of development the products were in. Information about the performance of the machines versus the performance specifications in the business plan was not available.

The Engineering status meetings were chaotic. Hay and Potter were not pleased with the lack of understanding of the status of product development. The Engineering staff who Potter inherited were not disciplined and lacked an understanding of the financial impact their failure to meet performance specifications would have on the financial performance of the product.

The Xerox financial performance bar for the return on investment for a new product was an IRR of 40 percent, which was a challenging goal!

Attaining product performance specifications was critical to achieving the placement and revenue targets in the business plan. The achievement of the UMC goal for a product was essential to generate product profitability when coupled with the leasing prices targeted in the business plan.

I suggested that we should not grant continued funding to a product that was not meeting its performance specifications; the funding should be limited to the estimated cost to reengineer the product to meet the specifications.

The products under development contained many components. I suggested that we needed reporting on the performance of each of the components in order to identify the root cause of the failure of the machine to achieve the overall performance objective.

Hay and my fellow directors agreed we needed a road map to bring discipline to the development process. Hay appointed me, as program manager, to lead the effort.

It was typical for Xerox to fund new product development from what I termed "goal line to goal line"—from the initiation of a program to the opposite goal line, which represented the product launch, and then scoring big with the achievement of positive cash flow. If Engineering needed more money, it was normally provided. There were no mileposts to measure performance goals, UMC goals or IRR.

I likened the need for mileposts to the safety need for signs posted at railroad crossings: "Stop, Look and Listen!" I suggested we not fund product development from goal line to goal line but insert milepost checkpoints at the 20-yard line, 40-yard line, etc.

We identified four phases of product development.

With the concept phase model, which Engineering described as a "breadboard model," the components could be spread out on a tabletop and were not connected. The objective was to determine that each of the components worked and could be engineered and connected to achieve a predefined performance goal.

The second phase was named the engineering model; it was an actual operating model but without housing suitable for marketing. The objective was to determine if the product could meet the performance goals outlined in the business plan. In order to advance the development, the model had to meet the performance specifications for image quality, speed, reliability and the UMC.

The third phase was labeled a manufacturing model and was a complete operating unit ready for launch to be built by Manufacturing—and it would meet the UMC goals.

The fourth phase, beta test units, were units produced by Manufacturing and placed with cooperating customers to determine reliability and customer acceptance.

On the completion of the second, third and fourth mileposts, the units were expected to meet multiple operating specifications such as speed and image quality. Manufacturing Engineering had to verify that the UMC target could be met in the production quantities specified in the business plan.

Marketing had to verify that the unit placement goals and the leasing prices contained in the business plan could be achieved.

Finance, working with Manufacturing, determined the investment required for the production facilities and equipment. Finance then ran five-year profit and loss statements and determined the IRR for the project.

If a product under development failed to meet any performance targets at the milepost review, the development was put on hold. Engineering and Manufacturing were required to identify the time and cost to correct the performance shortfalls. Funding was provided to complete the reengineering, and a new review date was scheduled.

Engineering personnel would have to be reassigned to work on other projects or reassigned to CDD with the understanding that they could be recalled when needed. This was a far better financial solution than committing funds for advancement to the next milepost when a product failed to meet performance goals.

We achieved discipline in product development. We published our procedures in a booklet entitled Phased Product Planning. McCardell attended one of our engineering review meetings and was impressed with our approach; he took several copies of the report with him.

We had two products to actively market. The first was a high-speed electronic copier/printer that required a dedicated coaxial cable for the point-to-point transmission of images. It was called Long Distance Xerography (LDX). We had several installations within the CIA, the FBI and NASA. Commercial applications included placements with aerospace companies and defense contractors. The cost of the dedicated coaxial cable made LDX expensive to operate. Placements were limited to customers with an urgent need for the high-speed transmission of documents.

We launched a facsimile machine to transmit images over a telephone line. The first product was slow; it required six minutes to transmit an 8½-by-11 document. The initial product required an operator for both the send and receive units. It was called the Xerox Telecopier.

ISD Engineering was designing a follow-on product capable of a three-minute transmission time with automatic receiving capability.

The launch was highly successful. The customer commitment was for a one-month rental at a very low price, so the sales cycle was very short. The sale could be approved by a local manager.

It was obvious to me that the telecopier could be marketed by the CDD sales organization. I recommended that it be released to CDD as soon as ISD Manufacturing could ramp up production.

ISD was stabilized and generating positive cash flow!

I had never been satisfied with the CDD sales training program; it was oriented toward product performance. ISD products enabled the customer to achieve reduced communication costs and improved efficiency.

The ISD products were much higher priced than the CDD products, the lease agreement was for one year, the products had to be integrated with products produced by other vendors and the purchase commitment had to be approved by both the IT manager and the Finance department. I felt we had to improve the skills of our sales force to achieve our revenue goals.

I contacted The Benefit Company (TBC) and requested a quotation for developing a sales training program for Xerox's exclusive use employing the concepts of their standard program. Bill Winiger had been promoted to Roy La Hue's staff at CDD to be in charge of sales training and management development. I asked Bill to work with me in outlining the specifications for the development of a Xerox sales training program for ISD.

TBC worked with Bill and me in developing several iterations of the program to which we recommended improvements and modifications. When the final program was approved, TBC requested a modest development cost fee and a royalty to be paid for each trainee who participated in the program. We negotiated a lower royalty fee and placed a cap on the aggregate royalties to be paid to TBC. TBC was also to be paid a fee for training the Xerox trainers.

Bill Winiger and I met with Roy La Hue and convinced him the TBC program would improve the skills of the CDD sales organization. La Hue agreed to pick up 90 percent of TBC's development cost. I introduced the plan to Ray Hay; the cost to ISD was modest, and he agreed to the implementation.

We were raising the performance bar and providing the skills to clear the raised bar.

I had now sponsored and contributed to the development of two initiatives that would improve Xerox's financial performance over the long term: Phased Program Planning for the planning and control of engineering development and the development of a superior sales training program employing TBC's concepts that would be utilized by CDD and ISD.

RAY HAY IS PROMOTED TO EXECUTIVE VICE PRESIDENT

McCardell appointed Hay as executive vice president responsible for CDD. John Glavin, who had been vice president of Corporate Planning, was promoted to president of ISD. I was disappointed that I was not given the assignment; I spoke with Hay about my concern. He informed me that Glavin had never held a line-operating position, and the company wanted to give him the experience of being an operating manager.

John Glavin was a highly talented individual; we shared a common value system, and I was comfortable working with him.

A few months went by; Bob Potter was promoted to Archie McCardell's staff as an engineering and technical advisor.

Xerox did not have access to an auditorium that would seat its senior management. The company used the auditorium of a small, private liberal arts college, St. John Fisher, when it wanted to assemble its senior management.

When we were instructed to assemble at St. John Fisher in the morning, we expected that the meeting would involve an announcement of a major organizational change. Organizational changes occurred frequently. If the meeting was scheduled in the afternoon, after the stock market had closed, we knew the purpose of the meeting would be to announce an acquisition.

One such meeting was organized to announce the acquisition of Scientific Data Systems (SDS) in an all-stock purchase agreement, with Xerox stock at a 50-percent premium to SDS's closing stock price on the day of the announcement.

I was an investor in SDS stock, and the transaction was very profitable for me. I did have a concern about SDS's balance sheet and how they were accounting for leased equipment.

Jack Rutledge organized a cocktail party at his home to introduce a small group of senior Rochester executives to the SDS officers. I spoke with the CFO of SDS about its accounting treatment of leased equipment. His answer made no sense to me; I was concerned. I did not have a good feeling about any of the officers I met; they were too slick!

Leon Berg, the ISD CFO, was transferred to SDS, reporting to the CFO to become the eyes and ears of Xerox corporate management within SDS. The mission of SDS was to maintain its position as a leading developer of scientific computers and initiate the development of business computers to be marketed under the Xerox name.

Berg began to uncover accounting irregularities. Customers of SDS equipment began canceling their leases in favor of more powerful, efficient computers being marketed by SDS's competitors. SDS could not develop a business computer. It turned out that SDS was a "house of cards." The business collapsed, the company was closed and Xerox had to take a huge asset write-off.

I added a new classification for thieves. I classified the SDS officers as brilliant thieves.

David Powell and I were the only remaining directors from the original team recruited by Hay to turn around ISD. I began to feel as though I was forgotten and left behind.

Glavin informed me that Archie McCardell was in Rochester and wanted to meet with me at three p.m. that day in his office.

John Glavin's Corporate Planning organization had identified the healthcare market as a major growth opportunity for Xerox. In particular, the role of preventive medicine was identified as an even higher growth opportunity within the healthcare market. Specifically, the plan identified the need for a more efficient device to serve a growing demand for blood analysis.

The market was dominated by a company whose device was a large tubular machine, cumbersome to operate, which employed wet chemistry with a shelf life of two hours when exposed to oxygen. Therefore, the machine had to be shut down and cleaned after two hours of operation. It was not capable of performing specific tests; it was a batch-operated device that performed 57 tests on each blood sample. It was expensive to start up and operate. Intraday blood analysis was not available. If an analysis had to be completed intraday, it had to be performed manually.

John Glavin's business plan called for the design of a device that would employ dry chemistry with an unlimited shelf life for 36 of the most common blood tests. The device should be capable of providing specific tests on demand at any time of the day.

The business plan identified the market as being hospitals with 500 or more beds and estimated the market would increase each year along with the rise in population. There would be increased demand for testing as preventive medicine began to play an increasingly larger role within the healthcare market. The market opportunity was significant.

The marketing concept was to lease the machines and sell the chemistry, which would be sold in a patented package design. No competitive capsule could function in the Xerox device.

The company had created a development organization, Medical Diagnostics Operations (MDO), in Pasadena, California, in 1967.

McCardell informed me that Bob Potter had organized an engineering audit team to evaluate the development status of the project. The audit report was one-and-a-half inches thick. McCardell presented me with a copy, asking me to review the report and meet with him at 11 a.m. the next day. He intended to appoint me as the general manager of MDO.

I returned home and read the report until I fell asleep at one a.m. I resumed reading the report that morning and completed as much as I could before departing for the meeting with McCardell.

My response to McCardell was that the major challenge to the successful development of the product was developing the dry chemistries and the critical path of the development program was the time required to gain Federal Drug Administration (FDA) approval of those chemistries.

I suggested that the replacement GM should be someone with a background in pharmaceutical development.

McCardell retorted: "Those people have been blowing smoke up my ass for 12 months! I want someone out there who I can trust. You are the man. Meet me in Pasadena Sunday night."

Xerox had a relocation policy that financed 90 days of temporary living expenses and travel-home expenses every two weeks for transferred employees. I informed Archie that I had been with the company for six years and this would be my third relocation. I asked to be able to take my family with me to Pasadena and for the company to finance temporary living until we found a home. He agreed. Xerox purchased our home in Rochester. We rented a house on the grounds of the Huntington Sheraton Hotel in Pasadena.

I had not been aware of the MDO development activity. I sought out Glavin and Potter to provide me with background on the situation.

Glavin informed me that Xerox had acquired Electro-Optical Systems (EOS) some years before. The EOS founder and major shareholder had retired and became a member of Xerox's board of directors. He named his protege, Sandy Sigoloff, as his successor at EOS.

When John Glavin made his presentation to the Xerox board of directors in 1967 identifying the business opportunity and requesting funding to start up the engineering development, the retired EOS director recommended to McCullough that Sandy was the best-qualified Xerox scientist to manage such an endeavor. McCullough accepted his advice, and MDO became part of the EOS organization.

John Glavin recommended recruiting an engineering manager from the pharmaceutical industry to lead the development.

Bob Potter informed me that Horace Becker, who had been the Engineering manager for the development of the 914 office copier and whom I had identified as a tough-minded, highly disciplined Engineering manager when I encountered him in meetings at CDD, was the leader of the Engineering audit team that audited the MDO development effort.

McCardell relieved Sigoloff of his responsibility for MDO and terminated the general manager of MDO on Monday morning. That afternoon, he introduced me as the new GM and informed the management team that MDO would now report directly to him.

MEDICAL DIAGNOSTICS OPERATIONS (MDO)

I was now a general manager with total responsibility for the success or failure of a complex electronic, mechanical and chemical operating system. I reported directly to the President and COO of the company.

I made the second fire-in-the-hole speech of my career; I was blowing up all of the standards of performance and personal attributes established by the previous management. I made it clear that management's loyalty was now to Xerox and not Electro-Optical Systems.

I announced that from that day forward, we were going to deal with reality. I wanted their best estimates of the resources, funding and time required to reach our development objectives.

I made an emphatic statement that if I discovered anyone who deliberately provided inaccurate information as to the resources, funding or time required to meet our objectives, they would be looking for a new employer.

I pointed out that the market potential for the product was significant. Our immediate mission was to identify the cost and schedule to develop the chemistries and the device. The development cost coupled with the investment in manufacturing facilities and equipment would determine whether our entry into the market could be rewarding.

We were burning cash at a rate of $20 million annually; this was a lot of money in 1969 dollars.

I had no knowledge of pharmaceutical development, the healthcare market or the financial criteria by which hospitals made investment decisions for the purchase of new equipment.

I had no fear. I was a quick learner; I recognized my deficiencies and would educate myself as we moved forward.

I did know how to plan for, control and measure the progress of engineering development programs.

I introduced Phased Program Planning to the management team and set a review date for each of the four engineering disciplines to identify the phase of development for each chemistry and each component of the device. This exercise would establish a starting point for the further development of each chemistry and each machine component. From that point of reference, we could determine the resources, funding and time required to advance to the next milepost.

The next day, three of the Engineering managers came to me independently to inform me that they had been ordered to lie in response to the inquiries made by Becker's engineering audit team. I called McCardell and informed him we could "deep six" (trash) the engineering audit report.

MDO DEVELOPMENT CHALLENGES

Chemistry: MDO employed 26 PhDs in chemistry, all of whom were recruited from the pharmaceutical industry. The business plan called for the development of 36 of the most commonly used blood tests. Four chemistries had been approved by the FDA.

MDO had a working relationship with two hospitals, one in Los Angeles and one in Detroit, in which we leased space adjacent to the hospitals' pathology laboratories. We created a pass-through window between the two labs. When the hospital completed an analysis on a blood test for which we had a chemistry ready for testing, the hospital staff would pass through a specimen of the patient's blood on which they had conducted their analysis and a copy of their analysis. Our staff then conducted a test using our chemistry and compared our analysis with the hospital's analysis. It was a pass/fail test.

The tests were then shipped to Pasadena, where MDO scientists analyzed the results to determine the next steps for modifying the chemistry to achieve an acceptable result. The chemistry development and approval process would be time-consuming, but it was critical to stay on the path for the launch of the product.

Electronics: The controlling element of the machine was a Digital Equipment Corporation mini-computer, model PDP-8, which at the time cost $18,000.

The challenge for electronics development was that programs needed to be written that would instruct and control the mechanical aspects of the device for inputting the patient information and the tests to be completed, the dispensing of the required chemistries for testing and the mixing of the blood and chemistry. The blended solution would then be analyzed by a spectrophotometer, which measured the intensity of light that was absorbed as it passed through the blood and chemical solution.

The spectrophotometer reading was then compared to a range of standards. The results showed whether the blood sample was in an acceptable range or outside the range, indicating the existence of a medical problem.

Mechanical: The mechanical design would involve the performance of three miniature robotic devices designed to dispense the chemistry, transfer the blood specimen into a vial, penetrate the chemistry capsule, mix the blood and chemistry and then dispose of the spent solution.

The reliability of the machine was a critical performance standard that had to be met. The unit manufacturing cost (UMC) of the device was a critical element to be achieved to ensure the profitability of the program.

Packaging: The design of the chemistry capsule had to be unique so that it could be patented. Furthermore, the capsule design had to achieve an ultra-low manufacturing cost. Our objective was to achieve a manufacturing cost, including the chemistry milling cost, the filling of the capsule and the cost of the capsule itself to be no greater than 25 percent of the selling price of the chemistry. The sale of the chemistry was to be a high profit-margin product.

The achievement of these goals would be difficult and would require creative engineering design and manufacturing efficiencies.

Marketing: MDO marketing was staffed with personnel from John Glavin's Corporate Planning group, who had identified the market potential for the product. We knew the targeted market for machine placements. The challenging aspect of marketing was identifying the equipment rental cost and the selling price for the chemistry that would reduce the hospitals' cost per test and achieve an IRR on the invested development capital equal to or exceeding 40 percent.

At this stage, the IRR was a moving target. We emphasized the reduction in the UMC of all elements in the engineering design.

Manufacturing: Production of the chemistries would require a separate, "clean" facility for the mixing and milling of the chemistries and the filling of the capsules. The experience of the MDO pharmaceutical scientists was in product development. We did not have anyone in the organization with pharmaceutical production experience.

MDO did not have anyone in the organization who was experienced in manufacturing engineering to ensure that the design could achieve the lowest possible UMC and the most efficient assembly process.

These two organizational shortcomings would have to be addressed.

MDO ORGANIZATIONAL CHANGES

There was no one in the organization assigned to the role of program management. I concluded that this was my role as the GM.

I recognized a very talented young man, Bob Verhey, a Dartmouth MBA, who was a financial analyst reporting to the controller. I needed his expertise and had him report directly to me. Verhey had two bright, young MBAs on his staff.

The first assignment I gave to Verhey was to determine the cost and time it had taken the various Engineering departments to achieve acceptable performance results in the development of a component.

I used this example: We have four chemistries approved by the FDA. We should know how many man-hours and how much funding would be required to secure the approval of each chemistry. Then we need to determine whether the cost and time of the most recent approvals were achieved more efficiently than the first chemistries to be approved.

The analysis would provide us with a baseline with which to measure the cost and time estimated by each engineering discipline to achieve the next milepost in the phased program plan.

Expenditures in time or money below the baseline would raise a red flag and initiate an inquiry to determine the cause. A red flag would also be raised for expenditures above the baseline.

I alerted McCardell of the shortcoming we had in Manufacturing Engineering and suggested he arrange for the transfer of a talented manufacturing engineer from CDD Manufacturing to MDO. This individual would discipline the Electronic, Mechanical and Packaging Engineering departments to design to reduce the manufacturing cost of the device. In the event we would require additional resources, we could purchase expertise from CDD.

McCardell arranged for the transfer of a talented, young manufacturing engineer to MDO.

Regarding the production of the chemistry capsules, we thought the early production could be produced by a fulfillment contractor until the volume increased to a level justifying constructing a plant and purchasing equipment.

The new manufacturing engineer and I visited several contract fulfillment companies. The most important thing we learned was that the uniqueness of the capsule and the need to achieve the exact dosage of the chemistry encapsulation was going to require us to design a customized packaging machine that would add to the equipment investment and the unit cost of the chemistry capsule.

The most talented Engineering manager, who immediately embraced the concept of phased program planning and exhibited an excellent sense of business acumen, was a young man by the name of Joe Sanchez. I promoted him to the position of product development manager.

Because the chemistry development was on a critical path to launching the product, we had to make the most efficient use of our human resources in that department. We focused on a series of questions:

✦ Can the development of the chemistries be classified as being easy, moderate and difficult?

✦ If so, should we focus our resources first on the extremely difficult chemistries to develop?

✦ Do we have sufficient human resources and the proper skill sets to complete the development in a reasonable time to meet the product launch?

We decided we would prioritize the development of the most difficult chemistries. We determined that we had the correct number of scientists and the proper skill sets to achieve our goals in a reasonable amount of time.

I identified an additional organizational shortfall: We did not have anyone monitoring reliability and disciplining the design of the electronic and mechanical components of the machine. Reliability was particularly critical in the design and operation of the robotic functions in the mechanical design and the interface with the spectrophotometer.

I asked Joe Sanchez to identify someone in Mechanical Engineering who could fill this role. The man he identified was a creative and astute engineer, but he had no experience in managing reliability design. I put him in touch with the CDD librarian and informed him that she would provide him with a set of books on the subject; he would be an expert in two weeks.

The organization I went forward with—staff and departments reporting directly to me—included Joe Sanchez, Product Development; Bob Verhey, Financial Analysis; Marketing; Manufacturing Engineering; Quality Assurance and the controller.

When I was attending The Basic School at Quantico, Virginia while dating Kathie, who was attending nearby Georgetown University in Washington, D.C., her roommate Peggy Davis was dating Leon Smith, an intern attending Georgetown's Medical School. The four of us would double date. Peggy and Leon were married in 1958. We became lifelong friends.

Leon became a highly respected specialist in internal medicine. He had been summoned to Rome to diagnose the Pope's illness. He traveled to Japan to diagnose the Emperor's illness. He also traveled to Russia to lecture on the diagnosis of internal diseases.

At the time I was appointed GM of MDO, Leon was the director of medicine at St. Michael's Hospital in Newark, the teaching hospital for Rutgers Medical School students. When I informed Leon of my responsibilities, he became ecstatic that Xerox was entering the health market. He wanted me to spend a month at his hospital learning everything about its medical procedures. I told him that I did not have that kind of time, but I hoped he and his staff could accommodate me for four days.

::::::::

On Monday morning, I was issued a white coat and attended the staff meeting of the hospital interns. Dr. Smith reviewed the status of each of the interns' patients and the changes in the patients' health that had occurred over the weekend. One intern had lost a patient, Mr. Jones. Leon quizzed the intern on what he thought was the cause of Mr. Jones's death. The group then moved to the basement and the morgue. Leon saw to it that I was in the front row. A staff member opened a refrigerated case and began to toss Mr. Jones' body parts onto a stainless steel table. He began to describe the effects of Mr. Jones' illness on his various body parts.

I had to exit the room. When Leon caught up with me, I explained to him that the most important education I needed was to gain an understanding of the hospital's cost to determine a patient's blood analysis. What were the labor costs involved in the setup, operation and cleanup of the equipment in use? I wanted to explain the operation of our device and obtain feedback from the pathologists to learn if our device would lower their costs and improve efficiency.

I also wanted to learn how the hospital's financial officer justified the purchase of new equipment. What other hospital personnel were involved in making the purchase decision?

I came away with a good understanding of how we would establish our pricing and the best method of presenting our pricing compared to the present method of operation in order to make the purchasing decision for the MDO device an easy decision for the hospital staff.

The four-day visit was highly successful; I was able to sharpen my saw!

I gained even more knowledge during visits to the pathology departments of the hospitals in Los Angeles and Detroit with whom we had working relationships.

My objective was to create four working engineering models of the electro-mechanical device to determine the level of operating specifications we had achieved. From this base point, we would be able to determine the time and money required to achieve the performance specifications for a manufacturing model. The electrical and mechanical engineers stated it would require seven months to design and build four of these models.

Chemistry development estimated that they could submit and gain FDA approval for four additional chemistries during the seven-month time frame required to develop four engineering models of the device.

Chemistry development was on the critical path for the product launch, which we estimated should be two years beyond the time we would have an engineering model that met all of the performance specifications.

The Austin Company of Cleveland, Ohio, had designed and constructed several manufacturing plants for Xerox in Rochester, New York. The company provided MDO with preliminary designs and cost estimates for the plant to manufacture the device and the "clean" factory to produce and package the chemistries.

The designer of the filling machines to package the chemistries identified the equipment and the process flow required to complete the packaging.

In November, we finalized all the information we needed to generate a comprehensive investment plan and make projections for the profit and loss and cash-flow statements for the endeavor.

We would be digging a $70 million cash pit before the enterprise generated positive cash flow. The development cost to date was an estimated $40 million, but we did not have to include this financial burden in our calculations as Corporate Finance considered the past investment to be a "sunk cost"— money invested in the past.

We ran 10-year projections for profit and loss and cash flow for the enterprise; the internal rate of return was 20 percent.

This was a reasonable rate of return for most corporations, but Xerox had alternate investments that could generate 40-percent IRRs.

The two major unfavorable cost variances we were experiencing compared to the original business plan were: 1) The before-tax profit on the sale of the chemistries was projected to be 50 percent in the original business plan, but the cost of the chemistry and the packaging costs were about twice the cost of the original plan estimate. The profit before taxes declined to 25 percent. 2) The UMC of the electro-mechanical device was 33 percent higher than the cost estimate in the original business plan.

Financial analysis, working with Engineering and Marketing, developed models of alternate investment strategies such as launching the device with fewer than 36 chemistries and entering the market with a manually-operated device using a limited number of chemistries. The IRR declined rather than improved. We discarded these strategies.

Bob Potter again asked Horace Becker to review our engineering development plan and our cost estimates. Becker gave high marks to our engineers and advised Potter and McCardell that CDD should adopt the Phased Program Planning for product development.

We delivered the MDO business plan to all of the interested parties the last week of November 1970. On December 8, 1970, my 38th birthday, the MDO team made our presentation to the executive committee of the Xerox board of directors in Stamford. The committee included Peter McCullogh, CEO; Archie McCardell, COO; Ray Hay, Executive Vice President and a board member; Joe Flavin, CFO and a board member and two board members with scientific backgrounds. Bob Potter also attended as McCardell's technical advisor.

The business plan was well-documented, and we responded well to the committee's questions.

I presented the bottom line of the MDO endeavor as being a high-risk opportunity that could be expected to generate a modest 20-percent IRR. I pointed out that the company had several business opportunities employing xerographic technology that were capable of generating IRRs exceeding 40 percent, and unless the board was interested in doing something for humanity, my recommendation was to shut the endeavor down.

The MDO team was excused from the meeting, and 20 minutes later we were recalled and met with a smaller group consisting of McCardell, Flavin and Potter. McCardell informed us that the executive committee had accepted our recommendation and commended the team for a job well done. McCardell swore us to secrecy until plans could be made for the public announcement. He scheduled a meeting with me for the next morning.

Potter and Flavin suggested they would have dinner with me to celebrate my birthday. I declined, suggesting I thought I should have dinner with my team. We had a lot to celebrate in addition to my birthday!

The next day, I met with McCardell, Doug Reid, Vice President of Human Resources, and Bob Potter.

McCardell outlined an extremely generous severance plan for all pay grades that included the reimbursement of relocation costs if their new job was located more than 50 miles from their existing home and the new employer would not pay for relocation. Xerox wanted to be known as a good employer.

McCardell relieved me and my staff from any responsibility for the termination and severance of the MDO personnel. Doug Reid would staff and implement the severance benefits.

Doug Reid would also staff the personnel for securing the offices and laboratories.

My assignment was to secure the scientific data, engineering drawings and engineering models to be packaged and stored in a bonded warehouse.

My second assignment was to determine if the development plans, formulations and engineering could be sold.

McCardell asked for my recommendations of talented people who should be retained within the Xerox organization.

I was instructed to rent a theater in Pasadena for a morning meeting. McCardell intended to preside over the meeting. He set a date in December that presented a conflict for me. I chose to speak to him in private about my conflict.

McCardell then excused Reid and Potter. He informed me that I was to receive a 30-percent salary increase and would be promoted two pay-grade levels. I was also awarded additional Xerox stock options, and in an unusual gesture for Xerox, I was awarded a $150,000 cash bonus.

I thanked him for the generous rewards. I informed him that I had plans to take my family to Aspen for our Christmas vacation on the day he had selected for the meeting announcing the closure of MDO.

Without hesitating, he said the company would arrange for a private jet to take the family to Aspen on the day following the announcement.

The implementation of the announcement of the MDO closing, the security of the offices and laboratories and the safety measures taken to protect the MDO employees were handled by Corporate Human Resources, and it was something to behold.

McCardell and I arrived at the theater 30 minutes prior to the announced time of the assembly. Doug Reid was present and in charge of the event. Ten private security officers dressed in black suits occupied the seats in the front row in the center of the theater. No one was going to be permitted to charge the podium and threaten McCardell or me.

Security personnel checked the names and identification of the employees as they entered the building. The press and outsiders were to be denied entrance. When all of the MDO personnel were present or accounted for, McCardell began the meeting.

Three ambulances with medical personnel onboard moved from positions several blocks from the theater and parked in front of the theater. We were prepared to administer to anyone who fainted or worse, suffered a heart attack, on hearing the news of the closure of MDO.

While the meeting was underway, security guards set up stations at each entrance to the MDO offices and laboratories. No one would be permitted to exit the facilities after the announcement with anything more than their personal belongings.

At the appropriate hour, a Xerox representative informed the personnel employed at the Los Angeles and Detroit hospital laboratories that MDO was closing, outlined their severance benefits and provided contact information for a Xerox representative to assist them in obtaining new employment. Security personnel boxed all of the equipment, papers and tests to be stored in the bonded warehouse in Los Angeles.

The event was completed without incident. The attendees were disappointed to learn that the endeavor was being canceled as everyone thought it was an exciting growth opportunity with which to be associated. The generous severance pay and the relocation policy were very well received.

McCardell had asked for my recommendations of MDO personnel who should be retained by Xerox.

I recommended Joe Sanchez, the MDO technical manager, who became the program manager for the development and launch of Xerox's first color copier. His performance in that role was superior.

I recommended Bob Verhey, the manager of financial analysis, and his two excellent MBA associates, who were transferred to CDD Finance.

I recommended the manufacturing engineer who came to MDO from CDD and did an excellent job for MDO. He returned to CDD Manufacturing and received a two-grade promotion.

I also recommended that the young mechanical engineer who we had asked to assume the role of reliability manager for the blood analyzer be retained. He accepted a position in the Field Engineering unit in CDD's Research and Development department.

We were aware that DuPont Chemical was engaged in research to develop a blood analyzer. The librarian at CDD discovered literature indicating that a Swedish company and a Japanese company were also developing blood analyzers.

I had several meetings with DuPont representatives who expressed an interest in purchasing our FDA-approved chemistries and our research. They declined to engage in due diligence; they said our asking price for the knowledge was too high.

After I conducted discussions with the Swedish representatives and learned of the technical design approach they were pursuing, I concluded they would have no interest in our dry chemistry.

The Japanese likewise expressed no interest in acquiring our chemistry development.

Joe Sanchez and I supervised the cataloging of all MDO research data and the packaging of the engineering models to be placed in a bonded warehouse. We closed the doors on the MDO facilities. Joe departed for Rochester, and I awaited word of my next assignment.

 *Bearings*

+ *Trustworthiness is the primary attribute of a successful leader. Promotions will come more rapidly and your rewards will be great if you are honest with your superiors, your financiers and the members of your team.*

+ *Develop your self-confidence by thinking through the resources, time and money you are going to require to meet your objectives. Be honest with yourself—deal in real numbers. Assess the risks involved in implementing your plan and then make your decision to "Go" or "No go!"*

+ *Raise the performance bar, and prioritize honesty in the work ethos of your organization. Teach the team how to clear the raised performance bar.*

+ *Courage trumps fear! As your self-confidence improves, you will have no fear of taking on assignments in which you have no knowledge and experience. Time will be an asset; use the time to educate yourself on the technology you will be employing and the markets you will be entering. Sharpen your saw!*

+ *Why do inferior leaders fail and revert to perfidious behavior? My observations are that they lack the intelligence to realize the need to acquire skills to effectively plan and control the activities of an enterprise to achieve goals and therefore fail to create a viable plan utilizing people, money and time to achieve the goals.*

♦ *They fall short of accomplishing their goals and then lie to keep the investment money flowing and keep their jobs.*

♦ *They do not have the courage to acknowledge that they are over their heads and ask for help.*

RETURNING TO THE MOTHER SHIP

Ray Hay asked me to come to Stamford to discuss some potential assignments.

Thomas Law, the managing director of the Rank Organization, which produced motion pictures in the United Kingdom, read an article in a scientific journal about the Haloid Company in Rochester, New York, which had developed machines that could make an original-like copy of a document using a patented process called xerography. Law exhibited astute foresight in seeking a joint venture with Haloid in 1956.

Haloid and the Rank Organization formed a joint venture partnership, owned 50 percent by each partner, named Rank-Xerox. It would manufacture and distribute xerographic products in Europe, Africa and Asia.

Haloid reserved the rights for manufacturing and distribution in Latin America.

In 1962, Rank-Xerox entered into a joint venture with Fuji Film, a Japanese photographic film company, to be owned 50 percent by each partner, which would manufacture and distribute xerographic products in the Asia-Pacific area, but excluded the English-speaking countries of Australia, New Zealand, India, Singapore and Hong Kong.

Hay, in his role as executive vice president, was the Xerox liaison officer with Rank-Xerox and served on its board of directors. The Xerox Latin America Division, responsible for the distribution of Xerox products in Central and South America, also reported to Hay.

Ray described two opportunities for my consideration. The first opportunity was to become the number-two man at Rank-Xerox. Hay had not yet worked out the scope of the assignment with the managing director of Rank-Xerox. He first wanted to determine my level of interest.

I was dubious about the role because I would be the only American on the management team, and if I was actually going to be the number-two man in the organization, there would be a number of successful British managers who would resent my insertion. Rank-Xerox was a highly successful business enterprise.

Hay emphasized the experience I would gain in international business. I asked for some time to think about it.

Hay then mentioned that if I did not want to go to Rank-Xerox, I could consider becoming the number-two man in the Xerox Latin America Division located in Stamford.

My impression of South and Central America was that they were not the end of the world, but clearly, you could see the end of the world from any point of land in the area. I immediately turned down the opportunity.

I had been out of the mainstream business for three years; I wanted to return to the mother ship.

Kathie and I discussed the Rank-Xerox opportunity and concluded that we did not want to take the children to live in England. I informed Hay that I was not interested in the opportunity; he responded that he would find me a position in CDD, the mother ship.

Archie McCardell had installed Jim O'Neil as the president of CDD. O'Neil had been the CFO of Ford Germany and reported to McCardell when he was CFO of Ford Europe. I never understood this appointment. Xerox was a technical company; the president of the mainstream business should have been someone who was innovative and had an engineering background. In my opinion, the appointment of a finance person whose orientation was to control an organization was a mistake.

I first met O'Neil on an American Airlines flight from Los Angeles to New York City when I was with MDO. He was traveling with a contemporary of mine when I was director of marketing with CDD, who introduced us.

American was flying the new Boeing 707 commercial jets on its transcontinental flights. In 1970, American had a piano bar in the rear of the first-class cabin. It consisted of six barstools located to the rear of the piano and two cocktail tables with three chairs along each bulkhead of the aircraft.

The three of us met in the bar for a drink. O'Neil began to impress me with his self-importance. I found him to be an arrogant person and took an immediate dislike to him. I never understood why he needed to impress me with his superiority.

O'Neil later called me. He did not ask me to come to Rochester to discuss a new position within the CDD organization. He offered me a position reporting to the director of marketing, a position I had been in three years before. It was three pay grades below my pay grade at the time, that of a division vice president. It was an insult. O'Neil explained to me that the position would enable me to reorient myself to Xerox marketing. I had been a branch manager, a regional manager and the director of product marketing; I could write the manual on Xerox marketing.

I refused the assignment. Three days later, O'Neil called and informed me that he was terminating my employment with Xerox.

I said some harsh and inappropriate words followed by, "You cannot fire me; I do not work for you. If anyone is going to fire me, it will have to be McCardell!" I hung up the phone.

I called both McCardell and Hay and asked for a meeting in Stamford at their convenience. They met with me separately. They had obviously rehearsed their responses. After I unloaded on them that O'Neil's offer of the position reporting to the director of marketing was not only insulting but totally unnecessary as my knowledge of Xerox marketing was far greater than O'Neil's would ever be, they each escorted me to their office door and informed me that I was going to work for O'Neil and that he would be back to me in a few days.

VICE PRESIDENT OF FIELD ENGINEERING

O'Neil called and offered me the newly created position of vice president of field engineering. The position was created by removing the Field Engineering organization from the Research and Development department and removing the technical service organization from Roy La Hue's sales department.

The new structure had to be the work of Ray Hay; O'Neil was not creative enough to have thought through the benefits of creating such an organization.

The Field Engineering organization within the R&D department was under the leadership of Ed Finein, a highly capable engineering manager who had responsibility for 800 engineers working on designing replacement components and parts for new and existing products to improve reliability and reduce our service costs.

Joe Trumpeter, who had been the service manager in the Los Angeles branch in 1964 when I was the branch manager, was now in charge of the 6,000-person national technical service organization.

The operating budget for this new organization was the largest line item on the Xerox profit and loss statement. We were expending10percent of Xerox's revenue. Only Manufacturing spent more money, and because the machines were rented and capitalized, that cost was recorded on the balance sheet as an asset.

O'Neil viewed technical service as a cost center, not an opportunity center. He expected me to control the costs of the department. He did not assign any objectives to be achieved. It was clear to me that he did not expect any creativity or innovation.

I relied on my Marine Corps training: If they do not give you a hill to take, create a hill! I intended to make Field Engineering a force.

O'Neil and I were not off to a good start.

I requested that Bob Verhey and the two analysts who worked for him at MDO be transferred to Field Engineering from Finance. I convinced O'Neil that to achieve cost reductions, I needed a financial analysis team reporting directly to me. He arranged for the transfer.

I was impressed with the amount of data that both Finein's and Trumpeter's organizations accumulated and cataloged. My objective was to determine how we could use this data to improve Xerox's profitability.

McCardell and O'Neil had populated CDD's senior management with Ford executives. Jack Goldman, a Ford research executive, was made the head of Research and Development, and Don Lennox, a Ford plant manager, was brought in to head up the CDD Manufacturing organization.

La Hue, the CFO of CDD, the head of Marketing and I were the only employees in management who had been at CDD three years before when I departed for ISD.

Joe Trumpeter's organization had performance data for every region, branch and individual service personnel within the branch, starting with the response time it took for a service person to arrive at a customer location after a customer called the dispatch office. We had information on the time and cost to perform emergency maintenance (EM) and preventive maintenance (PM) for each service person by machine, by branch and by region. We had ratios of the time individual service personnel spent on performing maintenance, traveling, administration and training. We knew the cost of service as a percentage of revenue being expended by territory, branch and region.

Trumpeter's organization had developed a secondary reporting system that employed 10 percent of the field organization, about 600 people, to complete an additional report for the installation of each new piece of equipment shipped from the factory. We were able to compare our actual time to install with the installation time used in the preparation of the annual operating budget.

The challenge we faced was how to use this information to improve customer service, reduce cancellations, reduce our operating expenses and improve the company's profitability.

I determined we could become a force in improving Xerox's profitability. We were going to raise the performance bar for field engineering and national service.

Our first encounter was with Manufacturing and their failure to assemble equipment properly. Trumpeter's organization had generated data showing that wiring and components were being installed improperly, which necessitated more time and money for Technical Service to install the equipment. The problems existed across all product lines. The data showed that 1) the assembly of machines was sloppy at best, and 2) manufacturing quality control (QC) was not performing its role in identifying these failures and taking corrective action.

Trumpeter's organization had monthly meetings with plant management, Manufacturing Engineering and QC. The data we provided to Manufacturing would enable them to identify the assembly station, the shift and the personnel who failed to assemble or install the component properly.

I attended these meetings. Lennox did not. Time went by, and the situation did not improve.

I invited Lennox to have lunch. I politely explained to him that his organization's inability to assemble equipment properly was costing the company millions of dollars. He asked me to explain what was occurring with the installations that were creating the increased costs for national service. He listened intently, and after hearing my explanation, he exclaimed, "Bob, what you are talking about is 'dealer prep!'"

I had observed my father's purchase of our first family car in 1946. The routine was for a buyer to select and pay for the automobile and return in three days to take possession of the vehicle and drive it away. The dealer performed maintenance on the car to make it operative before it could be delivered to the customer. The U.S. auto industry referred to this activity as "dealer prep."

The entry of Toyota Motors, the Japanese automaker known for its quality, into the U.S. car market in 1958 would cause Ford, GM and Chrysler to make significant changes to their manufacturing processes, but in the 1970s, they were still shipping uncompleted automobiles to their dealers.

I had to educate Lennox on Xerox's distribution practices. I informed him that we did not have a dealer network; we shipped directly to the customer from the factory via a private drayage firm. For the most sophisticated machines, we planned to have the machine operating properly within 20 minutes. I emphasized that the installation time was included in the operating specifications for the machine. Xerox was serious about customer satisfaction. We could not afford to have a canvas spread out on the floor outside a vice president's office, covered with components removed from the machine, with a technician working on perfecting the unit's operation for an hour and a half!

Lennox had never received any kind of orientation on Xerox's marketing strategy and the favorable relationship we had established with our customers. Furthermore, his boss knew nothing about Xerox's marketing strategy and therefore could not recognize Manufacturing's poor performance or provide direction to Lennox to correct the problem. The poor QC performance was not only tolerated at Ford; it was part of their culture.

Manufacturing's failure to assemble machines properly was costing Xerox millions of dollars of profits. Lennox assured me he would look into the problem.

Time went by with no improvement in Manufacturing's QC. I introduced the problem to O'Neil. He assured me he would correct it. Months went by, and the Manufacturing personnel attending our monthly quality meeting did not present any plans for improving Manufacturing's QC.

Whenever Ray Hay came to Rochester for meetings, he would arrange to have lunch with me and would ask what challenges I was facing. I outlined the problem with Manufacturing and the opportunity to improve profits if Manufacturing would face its QC problems and assemble machines properly.

That afternoon, I was summoned to O'Neil's office. Ray Hay attended, and Don Lennox, whose office was in the plant in Henrietta, was on the speakerphone. Hay informed Lennox that he wanted to see an action plan to correct the QC problems in two weeks and ordered Lennox to attend the monthly QC meetings with Trumpeter's people until Trumpeter was satisfied the problem had been corrected. Ray Hay was an action-oriented manager and an experienced Xerox marketer.

O'Neil was embarrassed. Lennox was annoyed. I became even more unpopular with O'Neil, but profits were improving, and Field Engineering was becoming recognized as a force.

THE TURNING POINTS IN MY RELATIONSHIP
WITH JIM O'NEIL

Jim O'Neil had a strange way of managing his organization. It was different from anyone for whom I had worked in the Marine Corps, PPG Industries or Xerox. He did not conduct staff meetings that included all of his direct reports. I was not included in meetings he conducted with Manufacturing and R&D. He did not conduct engineering reviews for products under development that included all senior management who could provide valuable input.

Ed Finein's engineers, who were working on the reliability and cost to service a new product referred to as the X5000, which when launched was expected to double Xerox revenues within three years, determined that the design for some mechanical and electronic components would fail at a rate that would double the service cost to maintain the machine compared with the cost to maintain our current products. National service was expending $70 million annually to maintain the current machines. This cost was 10 percent of revenue.

Finein's engineers, working with Verhey's analysts, determined the cost to service the X5000 was going be 20 percent of the expected revenue. The expense ratio in the business plan called for a service cost not to exceed 10 percent.

Finein informed me that the manager of Product Development within R&D had ignored his demands for a redesign. I suggested we have a meeting with the program manager. We presented our data concerning the high failure rates of components and the financial analysis that estimated the cost to maintain the machine would be 20 percent of revenue. He was reluctant to take any action.

I asked for a meeting with Jack Goldman, the head of R&D. He included his manager of Product Development. We made our presentation. Goldman's reaction was that a doubling of the service cost to service a machine that was going to double CDD's revenue was not a significant event, and he had no intention of initiating redesign activity.

I met with O'Neil privately. I used the technique of index modeling rather than using large numbers in the billions of dollars. I was able to illustrate that the extraordinary costs to service the X5000 were going to reduce Xerox's pretax profit margin by five percent.

I predicted this would result in a decline in Xerox's market value.

I informed him that Finein's engineers had created re-designs for a majority of the high-failure components that would require limited additional engineering to incorporate into the engineering model. Finein's recommendations were being ignored.

O'Neil understood the financial impact the high failure rates were going to have on the P&L and the stock price. He would call a meeting with R&D, Program Management, Manufacturing and Finance to implement the X5000 redesign.

I introduced him to the Phased Program Planning we had adopted at ISD and that I'd employed at MDO. He was impressed.

I also suggested he terminate the head of Program Management because he lacked the courage to fulfill the requirements of his position.

IBM was the primary computer vendor to Xerox, but when Xerox acquired Scientific Data Systems and announced to the world that SDS would be developing and marketing business computers, the relationship with IBM soured. IBM informed Xerox that they would continue to maintain the current equipment, but upgrades to the installed equipment and replacement equipment would not be available.

IBM then initiated the development of a line of copiers and duplicators to compete with Xerox.

In April 1970, IBM launched its first copier/duplicator product: a high-speed duplicator designed to penetrate the high-end volume of the copier/duplicator market. The image quality and speed of the machine were not a threat, but their pricing plan posed a serious threat to Xerox. The IBM pricing plan called for a monthly rental of the machine that was competitive with Xerox's pricing and a cost per copy that was also competitive with Xerox pricing. But, after generating 100,000 copies in a month, additional copies for the remainder of the month were to be free!

O'Neil called a meeting to discuss a response to the IBM pricing plan. La Hue, Product Marketing, Finance and Field Engineering were present.

The head of Product Marketing, a position I held three years earlier, kept pounding the table and exclaiming that IBM's behavior was irrational and predicting they would be out of business in a year. He suggested there be no response to the threat.

Joe Trumpeter's database had volumes of data on machine populations and further classifications by volumes of copies. I quietly asked Joe for the population of high-speed duplicators generating volumes in excess of 100,000 copies and asked Bob Verhey for an estimate of the revenue per copy. I made three swift calculations on my pocket slide rule and announced:

"Their behavior is not irrational. They desire to hinder our efforts to enter the business computer market and this pricing action has just reduced our free cash flow by an estimated $150 million annually.

"Marketing had better develop a plan to defend this market. Finein's organization will acquire several IBM machines and determine the failure rate of the machine in excess of 100,000 copies per month. We may find we have an advantage here in lower emergency maintenance (EM) requests in that high-volume sector. We can develop benefits for the customers that can be used by our salespeople to defend that population."

O'Neil just stared at me. He seemed to suddenly come to the realization that I possessed astute business acumen. Our relationship improved dramatically. He began inviting me to lunch; he invited me to play tennis after work. But we did not socialize. I kept my distance from him.

I had adopted an adage during my career: You cannot learn anything about improving your business standing at the base of the flagpole at corporate headquarters. An effective leader is in the field and in his factories engaging with the people who satisfy customers. The adage also extended to visiting with customers and vendors.

I insisted that Joe Trumpeter, Ed Finein and their direct reports spend time in the field.

Xerox had three branches in Manhattan. The travel expenses for each of the branches exceeded the budget, and the vehicle maintenance expense was the core cause. This was difficult to understand because a high percentage of the Manhattan service territories were composed of, say, 10 floors in a high-rise office building.

The national service personnel whose territories were in high-rise office buildings arrived in Manhattan via subway. Xerox rented space in each high-rise for the inventory of parts and the storage of the service personnel's tools. These service personnel had no need for an automobile.

No one at headquarters knew the cause of the unfavorable performance. I arranged for a visit to one of the Manhattan branches. The branch technical service manager could not identify the cause of the unfavorable variance from the plan.

My routine for visiting a branch was to request the assembly of 10 of the best service personnel for a meeting at 4:30 p.m.

On my way to the branch, I would stop and pick up two cases of beer to be available during the meeting with the service reps.

I would open the meeting with the statement: "We are here to learn how to improve our customer service and reduce our costs. Therefore, we want to learn what changes we should make in the conduct of our business that will improve customer satisfaction and reduce our costs."

The suggestions that came forth in these meetings were numerous and enlightening.

During our visit to New York, I asked the question: "How many of you use cars in your territories, and can you help us determine why the vehicle maintenance costs are so high?

The response from one employee was profound, "Sir, you provide us with black cars with black tires (white-walled tires were very popular on personal cars in the 1970s). The gang members in New York identify these cars as New York City detective cars, and they slash our tires. I have had to replace tires three times this year."

Joe Trumpeter had a section manager who managed our fleet of 5,000 automobiles. On returning to Rochester, we met with him and discussed how to either stop the leasing of black cars equipped with black tires or, if we were compelled to accept a certain number of these cars in our fleet, whether we could direct the delivery of black cars to civil neighborhoods like Beverly Hills in Los Angeles and Grosse Pointe in Detroit. The problem was solved.

On a visit to the Cleveland branch, Ed Finein was so impressed with the ideas put forth by a service employee—regarding the location and orientation of components in a particular model that would reduce the time to replace or repair the item—that on returning to Rochester, he created the position of technical associate in his department.

The associate would work in field engineering in the morning and in the afternoon attended the Rochester Institute of Technology, where Finein had worked out an exclusive program that enabled the candidate to obtain a degree in engineering. Finein would fill four associate positions over the next three months.

Each Xerox branch had a call center that was staffed with dispatchers who had responsibility for several service territories. Customers were provided with direct phone numbers to their dispatcher. The protocol was for the customer to call the center and request emergency maintenance for a specific machine. We did not have cell phones in the early 1970s. The dispatcher had no way of initiating communication directly with a service rep. The service rep called the center first thing each morning; the rep again called the center when he arrived at his first customer's location and again when he completed the maintenance.

The dispatcher recorded the time the request for service was initiated by the customer and the time the service rep arrived on location. This is how we measured response time, which we believed was essential for maintaining a high level of customer satisfaction. Our objective was to achieve a response time of one and a half hours or less.

Our response time objective played a critical role in the allocation of the number of service reps assigned to each branch and the branch's organization of territories. The machine population and the volume of copies generated by those machines had to be considered in the design of territories.

The dispatchers were provided with the identification of machines in their territories with the projected volume that would require preventive maintenance (PM) during each week. The dispatchers would then direct the service reps to plan for PM to be performed during the week.

On a visit to a Los Angeles branch, a service representative suggested during one of our after-work meetings that he knew his customer's needs and the critical times to perform a PM better than the dispatcher. He resented the dispatcher telling him how to manage his territory.

Service reps communicated with the call center either by using a pay phone or a customer's phone. There were no cell phones.

We had no capability for the customer to communicate directly with their assigned service rep. The Los Angeles service representative was not suggesting we eliminate the call center; he wanted the freedom to manage his territory. He was claiming ownership of his territory. Pride was at work here, and Trumpeter and I felt there might be an opportunity to improve customer satisfaction and possibly reduce the cost of our call centers.

We organized a task group that included one of our best branch technical service managers, the best service rep in the branch and one of Verhey's financial analysts from HQ. The objective was to develop a concept that would work and then try it in one territory. If we could make it work, we could roll the concept out nationally. Communication would be our biggest challenge, and I suggested that the Information Systems Division might be able to provide a solution. Radio dispatch was being used by police departments. I urged the task force to follow up on this.

We were breaking ground on a human resource concept to be known eventually as employee involvement (EI). We believed that if service reps could take ownership of their territory and manage it, their pride would escalate, they would be more productive, our costs would decline, customer satisfaction would increase and cancellations would decline. It would be a big win!

Roy La Hue's sales organization conducted two-day major account visits to Rochester in conjunction with Research and Development. The primary objectives were to solicit from the customers their future needs for improved communication and to show customers new products Xerox had under development and solicit input about enhancements for these products.

Ed Finein attended these customer meetings; I did not play a role in the visits.

Major customer visits included corporate customers the size of Dow Chemical, AT&T, General Motors and Chevron.

The General Service Administration of the U.S. Government, NASA, the FBI, the CIA and the U.S. Army, Navy and Air Force were invited guests.

On the occasion of a visit by the commandant of the Marine Corps, Leonard F. Chapman, Jr., and his staff, La Hue invited me to attend the formal farewell dinner. La Hue placed me on the left side of the commandant for dinner. La Hue occupied the seat to the right of the commandant.

During the dinner conversation, the commandant inquired as to the unit in which I'd served and the dates of my service.

I responded that I was a member of the 12th Marine Regiment, Third Marine Division, my service was from 1955 to 1957 and I had the good fortune to work for an outstanding commanding officer, Major Bill Siegler.

Later in the book, I will familiarize the reader with Major Bill Siegler, my commanding officer in the 12th Marines, who walked into my office, placed a file folder on my desk and stated, "Unfuck this!"

The commandant responded that Colonel William Siegler was a current member of his staff, and the only reason he did not visit Rochester was that he was retiring from the Corps. "We are conducting his retirement dinner tomorrow evening."

The commandant provided me with Colonel Siegler's direct line.

After the dinner, I gathered La Hue and Trumpeter and informed them of the management qualities of Bill Siegler and that he was retiring the next day. I said I wanted to extend him an offer of employment. La Hue and Trumpeter agreed. La Hue commented, "Find out where he wants to live, and we will make it happen."

I telephoned Siegler the next morning, introduced myself and told him about my conversation with the commandant the night before. We renewed our friendship. I told him I could offer him a management position in just about any major city in the United States. Bill informed me that he had promised his wife that on his retirement, they would take up residence in her hometown in North Dakota.

I do not remember the name of the town, but I do recall the closest Xerox branch was 200 miles away. I could not make it work. I thanked him for the excellent training and development he had provided to me some 13 years earlier and wished him good fortune in his retirement. Semper Fi!

From the time I first joined Xerox in 1962 and received my orientation to the company as the technical service manager reporting to Roy La Hue, the western regional manager, and then subsequently as branch manager in Los Angeles and regional manager in Detroit, I had been disappointed with the training facilities used for our technical service representatives.

Typically, we rented warehouse facilities, classrooms were partitioned off within the warehouse, there were no ceilings in the classrooms and fluorescent lights were hung from the ceiling of the warehouse. The environment was not conducive to a superior educational experience.

The students were housed in a local motel with a restaurant. They were provided with a daily per diem for their meals.

Because the motels were located in a warehouse district, there was no opportunity for the students to walk to a bar for a beer or to play a game of pool.

I felt the service reps deserved better treatment. The teaching environment was not up to Xerox's standards. Sales Training had entered into a long-term lease for the Sheraton Hotel in Fort Lauderdale, FL. The hotel was across the street from the beach on the Atlantic. Restaurants, bars and movie theaters were within walking distance of the hotel. Sales training was a pleasant experience. The service training was not a pleasant experience. I was now in a position to improve it.

Ed Finein's engineers who were working with R&D product development on the X5000 were also working with Joe Trumpeter's Training department to develop the training curriculum for the product. The X5000 would be employing a far more sophisticated level of electronics than had been used in Xerox's product lines. Trumpeter's training managers expected that training of representatives to service the X5000 was going to take eight weeks versus the four weeks required to train representatives on the high-speed duplicators we were then marketing.

We were faced with a potential 100-percent increase in our training costs for the X5000. We were operating five training centers in the United States. I formed a task group, led by Bob Verhey, to determine if we could sufficiently reduce our training costs by creating one national training center that could provide a satisfactory return on the investment in the center.

Verhey's task group's concept study revealed that the cost savings generated by having one national training center would provide an adequate return on this essential capital investment. The capital investment required for an essential need to support our business would not be required to meet the 40-percent IRR hurdle required for new products.

The transportation cost study revealed that Cincinnati would be the lowest-cost site followed by St. Louis and then Dulles Airport in northern Virginia.

Our design requirements were modest. We needed classrooms, laboratories for training and offices for the management and instructors. We required hotel rooms for the students, a cafeteria and dining facilities. I insisted on lounge facilities to include a library, TVs and space for ping-pong and pool tables. We also provided outdoor basketball and tennis courts.

We worked with Corporate Real Estate to determine the size of the site we would require and the estimated construction costs.

Corporate Real Estate determined that we would need 50 acres of land to accommodate the facility and provide the school with some degree of privacy. Furthermore, they determined that the lowest land and construction cost would be in northern Virginia.

We worked with Marriott International to determine the costs of operating the facility. Marriott's proposals confirmed that they could provide the lowest operating costs in northern Virginia.

We engaged a local real estate agent to locate suitable sites. We focused our search west of Alexandria, Virginia, which was west of Dulles Airport on Virginia State Road 7, also known as the Leesburg Pike. In 1971, this area was all farmland.

We made our investment presentation to Jim O'Neil and the CDD Finance group. I had three 50-acre parcels available for his consideration. He endorsed the concept and requested I arrange for a helicopter tour of the three sites I was recommending.

My first choice was a 50-acre site owned by U.S. Steel. It was zoned industrial, but on three sides of the parcel was residential housing that had been developed by U.S. Steel. O'Neil informed me that he did not want to risk having 500 Xerox technical representatives "raping, pillaging and burning" nearby residential communities. He instructed me to find a 100-acre site farther west on the Leesburg Pike. He wanted a buffer of land surrounding the school. We took an option on a 100-acre parcel.

We had to brief and gain the concurrence of Ray Hay, the executive vice president Jim O'Neil reported to, on the investment opportunity before going to Corporate for approval.

Hay embraced the concept but thought the training center should be located in Rochester, which he identified as being the technical Mecca of xerography.

I strongly objected to his idea. Although I was uncertain of how I should respond, I stated that the cost of the land, the construction and the operating costs of the facility were going to be higher in Rochester. I protested that 60 percent of our technical representatives resided in the southern portions of the U.S. We would have to have wardrobes of parkas, sweaters, wool hats, gloves and snow boots to issue to those representatives on their arrival in Rochester in the winter. My worst fear was that we would have to mail the clothing to them before traveling to Rochester and then have them send the clothing back to the school on their return home. Inventory shrinkage would be a major problem.

O'Neil stated that we should present northern Virginia as the preferred location to Corporate and that I should obtain all of the information I could put together to counter Hay's concept of locating the school in Rochester.

I never thought I would see the day when I was allied with O'Neil against my friend and mentor, Ray Hay.

I confirmed that the land, construction and operating costs would be higher in Rochester, and I obtained the average number of days the Rochester airport was closed each year due to bad weather between December 1 and March 31, which would disrupt our training schedules. We were prepared to counter Hay's idea.

AN OPPORTUNITY FOR GREATER RESPONSIBILITY

I received a call from an executive recruiter informing me of an opportunity for greater responsibility with a company in San Francisco. He immediately had my attention.

In November 1955 while serving in the Marine Corps, I spent 12 days in San Francisco awaiting transportation to Japan. For a boy who grew up in the Monongahela Valley near Pittsburgh, I thought I had died and gone to heaven. I wanted to live in that city.

::::::::

I met the recruiter in Washington, D.C. At the end of the interview, he identified his client as the Fibreboard Corporation, a paper and forest products company.

I began to review the company's financial statements. My assessment was that the company had been on an acquisition binge in the Forest Products division; the balance sheet was overleveraged, the company's cash flow was negative, profitability was declining and, if the current rate of negative cash flow continued, the company with no further sources of bank credit would hit the wall in about 90 days.

XEROX UNIVERSITY

O'Neil, the CDD financial officer, Trumpeter and I made the presentation for the one central training center to Corporate in Stamford. Peter McCullough, Archie McCardell, Ray Hay, Joe Flavin, the CFO and Harold Green, the head of Corporate Real Estate, attended the meeting.

We completed our presentation; Ray Hay was the first to respond, introducing his support for the concept but recommending the school be located in Rochester.

Peter McCullough interrupted him, stating, "Ray, we have too many of our assets located in Rochester. I prefer the northern Virginia location." End of discussion!

McCullough continued, "Bob, great concept and an excellent financial presentation and justification. I would like to expand on this concept. I believe we should create a Xerox University, a campus where we could conduct our sales, service and management training."

He turned to Harold Green of Corporate Real Estate and stated, "Harold, I want you to assume responsibility for the university project. Bring me a recommendation for several world-class architects to design the buildings and the campus."

He then addressed me: "Bob, you have the relationship with the real estate agent; I want you to obtain 1,000 acres of land for the campus. Work closely with Harold."

I met with the real estate agent in Washington. I have never seen a happier face than his when I told him we would require a thousand acres of land. We had to focus our search farther west on the Leesburg Pike.

A week later, the agent called to inform me that he'd found a 500-acre site that was for sale, located adjacent to a 2,000-acre site owned by IBM that was being held in their land bank. The agent thought that perhaps IBM would be willing to sell 500 acres of their land to Xerox.

I contacted Harold Green and gave him the parcel number of the IBM land; he responded that he would inquire about whether IBM would sell 500 acres of their land.

The next day, our agent called me and stated, "Something strange is happening down here. Someone is exercising options to purchase every large piece of land for five miles east and west of the 500-acre site I recommended to you, including that site."

I suspected that IBM was behind this activity. I informed Green; he called me back in 15 minutes to inform me that he had spoken with his counterpart at IBM and was told that IBM did not wish to have Xerox as a corporate neighbor and requested that we look elsewhere for a location.

Jim O'Neil was furious when I informed him of IBM's position. Green called and informed me that McCullough was angry and instructed me to locate a 2,000-acre site farther west.

We found a 2,000-acre parcel just outside the town limits of Leesburg, Virginia. Green and I walked the property with our agent. Green approved the site; Xerox purchased the property.

Leesburg is approximately 50 miles west of Alexandria, the original location of our search for the 50-acre property.

I was invited to San Francisco for meetings with Fibreboard representatives. The executive recruiter informed me that the meetings had gone well.

Still, I was concerned about the financial condition of the company. I was going to need superior financial analysis capabilities to discover the root causes of the poor performance. I spoke to Bob Verhey in confidence about my possible departure from Xerox and inquired if he and his two analysts would join me. All three of them agreed to come with me to Fibreboard. They were up to the challenge and eager to get back to California.

I received pushback concerning the hiring of Verhey and his analysts; I took the position that not accepting my proposal was a deal breaker. The company accepted my proposal.

I informed O'Neil of my resignation and asked to be relieved of my responsibilities in two weeks. I recommended that Ed Feinen be promoted as my replacement. I informed O'Neil that I had recruited Bob Verhey and his analysts to accompany me to Fibreboard and assured him I would not recruit additional Xerox employees. He was okay with this.

O'Neil said he regretted I was departing and encouraged me to reconsider.

Ray Hay flew into Rochester and encouraged me to stay with Xerox. He asked if I had examined the company's financial statements. He stated that the company might have to file for bankruptcy.

During the second week before my departure, Jim O'Neil's administrative assistant called and asked if I would set aside two hours to visit with David Kearns, a new hire on the corporate staff, who was being oriented to Xerox.

Kearns had been the vice president of Marketing with IBM. I told him about the role I had created for Field Engineering and how the organization was contributing to improving Xerox's profitability. I told him how we had raised the performance bar for the CDD headquarters and the field organization. I explained to him the critical role the organization was playing in raising the performance bar within Manufacturing and R&D.

After our meeting, he mentioned that he was aware that I had resigned. He went on to say that he had been informed at Stamford headquarters that I was considered to be a superior manager and a future leader at Xerox. He said he was impressed with my management style and urged me to reconsider my resignation.

I thanked him and said I thought the time was right for me to move on.

Ed Finein's and Joe Trumpeter's organizations were respected and were making substantial contributions to Xerox's profitability. Each associate in the organizations was proud to be a member of the team. Field Engineering had become a force. It had taken only 10 months to achieve that recognition!

Six months after my departure, David Kearns was named president and CEO of Xerox, replacing Peter McCullough, who moved up to chairman of the board. It was the second time that McCullough had gone outside the organization to recruit a senior officer. First, he recruited McCardell as president and COO, and on the second occasion, he recruited Kearns to be the CEO.

McCardell and Hay departed Xerox within months of Kearns' appointment. McCardell went to International Harvester as CEO and Hay to Ling-Temco-Vought (LTV) as CEO. LTV was a conglomerate engaged in aerospace, steel manufacturing, pharmaceuticals and sporting goods.

Within three years McCardell and I would be unemployed, and Hay would be forced to place LTV into bankruptcy.

Bearings

✦ *Whenever you are given responsibility for an organization, never accept the status quo. Observe, measure and recognize substandard performance.*

Initiate change; act and raise the performance bar. Knowledge is power.

✦ *When you are appointed to a senior level of management, you not only have the responsibility to improve the performance of your organization. You have an obligation to stimulate improved performance in your peer management organizations. This activity requires courage!*

✦ *If you find yourself in the position of working for a supercilious boss, set your own goals and achieve superior results. In time, you will be recognized as an elite performer and hopefully, bring about change in the management practices of your boss.*

✦ *Take care of your people. Provide them with training and education, provide them with career advancement opportunities, compensate them well and provide them with a comfortable work environment. Allow your people to take ownership of their responsibilities. Create an elite organization, one in which they will be proud to serve.*

✦ *Take care of yourself! Exercise and maintain a healthy diet. An effective leader requires stamina and clear thinking to achieve superior results. Your people are counting on you; they have entrusted you with their careers. Maintain your good health.*

HERITAGE AND MY EARLY LIFE

I was born and raised in Swissvale, Pennsylvania, a suburb of Pittsburgh on the Monongahela River. From Swissvale to McKeesport, a distance of 16 miles, the Monongahela was lined on both sides with steel mills. Located on the east side of the river, Swissvale was the home of the Currie Furnace Mill, which extended into the neighboring community of Rankin. The Edgar Thompson Works of United States Steel (USS) was located in Braddock; the mill covered 176 acres. Steel mills are mammoth structures. A blast furnace is eight stories high, and the smallest of mills operated four furnaces.

On the west side of the river, the USS Homestead Mill covered 258 acres. At one time, it was the largest steel mill in the world. During WWII, the U.S. government executed the right of eminent domain and acquired 8,000 residences to provide acreage for expansion of the mill.

Eleven steel mills were operating between Swissvale and McKeesport. In 1942, during World War II, these mills produced more steel than at any other location in the world. The mills operated 24/7s producing the steel to build the ships and tanks required to win WWII.

The prevailing winds were from west to east. Steel production generated smoke and soot, a black carbonaceous substance produced during the imperfect combustion of coal in the blast furnaces, which descended on the communities located east of the mills.

Because of that soot, the Monongahela Valley was described as: "Hell with the lid off!"

The electric clothes dryer had not yet been invented in the 1940s, yet in the Monongahela Valley, laundry could not be hung outside to dry as it would become black from the falling soot. Clothes were dried on clotheslines strung back and forth across residents' basements. Swissvale was a dirty community; the air was unhealthy to breathe.

I was born in 1932 during the height of the Great Depression, but the event that dominated my childhood was WWII. On Sunday, December 7, 1941, when the Japanese attacked our military bases in Pearl Harbor, Hawaii, it forced the United States into the Second World War. I hung maps of Europe, the Middle East and Asia on my bedroom walls. I placed pins in the maps locating our early defeats and eventually our victories. I kept a daily journal of the events for each theater of the war.

On Fridays, schoolchildren would bring coins to school to purchase War Stamps. Ten-cent stamp books contained enough pages to accumulate 250 stamps, and when the book was filled, it could be exchanged for a $25 War Bond redeemable with interest at the end of the war—assuming we would win!

My father was employed by Bell Telephone of Pennsylvania.

He was the youngest of seven children and the only male in the family to receive a college education. His three brothers worked in the steel mills. He was extremely fortunate to be employed during the Great Depression.

John McLaughlin, my grandfather, had immigrated from Ireland in 1880. I have no memory of him; he died when I was two years old.

Ellen Claugherty, my grandmother, immigrated to the United States from Ireland in 1882. She married John McLaughlin in 1886. My grandmother could not read or write, but she was a shrewd businesswoman. She acquired residential real estate in Swissvale and Rankin. She saw to it that her three daughters received college educations, an extraordinary accomplishment for the times.

My mother, Louise Hodder, and her family immigrated to the United States from Newfoundland in 1923. She was 17 years old and the oldest of eight children.

James Hodder first emigrated from England to Newfoundland circa 1816. He settled in Twillingate, married, and with his wife, had two sons, George and James. James married Susan Linfield and had eight children. My mother's father, Alexander, was the youngest child in the family.

Alexander's father, "Skipper Jim" as he was called, was a fisherman; eventually, he became the owner of a small fleet of fishing vessels that were skippered by his sons. He owned a wharf and a general store.

In the spring when the ice melted in the Twillingate harbor and the North Atlantic was navigable, the fishing fleets would set sail for the ice fields 300 miles to the northeast to participate in the seal fishery. These vessels had no auxiliary engines, and navigating through the ice floes was dangerous.

On returning from the seal fishery, Skipper Jim would refit his vessels and set sail for the waters off the coast of Labrador to fish for cod. The Labrador fishery would end in September.

After the close of the fishing season, Skipper Jim would engage in "coasting" until October. He would sail the east coast of Newfoundland and venture south as far as Halifax, Nova Scotia, trading his summer catch of dried cod for dry goods and tools, which he then sold in his general store.

Skipper Jim's children began to emigrate to Braddock, Pennsylvania. Alexander remained in Twillingate to help his father with the fishing fleet and the general store.

Alexander married Annie Gillett in 1905; she was the ninth child in a family of 11 children. Annie's father, George Gillett, owned three large clipper ships and operated a prosperous trading business.

Alexander purchased a three-masted schooner, which he captained, and named the ship The Alexander G. He transported cargo from the east coast of Newfoundland to St Johns, Newfoundland, Halifax and Boston.

He lost the ship in a violent storm in 1923. All hands survived. The ship was not insured, and Alexander was financially ruined. He followed his brothers to Braddock and took up the trade of masonry; he became a bricklayer.

Alexander's brother, Titus, lived in Swissvale. Louise would visit her cousins in Swissvale and on one visit was introduced to Joe McLaughlin. My parents were married in 1930.

I was dyslexic; it was very difficult for me to read, and I struggled in school. I was not physically coordinated, and in any sandlot "pickup" game, I would be the last player chosen by the two captains. In baseball, I would be placed in right field where I could do the least defensive damage. I always batted last. In football, I would never handle the ball. "McLaughlin, you block!"

The one athletic endeavor for which I received coaching was swimming. My mother insisted that I learn to swim. She was aware of the many drowning deaths of fishermen in Newfoundland and lost a brother to drowning in the Monongahela River after his sailboat capsized.

I became an excellent swimmer; the ability to excel at a sport improved my self-confidence.

I was a Cub Scout and a Boy Scout; our Boy Scout troop leader was a devoted outdoorsman who arranged several camping trips in the wilderness each year. I became very confident in my ability to survive in the wilderness.

I attended Boy Scout summer camp each year. In my third year, I qualified for a position as a junior counselor, and the following year I enjoyed a paying job as a senior counselor. These assignments were my first leadership experiences, and I enjoyed the role.

Because of my swimming ability and the ease at which I passed the test for my life-saving merit badge, I was also offered a paying job as a lifeguard. I enjoyed the responsibility.

In the summer of 1949, I received a driver's license; I was mobile! Two events occurred during that summer that influenced my maturity.

In the 1940s, department stores were required to have a nurse's station to treat customers and employees who might become sick or injured. Florence McLaughlin, my father's sister, was a registered nurse employed as the head nurse at the nurse's station in Kaufmann's department store. Edgar Kaufmann, the owner of the store, was in poor health, and Florence also served as his private nurse. She accompanied him to his summer home, Falling Waters, designed by Frank Loyd Wright, in Mill Run, Pennsylvania, and on his many trips to Europe.

Her involvement with Edgar Kaufmann introduced her to a level of society far above her modest roots in Swissvale.

It was at this higher level of society that she met and eventually married Stanley Rogers, president of the American Shear Knife Company, which manufactured huge knives to cut steel beams. When the United States entered WWII, the U.S. government allotted millions of dollars to Stanley Rogers to expand the capacity of his factory. After the conclusion of WWII, the U.S. was the only source of steel in the world. Most of the mills in Europe and Japan had been destroyed during the war. Stanley became a multimillionaire.

In the summer of 1949 and again in 1950, Florence asked me to drive her and her two sisters, Mary and Elizabeth, to The Homestead, a resort located in Hot Springs, Virginia. Florence purchased the proper clothes for me. I met my aunts for a formal dinner each evening; during the day, I was on my own. I enjoyed all of the activities the resort offered, including lessons in golf and tennis.

Florence's objective was to motivate me to be successful. She told me,

"This can be yours if you are willing to work smart and hard… Strive to succeed!"

I had no idea how I was going to succeed, but the seed of desire had been planted. Florence was the first of three people, besides my parents who had a tremendous influence on my development.

My mother's brother, Clinton, was a bricklayer by trade. He formed his own company, The Hodder Construction Company, which specialized in the replacement of refractory fire brick in blast furnaces. I went to work for Clint as a laborer. He was a tough taskmaster. My mother made it clear to me that failure was not an option.

The mill management demanded to have the blast furnaces back online as soon as possible. Laborers entered the furnaces while they were still hot, erected scaffolding and began to tear out the old brick from the top to the bottom of the furnace. It was hot and dirty work. We had no dust masks; we tied bandannas over our mouths and noses to keep out the dust. The worksite was then ready for the bricklayers. The laborers brought in the refractory brick and mortar, and as the bricklayers progressed, we would erect the scaffolding so the work could continue to the top of the furnace.

I worked for Clint every summer until I graduated from college. The work was hard, the union pay was good, and it was valuable experience. I learned how to work!

I began to read books on the lives and accomplishments of Andrew Carnegie and Henry Clay Frick, the industrialists who developed the coal and steel empires that made Pittsburgh the world's largest producer of steel. I wanted to become an industrialist.

Bearings

- *You can start from nowhere and be the last one chosen for teams but eventually become a recognized leader.*

- *Early in your journey, choose one or two objectives, no matter how vague, to strive for.*

- *Develop a work ethic, learn from tough taskmasters, learn to excel.*

- *Excel in your education.*

- *Read, broaden your horizons, adopt heroes.*

- *Family is of paramount importance; family provides the foundation for your value system.*

MY RITE OF PASSAGE

I graduated from high school in 1950 and was accepted by Purdue University in West Lafayette, Indiana. I was unprepared for college. I did not know how to study. I was undisciplined. I flunked four of the five courses in which I was enrolled during the first semester and was required to repeat those courses in the second semester. Purdue's grading system was based on a 5.0 GPA. I was required to achieve a 3.5 GPA in the second semester, and if I failed to do so, I would be asked to depart the university.

I achieved the 3.5 GPA and was able to continue my education. During the second semester of my freshman year, I was invited to join the Sigma Alpha Epsilon fraternity. I was able to live in the fraternity house in my sophomore year and was elected president of the fraternity.

North Korea invaded South Korea in late June 1950; the United States came to the aid of South Korea and was again engaged in a war. Purdue was a land grant university, and all male students were required to participate in a Reserve Officer Training Corps for two years. I chose the Air Force ROTC. All males of ages 18 to 25 were required to register with the Selective Service. Conscription, more commonly referred to as the "draft," was conducted to enlist males into military service.

If you were enrolled in college, you could be deferred from military service until your graduation.

The Naval ROTC unit at Purdue was a prestigious four-year program. Most of the midshipmen were on scholarships. Upon graduation, the midshipmen were commissioned as ensigns in the U.S. Navy or as Second Lieutenants in the U.S. Marine Corps.

In the 1950s, Purdue was a "dry" campus; no alcoholic beverages were permitted to be consumed on campus. There was only one beer bar in West Lafayette, and the drinking age limit was strictly enforced. Across the Wabash River in Lafayette, however, there were plenty of bars where IDs were seldom checked.

The faculty advisor to our fraternity was Lieutenant Colonel Don M. Beck, the CO of the Naval ROTC unit and a highly decorated WWII Marine. Colonel Beck would periodically meet with me as president of the fraternity. Our meetings took place on Saturday nights, and we would throw down several beers. So much for the "dry" campus.

Colonel Beck introduced me to the Marine Corps Platoon Leaders Course (PLC). Officer candidates would attend training for six weeks in the summer following their sophomore and junior years. Upon graduation, the candidates would be commissioned as second lieutenants and attend Basic School in Quantico, Virginia.

Beck convinced me that I would not be happy being drafted into the Army, Navy or Air Force upon graduation.

I completed all the application paperwork for the program; the next step was to take the physical exam. Beck arranged for a Navy doctor to conduct physical exams on a number of candidates for the PLC program.

The doctor who examined me summoned Beck and me and informed us that he had to disqualify me as I had checked off a box that disclosed I had a "trick knee," the result of a cartilage tear incurred playing sandlot baseball that had not healed properly and caused significant instability.

Colonel Beck asked to see the medical report. The doctor passed the report to him. Beck tore it in half and threw it in the wastebasket. He informed the doctor, "You have never seen McLaughlin!"

The doctor protested. "Colonel, he will be leading 42 men, and if his knee collapses, they will be without a leader."

Beck responded, "We will take care of his knee!"

Beck dismissed the doctor and told me he would have another doctor on campus in a month. He then commanded, "You do not have a trick knee!"

I passed the second physical. I endured a great deal of pain during the first summer of PLC training as a result of the long marches and the constant running. But I never had a knee collapse during my active duty. Exercise cured the problem!

Colonel Beck recommended that I begin running every day and engage in strength training at the gym.

In June of 1952, I received a package of orders and instructions as to how to proceed to Quantico to participate in the PLC program.

We were instructed to arrive at Union Station in Washington, D.C., at an appointed hour. I found myself part of a 50-man group of PLC candidates. The sergeant who welcomed us was cordial and politely asked us to walk with him to the train. We strolled out to the train platform. It would be the last stroll we would take for the next six weeks.

The descent from the railcar onto the platform at the Marine Corps Base Quantico was horrifying! A drill instructor (DI) greeted me wearing a campaign hat, a broad-brimmed hat similar to those worn by the Army cavalry in the Western frontier in the 1800s. A matte black Marine Corps emblem, the Eagle, Globe and Anchor, was in the center of the hat. The brim came within a quarter of an inch of my forehead, but it never touched my person.

In a loud voice, the DI informed me that I was a miserable civilian unworthy of being a Marine. He then declared, "Your ass now belongs to me, and I intend to make you into a Marine. Now, get your ass over to the parking lot and fall in as instructed by the sergeant! Move!"

We were boarded onto buses and driven to Camp Upshur deep in the confines of the training reservation. That afternoon, we were issued our fatigue uniforms, underwear, socks and boots and were marched to our barracks.

Inside the barracks were mattresses, pillows, sheets, pillowcases and a blanket on each bunk. I grabbed an upper bunk; my Boy Scout training had alerted me to the fact that it was more enjoyable to stare at a ceiling than to stare at the springs of a bunk above. I also chose a bunk next to a door to be close to an exit.

The first instruction by the DIs was to illustrate how to make a Marine bed. The blanket was to be so taut that a quarter dropped from a height of 12 inches above the blanket would bounce three inches. I noticed that it required the efforts of two DIs to make the blanket taut and suggested to my bunkmate that we should work together in making our blankets taut.

The following morning, when the bunks were inspected by the DIs, if one bunk failed to pass the three-inch bounce criteria, all bunks were stripped and you started over. In short order, everyone was working in pairs.

The second instruction of the afternoon was devoted to marching. The DIs wanted our heels to dig in, and they wanted to hear one synchronized thud of 42 heels hitting the pavement in unison for every step we took!

We marched off to the mess hall for our evening meal and came to a halt outside the mess hall. Each platoon in the camp had a designated time to eat, and our platoon had to wait until another platoon exited the mess hall before we could enter.

The DI allowed us to stand at ease, but he said there was to be no talking.

Some began to talk anyway. The DI pulled them out of the ranks and instructed them to lay in the street in front of the platoon. Four candidates were in the street when it was announced we could enter the mess hall.

The DI informed us that when he gave the command "Forward march," no one was to miss a stride, and he wanted to hear 38 heels hitting the pavement or the bodies lying in the street. He observed the movement of the platoon over the bodies, and anyone he found breaking stride would be placed on the pavement in front of the platoon when we departed the mess hall. He had our attention!

No one ever spoke again after being instructed to be silent.

The first night was exasperating! Stupidity prevailed; it was a long and painful night.

First, dressed in fatigues, we were instructed how to enter a bunk by the numbers. In my case, occupying an upper bunk, I was expected to enter the bed between the sheets on the count of five and to be asleep on the count of six.

The DI ordered us to get undressed and enter our bunks. He returned in 10 minutes and turned off the lights.

Another 10 minutes went by before he returned. In the darkness, he inquired, "Are all of you people asleep?"

Some idiot responded, "No, sir!"

The DI ordered, "Everyone out of your bunk; fall in at attention at the foot of your bunk!"

The DI, wearing his campaign hat, his back ramrod straight, walked down the center of the barracks, eyes forward. When an irregularity caught his eye, he came to a halt, executed a sharp right or left turn and stepped forward to face his victim.

The first candidate to suffer abuse was stark naked! The DI inquired whether the candidate was "queer." Before the candidate could respond, the DI continued, reciting the federal law that no matter how slight the penetration, sodomy was a federal offense and was punishable by imprisonment for up to 10 years.

He continued his walk and came to a halt at the next offender, who was wearing a pair of yellow pajamas with small bears decorating the garment.

The DI inquired whether the candidate's mother had suggested he pack his PJs. The response was, "Yes, sir". The DI responded, "The Marine Corps does not recruit mama's boys. If the Marine Corps wanted you to sleep in PJs, we would have issued you PJs today."

Both men were marked. They would receive special attention from the DIs for the next six weeks.

Then the DI announced that it was obvious that the platoon could not sleep because we were not tired. What we needed was exercise. He commanded the platoon to get dressed and to fall out on the company street. We marched to the parade field and completed 20 laps at a full run around the field.

We returned to the barracks, climbed into our bunks and the DI turned out the lights. Ten minutes later, he entered the darkened barracks and again inquired if everyone was asleep. Again one idiot replied, "No, sir."

We went through the same punishment of 20 laps around the parade field.

We returned to the barracks; lights out. Ten minutes later, the DI entered the darkened barracks and inquired if his people were asleep. No one spoke up, but one candidate giggled. Once again, we were dressed and on the parade field completing 20 laps.

Again, the DI entered the barracks and inquired, "Are you people asleep?" No one spoke. No one giggled. It was now 0100 hours! Reveille would be at 0500 hours. It was a short night.

On the second day, we were issued our M1 rifles and were instructed on field stripping and cleaning the weapon. Rifle inspection was conducted every morning at 0530 hours. It is not difficult to clean a weapon, but some people could not seem to master the task. They became marked individuals, and the DIs would focus their attention on them.

On subsequent inspections, it did not matter if a candidate's weapon was perfectly clean. The DI was going to find a speck of dirt. When the DI returned the weapon and asked if the private could see the dirt, if the individual responded, "No," the DI commanded, "Drop and give me 20 push-ups!" Their lives became miserable.

We were introduced to close-order drills, which consisted of marching in formation to a cadence while commands were issued by the DI, e.g.

"Right, FACE; Forward, MARCH; Right Turn, MARCH; To the Rear, MARCH." At the same time, marching commands were given indicating the position of your weapon, e.g. "Right Shoulder, ARMS; Left Shoulder, ARMS."

It was difficult that first week. I was surprised by the number of candidates who did not know their right from their left. When the commands were given in rapid succession, such as two sequential commands of "To the Rear, MARCH," some got mixed up and stumbled into others. They were pulled from the ranks and given a punishment of 20 laps around the parade field with their rifle at high port.

I had been exposed to close-order drills during the two years of Air Force ROTC at Purdue. I did not find it difficult to adapt to the intense drilling.

Normally, there were six platoons on the parade field. There would be 15 people completing their punishment on the track surrounding the field. DIs were stationed around the track to ensure the runners were maintaining a fast pace.

The objective of the close-order drill in the Marine Corps is to instill a rapid response to an order. We would complete hours of this drill each day. I hated it! It was boring.

Calisthenics was a daily drill; by the end of the third week, I could easily do 20 pushups.

The obstacle course was a challenge. The 20-foot rope climb was beyond my capability. A candidate had to complete the rope climb hand over hand, touch the top of the wooden structure and then lower himself hand under hand back to the ground. The DIs supervising this obstacle were looking for progress. If they felt you were giving your best effort and making progress from week to week, they would release you from completing the task and instruct you to continue running the course.

Chinese log drills were the most exhausting of all the exercises. The platoon was broken into teams of six; all members of the team were about the same height. One member was designated as the leader and called out the commands.

Telephone poles had been cut into 18-foot sections. Each team completed six over-the-head presses with the pole and then ran 50 yards across the field and passed the pole to another team of six. The team transferring the pole was allowed to collapse on the ground and rest until another team returned with the pole, and the exercise was repeated. This drill would go on for an hour.

It was called a Chinese log drill because the team leader for the initiation of each overhead press and the initiation of the run across the field to transfer the log issued the command, "Gung Ho," which is Chinese for *Pull Together* and the enthusiastic battle cry of the Marine Corps.

Pugil stick fighting, which was taught to promote aggressiveness, was also challenging. I could hold my own competing against someone of my own weight, but when fighting against someone of a heavier weight, I would be driven to the ground in short order.

Forced marches with a full pack consumed a great deal of time beginning in the third week. The initial march was five miles, the next week the distance increased to10miles and on the fifth week, the distance increased to 20 miles. These marches were conducted off-road over difficult terrain.

Often we were running in single file. When you came to an obstacle like a stream crossing, where you had to break stride to maintain your balance, a gap would open up between you and the candidate in front of you.

There were always four DIs on the far side of the stream, and as you emerged from the stream, one of them would run alongside you for 10 yards orally lashing you for allowing a gap to develop between you and the candidate in front of you and ordering you to fill the hole. "Move!"

I am going to relate a tale that illustrates the development of my self-confidence during the six-week program and my willingness to assume risk. It requires courage to assume risk, but if you can achieve a favorable outcome, you become more resilient and confident to take on additional risk.

Being placed on report involved severe punishment for violation of a cardinal rule of discipline. The punishment consisted of falling out on the company street with your rifle and an entrenching tool (a small spade) at dusk. A DI marched the daily group of offenders out through the main gate and into the woods about a mile away where it was pitch-black. The offenders were instructed to dig a trench long enough to accommodate their rifle, place the rifle in the trench and cover it with the dirt.

The offenders were then marched back to camp. They were reminded that they had to be present for roll call just before the command was given for lights out, there would be a rifle inspection at 0530 hours the next morning and no lights were allowed to be on in the barracks after "lights out."

Each individual made his way out the gate, and the group assembled at a location where they thought the rifles had been buried. It took a considerable amount of time to find the location, and everyone participated in the search until all of the weapons were recovered. Cleaning the weapons took place in the heads, which were illuminated at night with a single light bulb hanging in the center of the head.

You wanted to avoid being placed on report. The punishment was pure misery!

It was during a two-day, overnight forced march that we were given a break. I was leaning against a tree and had leaned my rifle against it. A member of our platoon brushed against my rifle, and it fell to the ground. An M1 rifle makes a distinct noise when it hits the ground. A DI heard that noise and confronted me, informing me that a Marine never drops his weapon—a cardinal rule. The DI was not from my platoon. He wrote down my name and serial number and placed me on report for the evening when we returned to base.

I gathered the courage to protest.

The DI responded, "Private, let me tell you something about life. Shit flows downhill, and right now you are standing at the bottom of the hill!"

This was a profound revelation. I made a vow to make my way to the top of the hill. I also vowed to avoid the punishment of burying my rifle when we returned to base.

The DIs rotated the tasks of taking charge of punishment details that involved members of multiple platoons. I was hoping that a DI from another platoon would be in charge of this night's detail. As the candidates to be punished gathered on the company street, I kept moving to the end of the forming column in order to be the farthest away from the woods. When the DI appeared, he was from another platoon; he had never seen me. He gave the commands to form the group into a column. I noticed he did not have a piece of paper with our names on it; he did not take a roll call. He did command that we count off. I was number 16. He seemed happy with the count.

He began marching us to the main gate. The DI was at the head of the column. I was the last man in the column, and when he gave the order for a right turn and was out of sight behind a Quonset hut, I did a 180-degree turn, raised my rifle to high port and began running. I had observed that as long as a candidate was running, a DI never stopped him. However, if you were walking and encountered a DI, you would be challenged to identify yourself and disclose the purpose of your wandering.

I ran around the camp for 20 minutes and then returned to my barracks. Everyone was either cleaning his rifle or shining his boots. I stowed my rifle in my locker and undertook the task of shining my boots. I blended in with the platoon.

I took a calculated risk and got away with it!

You did not want to fall behind on a forced march. Some people did; they could not keep up. Punishment was severe. If a candidate was unable to continue the march and had to be returned to base in a truck, he was gone the next day.

There was no ceremony involved in withdrawing from the program or being asked to resign. When we returned to the barracks at the end of the day, the mattress of the expelled candidate would be rolled up on his bunk, and his locker and footlocker would be empty.

The objective of the six-week program was to break you mentally and physically—to wash you out of the program. I recall that the mattresses of four candidates, representing about 10 percent of the candidates in our platoon, were rolled up during the program. They were victims of FTA—Failure to Adapt.

I developed perceptive skills that were necessary for survival. I became acutely aware of what was going on around me. In any given situation, I envisioned what was going to happen next. I developed a sense of readiness; I was always prepared and on my toes. I discovered that it was easy to excel!

The experience activated circuitry in my brain that had been dormant.

The ethos of the United States Marine Corps changed my life. The summer of 1952 at Quantico was my rite of passage.

✺ Bearings

✦ *A wise man once told me that the Rite of Passage is the event in one's life when you are no longer a drag on your community; you become a contributor, adding value to your community.*

✦ *The Marine Corps boot camp was my Rite of Passage; it was a stress test that activated circuitry in my brain that had been dormant for 20 years. I survived the test and became a contributor. I am not suggesting that everyone join the Marine Corps to complete their Rite of Passage. As an example, you can achieve this milestone by completing a challenging college education.*

✦ *Whatever challenge you choose to take to complete your Rite of Passage, you must extend yourself to succeed, your resolve to succeed must be tested and you must distinguish yourself from others in your community.*

✦ *Develop your perceptive skills, be alert, listen, observe what is taking place in any given situation and orient yourself to take action!*

✦ *Leadership requires taking calculated risks! Take risks; if you are successful, you will gain confidence. If you fail, determine why you failed and be resilient. Try again. Do not give up. You will make mistakes. You must continue to advance toward your objective.*

✦ *Avoid pain, avoid losses, THINK about the actions required to achieve the state of affairs you desire to achieve, your objective, and evaluate the RISKS before taking action. If you think you can achieve your objective, pull the trigger. ACT.*

GRADUATION, COMMISSIONING
AND EMPLOYMENT

When I returned home after completion of the six-week PLC program, I went to work for my Uncle Clint until I returned to Purdue. No one had to instruct me on what to do. I was alert to what was happening in my environment and took action. I anticipated when bricks, mortar or scaffolding were needed.

My junior year at Purdue, I knocked the cover off the academic ball! I achieved fives in every course I took. This performance enabled me to take advanced classes in the second semester of my junior year.

I taught myself to overcome dyslexia and learn to read. Time magazine was the best news periodical of the time. It employed excellent reporters who covered a subject with superb thoroughness. I forced myself to read Time articles and to understand each sentence. I would then ask my roommate to quiz me on the story. It worked!

In the classroom, I was alert and listened intently to the professors. I was acutely aware of their expectations, and I was able to perceive the vital information in the textbooks to achieve superior grades on the tests and pop quizzes. Learning became easy for me. I excelled academically.

My meetings resumed with Colonel Beck, and I developed a strong bond with him. Colonel Beck was the second person, after my Aunt Florence, who made a significant contribution to my development.

In the fall of 1952, Dwight D. Eisenhower, who pledged to the American people he would stop the war in Korea, was elected President of the United States.

During my second summer session of the PLC Program, on July 27, 1953, the United States, the People's Republic of China, North Korea and South Korea signed an armistice agreement that brought about the cessation of hostilities in the Korean War.

The armistice was not a peace treaty and as of this writing in 2022, a peace treaty among the combatant nations has not been agreed upon.

The second summer at Quantico was easier. The objective of the training was not to break you; we had survived the first six-week session, and I assumed we were being accepted as Marine officer candidates. The emphasis was on education; squad tactics and weapons familiarization were the primary topics

However, the program was not a walk in the park! The morning rifle inspections continued. Calisthenics were conducted daily, including the Chinese log drills, which were conducted once a week. The close-order drill continued. Forced marches were conducted every week.

Every Marine is trained as a rifleman. Whether you are assigned as a baker, a truck driver or a radar operator with a Marine Air Wing, you are first a Marine rifleman and, if required, you can be introduced into a Marine infantry platoon to save the day!

We received hours of classroom instruction on squad-level tactics and then spent days in the field practicing both offensive and defensive tactics. The position of squad leader was rotated for training purposes. There were multiple training sites for each type of tactical problem, and each site was located in a different terrain environment. When the squad leader position was rotated, the new squad leader had not participated as a rifleman in an attack or defense in a similar situation; the terrain environment was completely different. It was an immense challenge. Each squad leader was evaluated on the execution of his plan; the critiques could be brutal.

We spent days on the firing range and were trained in marksmanship. After several days of training, we fired our M1s at targets for familiarization but not for record. We would fire for record during Basic Training.

We were trained in the use of BARs and the .30 caliber machine gun. We fired both weapons for familiarization.

We were trained in the operation of 60-millimeter mortars. The DIs oversaw contests between mortar teams to see which team could hit the abandoned tank located in the impact area. Interjecting fun made the training more enjoyable.

I returned home and went to work for my Uncle Clint in the blast furnaces.

I continued to excel academically in my senior year. I was able to take elective advanced courses and focused on English composition. I determined that if I wanted to be a leader and have my ideas and plans accepted, I would need to be an effective communicator.

I took a course in newspaper writing. My second English composition course required each student to write a total of 8,000 words. The minimum submission was 1,000 words, and the subject of each submission was the student's choice. There was no classroom attendance. We delivered our manuscripts to the professor's mailbox. The marked-up and graded manuscript was returned in a special mailbox outside the professor's office. I had one meeting with the professor during the course.

I was developing a superior value system; I had a high regard for country and family, I was ambitious and I had some vague ideas about accumulating wealth.

I read Ayn Rand's Atlas Shrugged and Peter Drucker's The Practice of Management. Both books would become my personal bibles and guided me throughout my career.

The Marine Corps was aware that I had to return to Purdue in September 1954 to make up the credits I had failed to achieve in the first semester of my freshman year. I could have made up those credits by attending one or two sessions of summer school, but I needed to work during the summers to earn money to contribute to the cost of my education.

I was scheduled to graduate in December 1954, and I was to report for active duty in the Marine Corps in January 1955.

The summer of 1954 was the first summer I worked the entire summer for my Uncle Clint.

On Labor Day of 1954, my best friend, Reese James, stopped by the house. Reese was enrolled in the NROTC program at Villanova University, and his roommate, Andrew Higgins, who lived in Mt. Lebanon, an affluent suburb of Pittsburgh west of the Monongahela River and thus free of the smoke and soot from the steel mills, was hosting a party that evening. Reese asked if I would like to come along.

I met Andrew's sister, Kathie Higgins, at that party. I was very impressed with her intellect and beauty. She was to begin her sophomore year at Georgetown University in Washington, D.C., in the fall of 1954.

We had our first date on Christmas Day that year, and I invited her to be my date at a New Year's celebration. We dated frequently on the weekends during the time I was attending Basic School at Quantico, which was only 40 miles from Washington, D.C. We feel deeply in love.

In July 1955 at Andrews Air Force Base, I proposed marriage to Kathie, and she accepted. The 1954 Labor Day party in Mt. Lebanon was the luckiest day of my life!

During my final semester at Purdue, I was introduced to Alice Fay, who lived in a nice suburb of Pittsburgh. It was during our Thanksgiving vacation that year that I called her and asked if she would like to have dinner.

When I arrived at Alice's home, I was greeted by her father; he informed me that Alice was not quite ready and invited me to sit down in the living room. He began to inquire about my background and then questioned me about my value system and goals for the future. The conversation went on for 15 minutes, and I realized I was being interviewed. I learned that he was the Chief Financial Officer (CFO) of PPG Industries, a Fortune 100 company headquartered in Pittsburgh. He was also a Purdue graduate!

Robert Fay asked if I would come to his office for further interviews over my Christmas vacation. I explained to him that I was to report for active duty in the Marine Corps in January, but that did not concern him.

I assumed that Alice had informed her father of my reputation at Purdue. Her father was looking to employ talented people and most likely asked Alice to delay her appearance for 15 minutes to give him time to size me up.

I called Mr. Fay when I arrived home for Christmas and met him in his office, where he introduced me to Stan Williams, the director of Financial Analysis reporting to Mr. Fay.

Following my interview with Mr. Williams, Mr. Fay offered me a job as an analyst reporting to Stan Williams. I responded to Mr. Fay that I expected to receive my orders to report for active duty any day; I expected that the date to report for active duty would be in early January.

Mr. Fay responded, "We are looking for talented people. Join us on January 5; it is okay with us when you must depart. Your job will be waiting for you when you return!"

I was very fortunate to meet Mr. Fay. I have always encouraged my family members to avoid spending time merely sitting on their front porches. I motivated them to be active and engage in the community. The more exposure you can get, the greater your chance of being discovered. This orientation is an example of the leadership attribute of being aggressive.

My mother pinned on my Second Lieutenant gold bars at the Allegheny County Marine Corps Recruiting Office on December 27, 1954. I was in a dress blue uniform; the American flag and the Marine Corps emblem were prominently displayed. I was now a certified leader!

I was employed at PPG Industries for five days before reporting for active duty.

 Bearings

+ *If you have a disability, overcome it! Conduct research; others have experienced the same disability and have most likely published articles about their experience in overcoming the handicap. Create your own regime to train to overcome your disability.*

+ *Education is so important. Learn to excel. Never stop learning new skills; it is a lifetime commitment. I will devote a section of the book to continuing education entitled "Sharpening your Saw."*

+ *Be active in your community. Do not spend your free time sitting in a rocking chair on your front porch. Be involved in your community! Engage and be recognized! You never know who you will meet— possibly a mentor or your future wife or husband.*

UNITED STATES MARINE CORPS

 BASIC SCHOOL, QUANTICO, VIRGINIA

Basic School was conducted at Camp Upshur. I was surprised as I expected we would be housed in brick-and-mortar barracks on the main base in Quantico.

We were housed in Quonset huts, 42 men to a barrack. Just like at the PLC summer camps, we had a footlocker and a standing locker. The platoon head was adjacent to the barracks. It was stoic living!

Basic School did have its own entrance into Camp Upshur—a curved, triangular sign in scarlet and gold hung above the entrance. It read: "Esprit" across the top, "Leadership" along the left side and "Knowledge" along the right side.

We had our own mess hall and classrooms.

Studying was difficult. We did not have a study hall. We did not have desks. We did not even have chairs! The only available seat was our footlocker, but you could not place your footlocker against a wall and lean back because the walls of the Quonset hut were curved. The best each of us could do was to sit on our footlocker and place a pillow between our back and the post supporting the upper bunk.

The 1-55 Basic School Class was organized as a battalion consisting of three companies, each of which was made up of three platoons. There were 378 lieutenants in the class. All of the unit's commanding officers and instructors were officers who had served in WWII and Korea.

Basic School was an eight-month program.

It was made clear to us that a Marine commission brings with it a special responsibility for the people we would command.

Trust!

We were indoctrinated to push beyond preconceived limits.

Raise the performance bar!

The instruction stressed action based on sound tactical decisions and rewarded offensive thinking and a proactive mindset.

The focus of the training was on platoon tactics, both offensive and defensive. We attended hours of classroom lectures and then went into the field for daylight training. Once we had mastered the implementation of the tactics in daylight, all training exercises were conducted at night.

The training in offensive tactics started with the neutralizing of a single objective, such as an enemy bunker, and graduated to the attack and occupation of a fortified hill.

Defensive tactics began with the securing of a captured enemy position by one squad while the other two squads pursued the retreating enemy.

The ultimate defensive training was devoted to establishing a permanent main line of resistance (MLR) in which a platoon interlocked in a defensive position within a company.

Once we had mastered platoon tactics, the training shifted to company tactics with three platoons acting under the command of a company commander.

Map-reading and using a compass were critical parts of our training.

Effective communications are essential to any military victory, and we spent a great deal of time learning the operation and repair of communication equipment.

Our introduction to the subject of intelligence began with this short but effective recital:

"The road to hell is paved with the bleached bones of second lieutenants who failed to put out scouts!"

I never forgot the training I received on the need to gather intelligence on the strength of your enemy and later transferred this thinking to my civilian life. In business, I stressed to my associates the need to estimate the financial strength of our competitors. I wanted to know our competitors' cost to produce their product and then determine the cost we had to achieve to effectively compete on price and gain market share.

We were instructed in the use of a plastic explosive known as C4. It was a malleable substance that could be formed around a structure; it was safe to handle as it could only be exploded using an electric detonator. It was ideal for destroying bridges and collapsing telephone poles or trees across a road to set up an ambush.

"Fire in the hole!" was announced before detonating the explosive.

We were instructed in the tactical use of heavy weapons—the 60-millimeter and 81-millimeter mortars. Officers were qualified to operate these weapons and to call in fire in live-fire exercises.

Officers were also trained in the employment of artillery and close air support. Once we learned the fundamentals for calling in this support, our training moved to the artillery range, where we called for fire on targets located in the impact area. Map-reading and determining the coordinates of the targets were essential for calling in effective fire support.

::::::::

We participated in four-day field exercises in which we executed both offensive and defensive tactics. The utilization of helicopters for rapid deployment was introduced into this training. We were taught how to coordinate the use of tanks in securing an objective.

The instructors introduced chaos into each exercise, and the designated platoon leader had to respond with an impromptu plan to recover and take the objective.

The Basic School training coupled with the introduction of chaos, which forced us to act and improvise, provided a solid leadership learning experience.

We were continually being evaluated and measured.

We participated in classroom activity, learning the essentials of the Military Code of Justice in case we were called upon to prosecute or defend an enlisted Marine in a summary court-martial.

The 20-mile marches over difficult terrain were conducted every two weeks.

When in camp, we were free to leave Upshur in the evening, though not many people did. Fatigue became a factor; either you were so tired, you had no desire to depart, or more likely, you had to prepare for an exam in the morning.

We did have an outdoor beer garden we called a "slop chute" where you could throw down a beer, but I never saw anyone have more than two beers there.

On Friday nights, I would drive to Washington to spend the weekend with Kathie. The best place to stay was the Transient Officer's Quarters (TOQ) at Anacostia Naval Air Station (NAS). Guests were provided a private room with a tiled bathroom down the hall. We had the use of an officer's mess for meals. It was living in luxury!

If accommodations were not available at Anacostia, the fallback location was the Willard Hotel on Pennsylvania

Avenue, which offered a discount to Marine officers on the weekends.

Kathie and I would have dinner at Martin's Tavern in Georgetown on Sunday evenings. It was our favorite watering hole. We have fond memories of Martin's and make a point of dining there on our visits to Washington, D.C.

The ultimate in luxury in Washington was the officer's club at Andrews Air Force Base. The club consisted of tiered seating around a dance floor, and on weekends, an orchestra played for our enjoyment. It was in the same class as an elegant nightclub. The evening that I proposed marriage to Kathie, there were strolling violinists in the dining area. Romantic!

Back at Camp Upshur, we qualified for record with the M1 rifle and the .45 caliber automatic pistol.

We were taught how to escape if we were taken prisoner. If escape was not possible, we were trained on how to survive as a POW. The North Koreans had employed brainwashing of POWs during the Korean War to dissuade them from the values of democracy in the hope that they would reject repatriation at the time of the armistice. We were taught how to endure the brainwashing.

As graduation approached, we were given the opportunity to request a military occupational specialty (MOS), e.g. infantry, artillery, tanks, engineering, air wing, embassy duty or sea duty, and a preference for a duty location, e.g. any of the three Marine divisions in the Fleet Marine Force—1st MARDIV (Marine Division) at Camp Pendleton, California, 2nd MARDIV at Camp Lejeune, North Carolina or 3rd MARDIV in Japan.

Every Basic School graduate was a qualified infantry platoon commander.

I requested infantry and assignment to the 3rd MARDIV in Japan.

I was assigned to artillery school at Quantico and then to the 12th Marine Regiment, 3rd MARDIV, in Japan.

ARTILLERY SCHOOL

The school was conducted on the main base at Quantico. Each participant had a room that included a single cot, a desk and chair, a closet and a dresser. Real living!

The commanding officer of the school was a Marine major who was a "Mustang," slang for an enlisted man who received a battlefield commission during WWII. Mustang refers to the horse that can be captured, tamed and saddle-broken but still retains a wild streak. Our CO's wild streak would be exposed to us before our graduation.

The major was highly decorated; he had five rows of medals and campaign battle ribbons. He was casual in his approach to teaching and possessed a great sense of humor.

The composition of an artillery battery team consists of three entities. A forward observer (FO) communicates the target location to the Fire Direction Center (FDC) and then issues commands adjusting the fire of one gun until the gun is on target. The FO then calls for Fire for Effect, and all six guns in the battery respond. All lieutenants were trained for this role during Basic School.

The FDC calculates the firing data that would be entered into the guns. The raw data used in these calculations include the range, trajectory, fuse settings, propellant charge, weather and wind direction, all of which are used to calculate the setting for the traverse and elevation of the muzzles of the guns.

A battery consists of six guns; each gun had a crew of eight.

We trained on 105mm light howitzers and 155mm heavy howitzers.

The course was six weeks in duration and involved substantial classroom work focused on the calculation of firing data to be generated in the FDC.

The lead instructor was a master sergeant; he was assisted by three staff NCOs (non-commissioned officers).

We did not have computers; all of the FDC calculations were completed using circular slide rules. I had been trained in the use of a conventional, horizontal slide rule at Purdue, so I was a quick study on the calculation of FDC firing data.

During live-fire exercises on the artillery range, we would rotate positions between performing as the FO, working in the FDC and participating in the operation of the guns.

I developed a friendship with David Ballash, who lived in Berkeley and was a graduate of the University of California, Berkeley. David was married; his wife was employed and was living with David's parents in Berkeley since David had departed for Basic School.

The day before our graduation, we received a new set of orders. The officers assigned to the 1st MARDIV at Camp Pendleton and the 3rd MARDIV in Japan were to attend Naval Gunfire School in Coronado, California. I expressed my displeasure to the major, who responded that Coronado was the most cherished duty station in the Corps.

I responded to him that I had been in training for nine months and wanted to get to work!

The graduation ceremony was to be a live-fire exercise in which the students performed all of the functions of the battery.

The Commanding Officer of Marine Corps Schools, a one-star general, and his staff of four bird colonels were positioned on the observation post (OP) to observe the accuracy of the fire on the targets.

The FO ordered the first fire mission. One gun in the battery fired for accuracy, and the FO adjusted the fire until the gun was on target. The correct firing data was then communicated to all of the guns in the battery, and the FO gave the command, "Fire for Effect" (FFE).

When the battery fired. the FDC communicated to the FO the standard alert, "On the way." It would take 45 seconds for the rounds to strike the target. The general and his staff raised their binoculars to their eyes to observe the accuracy of the shelling.

The sound of an artillery shell exploding sounds like "whump"; there were five loud whumps on or close to the target. At the same time, there was a loud whump to the far left where the sixth round hit a macadam road outside of the impact area!

The command from the Observation Post (OP): "Freeze the Guns!" The gun crews formed a column in front of the guns. No one was to change the settings on the guns.

The FO informed the major that the general and his staff were on their way to the battery position. The major ordered the FDC personnel to form a column outside the FDC tent.

There would be an investigation to identify the gun with the improper data that sent the round outside the impact area.

The general's jeep came roaring into the battery position at high speed; it was bouncing on the rough terrain and stirring up clouds of dust.

The general leapt from his jeep and charged toward the major, who called the class to attention.

The general administered a royal ass-chewing. From where I was located, I could hear portions of his rebuke: "...you can't teach Marines how to shoot a 105 howitzer...blow up a macadam road...waste of taxpayer's money...what the hell is going on?!"

When the general paused in the delivery of his tirade, the major interjected: "Sir, that round was alright when it left here!"

Fifty-five second lieutenants doubled over in laughter. The major quickly brought us back to attention. The general was now furious.

A one-star general was not going to successfully rattle the cage of a 17-year veteran mustang major! The event ended the graduation ceremony; we packed up and returned to base.

I wanted to get out of Dodge. I had my orders and departed for Washington, D.C., early the next morning.

I spent the weekend with Kathie. We had decided to postpone our marriage until after her graduation from Georgetown University in June 1957. The critical issue in making the decision was the fact that the university would not permit married students to participate in the Bachelor of Science/Nursing program.

In addition, the Marine Corps did not allow wives to accompany husbands deployed with the 3rd MARDIV because dependent housing was not available in Japan.

It was the right decision! We said our goodbyes, and I drove to Pittsburgh.

I put my personal life in order, sold my car and made the rounds of saying goodbye to my family and Kathie's parents.

I flew to Los Angeles. In 1955, there were no direct flights. The TWA Constellation flight made stops in Indianapolis, Kansas City and Denver before arriving in Los Angeles. I then boarded a train for the journey to San Diego and the Naval Amphibious Base (NAB) at Coronado to attend Naval Gunfire School.

NAVAL GUNFIRE SCHOOL

The course was short—only three weeks. Naval gunfire is used to support Marine Corps amphibious landings. All of the calculations to direct the firing are calculated in the Combat Information Center (CIC) aboard the ship. Our role would be that of a forward observer: to identify targets and adjust fire. Naval gunfire has a low trajectory compared to artillery fire, which utilizes a high angle of trajectory.

Our CO was a mustang major with five rows of medals and campaign ribbons.

We were taught to be highly selective in the choice of targets in which naval gunfire could be effective.

Dave Ballash's wife, Shirley, joined him on the weekends; she was a very nice person and on several occasions, the three of us had dinner together.

The last three days of our training was a live-fire exercise. We boarded a destroyer in San Diego Harbor and got underway for San Clemente Island, a live firing range located 40 miles off the California shoreline.

We spent the morning in the CIC of the ship learning how the firing data for the target locations we would be identifying would be calculated.

San Clemente Island was 56 square miles in area; the Air Force maintained an emergency landing strip on the island. We brought a cook and all of our food with us from the NAB; the major had also requisitioned10cases of beer, which made the nights more enjoyable.

The Air Force provided two personnel carriers for the journey from the dock to our barracks, which consisted of a sleeping area with 10 double bunks, a large head and a dining area consisting of several picnic tables and a kitchen.

The boys from California requested the major's permission to hike down to the ocean and dive for abalone. They had anticipated there might be an opportunity to take part in this sport and had brought along with them their bathing suits, diving masks, fins and crowbars

The major gave them permission and explicit orders to stay out of the impact area. From our location 2,000 feet above the ocean, the descent and the climb back up the hill were extremely difficult. The group returned with sacks of abalone, which they extracted from their shells and then began pounding with hammers to tenderize the fish.

I had never seen food prepared by softening it with a hammer and felt I would not participate in the feast. Our cook sautéed the floured abalone in butter. I tried it, and it was delicious—a delicacy! Travel provides a broad learning experience.

The next morning, we descended a ladder into a reinforced concrete bunker and secured the hatch. The wall facing the impact area had slits for observation to locate targets. Each observation post had its own radio equipment. We provided the coordinates of the target to the CIC and then adjusted the fire on the target. The major coached each student in the identification of targets and the adjustment of their fire.

In the afternoon, we had free time. We were told to bring reading materials with us.

After lunch on the third day, we packed up and rejoined the ship.

On returning to Coronado, those of us who were assigned to the 12th Marine Regiment received our orders to proceed to The Department of the Pacific in San Francisco and request transportation to Japan.

Dave Ballash invited me to stay with his family in Berkeley rather than at the TOQ on Treasure Island. It was a kind gesture on his part.

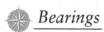 *Bearings*

◆ *Training is so important! I urge you to use every opportunity to train those in your organization. Set aside the time; the investment in training will result in improved performance.*

◆ *Remember that when you are being trained, you are being measured. Excel! Distinguish yourself!*

We reported to The Department of the Pacific and had our orders stamped. We were provided with a telephone number to call at 0900 hours each morning to determine if transportation was available that day. We expected to be in San Francisco for no more than two days.

Dave's parents' home was located atop the Berkeley hills; the view from the living room window was of San Francisco Bay and the Golden Gate Bridge. In the early morning, the bay was covered with fog; the north and south towers of the Golden Gate Bridge, painted bright orange, pierced through the fog. It was a beautiful sight.

Dave's father was an executive with Chevron.

Dave knew of all the good watering holes in the Bay Area. Our daily routine included phoning in to the Department of the Pacific, and when transportation was not available, we drove to Richmond, boarded the car ferry to San Rafael and then drove south to Sausalito to Zack's restaurant and bar.

At Zack's, we would drink beer and play shuffleboard for 10 cents a game until lunchtime. After lunch, we participated in the turtle races. The races involved miniature turtles whose shells were painted different colors. You picked a turtle and placed your bet.

There were two concentric circles outlined on the restaurant floor. The diameter of the inner circle was the diameter of the plastic cake cover that was placed on the circle to confine the turtles until the start of the race.

The outer circle was located two feet from the center of the inner circle and served as the finish line.

When the bets had been placed and covered, the owner lifted the cake cover, and the race was on; the first turtle to cross the outer circle was declared the winner.

Dave's mother prepared delicious dinners each evening, and after dinner, Dave, Shirley and I would venture into the North Beach district of the city and listen to some great jazz.

This routine went on for seven days. We ran out of money. Officers were permitted to carry their pay records with them when traveling to new assignments. Dave and I visited the paymaster at the Department of the Pacific and requested that he provide us with the funds due to us through November 30, 1955.

He was reluctant to do that; he limited the disbursement to seven days of pay. We were faced with a decision. Either we cut back on the beer and betting on the turtle races or we would have to cash a check on our bank accounts. We chose the latter!

The November weather in San Francisco was beautiful. The Bay Area was beautiful.

A young man who had grown up in the Monongahela Valley—Hell with the Lid Off—thought he had died and gone to heaven. I vowed that I would live there.

On the 12th morning, we were advised that transportation was available that evening. We flew out of Alameda NAS aboard a four-engine Mars flying boat, the largest flying boat in the world, which carried 250 passengers. Production during WWII had been limited to seven aircraft.

The cruising speed of the Mars flying boat was 190 mph. The flight to Pearl Harbor in Hawaii would take 13 hours! I thought we would never get there. The flying boat seemed to maintain its altitude but never move forward. We landed in Pearl Harbor and were bussed to Barbers Point NAS on Oahu. We spent four days there awaiting transportation to Japan.

Each day, we took a taxi into Honolulu to the Royal Hawaiian Hotel, which provided a changing room with lockers for servicemen. We spent the day on the beach before returning to Barbers Point.

Our flight from Hickam Field in Hawaii on a Military Air Transport Service (MATS) aircraft would be direct to Tachikawa AFB outside of Tokyo, with a refueling stop on Wake Island.

My mother died in 1999. When Kathie and I were cleaning out her apartment, I discovered several boxes containing every letter I had sent to my parents from Purdue, Marine Corps bases and during the early years of our marriage when we lived in North Carolina and California.

The only correspondence I retained was a postcard I had sent from Wake Island dated December 1, 1955. The front of the card was an aerial view of Wake Island; the reverse side contained the message:

"Island is still scarred from its "Finest Hour" some 14 years ago. 2/3 of way over. Eight more hours to Tokyo and to "work." I hope! Love, Bob"

We landed at Tachikawa AFB, outside of Tokyo, and were bussed to Yokosuka Naval Base at the entrance to Tokyo Bay, 40 miles south of Tokyo.

Our route took us through the industrial area of Yokohama, which during WWII was the steel-producing center of Japan. It was a short ride through the industrial area; the steel mills in the Monongahela Valley covered 16 miles on both sides of the river. I mentally shook my head and questioned how the Japanese government could have ever thought they could defeat the United States.

The 12th Marine Regiment was encamped at North Camp, located 10 miles outside of Gotemba at the 3,000-foot level of Mt. Fuji. North Camp was a 300-acre military facility that included a 34-acre live-fire range and 50 acres of maneuver area.

The next morning, our Navy hosts provided us with a driver, a jeep and a cargo trailer for our luggage to take us to the train station. They also provided a helpful travel schedule for each daylight train departing Yokosuka for Gotemba with instructions for the two transfers necessary to reach Gotemba. The transfer instructions included the name of the station before the station in which we were to make the transfer, the time of arrival at the transfer station and the platform number and arrival time of the train we were to connect with.

We were met at the Gotemba station by a driver with a cargo trailer from the 12th Regiment to take us to North Camp. It was a cold 10-mile drive; there were three feet of snow on the ground.

We submitted our orders to the Regimental Adjutant, who introduced us to the Regimental Commanding Officer (CO). He welcomed us, outlined the standards of performance he was expecting of us as officers under his command and reminded us of our special responsibility for the Marines we would be commanding.

He informed us that the living conditions at North Camp were spartan but expressed his confidence that we would survive.

We were shown to our quarters, which was a tent erected on a concrete slab. Each tent accommodated four officers; the furnishings included a cot, an armoire, a card table and four chairs. There was a potbelly stove in the center of the tent and a large wooden container filled with wood for the stove.

A single light bulb hung over the card table.

We were introduced to our Japanese house boy, who would clean the tent, wash and iron our clothing and maintain the fire in the stove. The head was located in a very large tent that included a large gang shower; it was located just 15 yards from our tent. The water was hot!

The regiment hired Japanese labor to keep the wooden walkways between the tents and the head and the tents and the officers' mess clear of snow in the winter and mud in the spring.

We were issued long underwear, sweaters, wool shirts, winter gloves, wool hats and winter liners for our field jackets. We were also each issued a sleeping bag and two blankets. We slept with our wool hats on!

I was prepared for sleeping at North Camp as the winters in Indiana had been cold! The SAE house at Purdue was home to 60 members of the fraternity. The rooms had been small, and the furnishings were limited to two desks, two dressers and a closet. There was no space for beds. The third floor of the house was dedicated to a dorm with 30 double bunks. The windows and the two doors leading to the outside fire escapes were kept open all year. Each member provided his own sleeping gear, including a sleeping bag, two blankets and a wool hat—just like in Japan.

My battery commander was a highly decorated mustang captain who commanded a "tight ship." He was a good teacher who I respected. I severed as the battery's Executive Officer (XO). Sometimes when on maneuvers with an infantry battalion, he assigned me his role of interfacing with the infantry battalion CO commander and commanding the battery to support the infantry advance. It was excellent training.

Training went on endlessly. The CO measured every variable connected with the performance of the battery. He carried a stopwatch and measured such things as the time to complete a fire mission from the time the FO communicated the target location until the target was bracketed with fire and the FO called, "Fire for Effect!"

CSMO is a command acronym for Close Station Marching Order, which translates to "The fire mission has ended, haul ass, pack up and form up to move out!" The guns had to be prepped for transport and the trails collapsed and physically moved and hitched to a 6x6 truck. Ordnance, powder packs, equipment, radios, tents and camouflage covers had to be uploaded into trucks.

The FDC had to be broken down and uploaded into trucks. Each truck was loaded and unloaded by the LIFO method: last in, first out. Every piece of equipment had a specific location on each truck. The battery had to be ready to provide fire support at the new location as soon as possible. Everyone had to know his job and perform it automatically.

The section chief of the last truck to form up in the convoy would receive a royal ass-chewing from the first sergeant.

The CO received instructions for the best possible location for the new firing position from the battalion operations officer and was provided an NLT, no later time, when the battery was expected to be ready to conduct fire missions at the new location.

The CO formed up the advanced party and moved out to reconnoiter the assigned area to determine the best location for the battery based on the azimuth of fire required to support the infantry advance. The CO would lay out the position of the aiming circle, the location of the guns and the FDC and the establishment of the defensive perimeter to provide security for the battery.

As the XO, I was responsible for moving the convoy to the new location. We placed machine guns in the turrets of the trucks for defense in case we were ambushed en route. I was in the lead vehicle of the convoy serving as the "pacesetter." The gunnery sergeant was located within the convoy and maintained convoy discipline, ensuring that a proper distance was maintained between the trucks and that the trucks were keeping up the pace. He dealt with any truck experiencing a mechanical failure.

When we arrived at the new firing position, the CO there activated his stopwatch. The advanced party provided guides who led the gun trucks and the FDC truck to their assigned locations. Instructions were given for the location and manning of the defensive perimeter. The FOs were already with the infantry battalion we were supporting.

When I announced "Ready to Fire," the CO would stop his watch. We hoped we had beaten our best time for Ready to Fire. We had to be ready before the NLT that had been imposed by the battalion.

We were always training under emergency conditions. The battalion would introduce chaos into the operation; e.g. with the introduction of an ambush en route, the mechanical failure of a vehicle, a radio being placed out of commission or the CO being killed in action (KIA). On various exercises, key personnel, e.g. the XO, the first sergeant or the gunnery sergeant, would be KIA. The battery responses to these setbacks were measured and reviewed.

Most of our training was completed at night. The thinking was that if we could perform the tasks at night, daylight execution would be a "walk in the park"!

When we arrived at the firing range for a live-fire exercise, Japanese scavengers would be in the impact area both day and night searching for unexploded ordnance, which they would collect and sell to scrap dealers.

At night before initiating fire, we fired illumination rounds to light up the impact area. Spotters used binoculars to identify scavengers. The battery employed Japanese interpreters on all live-fire exercises to announce over a public address speaker that a live-fire exercise was about to begin so the scavengers should evacuate the area. This would take time.

I never understood the economics of the scavenger activity. It was a high-risk endeavor. I often wondered who would defuse the ordnance. Did an ex-Japanese Army ordnance officer reside in the nearby village?

When in camp, we trained enlisted personnel. There was always a requirement to train new arrivals. Corporals and sergeants had to be instructed on new skills to prepare them to assume greater responsibilities.

We would isolate tasks and go through dry runs to determine if we could introduce new procedures to reduce the time to perform the task.

We were constantly raising the performance bar!

The CO asked me to train our corporals and sergeants to perform as FOs and have them ready to call in fire at the next live-fire exercise. I suggested we begin the training in a classroom environment and first teach them map reading and compass use. He agreed. I made the learning process entertaining; I wanted the students to enjoy the training.

Before the live-fire exercise, I instructed the students to go to Regimental Supply to obtain a folding canvas seat, a clipboard to write on and a supply of pencils. I wanted them to be comfortable during the coaching sessions and to be able to take notes, which would improve their skills.

My CO recommended me to the battalion CO and the other battery commanders in the battalion. In a battalion table of organization, the position of trainer does not exist; I became the de facto trainer. I had distinguished myself!

I wrote to the Purdue Placement Office requesting that they inform me of any corporation recruiting for personnel with my degree for location in San Francisco. The Placement Office identified the personnel managers of Chevron and Kaiser Engineers. I wrote to both managers and requested an opportunity to schedule interviews on my return to the United States in January 1957. Both managers responded, requesting that I provide them with one week's notice to give them time to set up interviews.

Spring arrived on Mt. Fuji. All of the newcomers to the regiment were eager to climb Mt. Fuji, but the snow had not melted at the top to permit the ascent. We were informed, however, that many of the resorts at the middle elevations were open. Several of us took a bus from Gotemba to a resort that was open. I had a private room, although the bed was just a mattress on the floor, as well as a bathroom and access to the hot tub and a massage. The restaurant had several American dishes on the menu. It was grand living! We did a lot of hiking in beautiful forests with no field packs.

On my return to North Camp, I was summoned to the regiment adjutant's office and informed that the 3rd MARDIV was to be relocated to Okinawa, and I was to be the 12th Marine Regiment's advanced party representative, responsible for preparing our assigned camp for the regiment's occupation.

My orders read that I was to report to a colonel at a location in Okinawa. Further on, the orders stated that I was to be detached from the regiment the next day!

I asked the major how I was to get to Okinawa. He gave me a bewildered look and said, "I would go to Atsugi."

I was aware that several squadrons of the 3rd Marine Air Wing were stationed there; the main body of the Wing was in South Korea.

I asked the major, "Where is Atsugi, and how do I get there?

The major rose to his feet and, pointing to the door, said, "Lieutenant, you are a commissioned officer in the United States Marine Corps. I do not have time to wet-nurse you by arranging your travel to Okinawa. Get out of my office and report to Okinawa!"

I was on my own. I remembered that the Navy had treated us very well on our arrival at Yokosuka and the splendid train guide they had created for the train trip up the mountain to Gotemba. I would travel to Yokosuka and have the Navy arrange for my travel to Okinawa.

I went to my tent, packed my footlocker and paid off my share of our house boy's wages. He advised me, "Okinawan 'boyson' steal!" I made a mental note of that intelligence.

I called the motor pool, requisitioned a jeep and drove to Regimental Supply. I delivered my footlocker with instructions to ship it to my new address in Okinawa and returned all the winter clothing I had been issued on arrival except what I was wearing.

I then stopped by the regiment HQ and recruited one of the Japanese interpreters we employed. We drove to the Gotemba railroad station, where I instructed the interpreter to create a guide similar to the Navy guide we had been provided for the journey up the mountain to Gotemba. I requested that he compile a similar guide for the connections I would have to make for an 0820 departure from Gotemba to Yokosuka the next day.

On my return to North Camp, I arranged for a call to the Yokosuka Naval Base and requested a pickup at the train station on my arrival.

That evening I paid my officer's mess bill. I said goodbye to my "skipper" and thanked him for everything he had taught me. The Regimental CO dropped by my table at dinner; he expressed his confidence in me to make the camp ready for the regiment and wished me good luck. I departed for Yokosuka the next morning.

The Navy base at Yokosuka was the largest U.S. Navy installation in the world in 1955 and HQ for the U.S. Navy's Seventh Fleet. I reported in to the TOQ, had my orders stamped and requested air transportation to Okinawa. I was instructed to check in at the front desk each morning at 0900 to determine if transportation was available.

The journey from Coronado, California, to North Camp, Japan had taken 20 days—not very efficient. I hoped my transportation to Okinawa could be completed more quickly.

Yokosuka was a typical Navy town; the streets outside the main gate were lined with saloons and tattoo parlors. You could buy anything you desired in Yokosuka. I went into town the first evening, returned to base and spent the remaining days at the officer's club.

Transportation was available on the fourth day. The Navy provided me with a car and a driver for the journey to Tachikawa Air Force Base.

I reported in to the TOQ and the procedure was the same: check-in every morning at 0900. Tachikawa AFB was a 20-minute train ride from downtown Tokyo. I took the train into Tokyo on the first day. I traveled in civilian clothes.

It had been 11 years since the end of WWII, and the economic recovery had been dramatic. The city had been leveled during the war, but in 1956, skyscrapers had already gone up in the downtown area. Land was very expensive; bars were built vertically with multiple floors connected by an elevator, and each floor had its own band providing entertainment.

The Army Post Exchange (PX) was located in a five-story building; every type of merchandise you could imagine was available for purchase. The PX was similar in size to Kaufmann's department store in Pittsburgh, although the prices were much lower.

The PX had a shipping department that handled shipments to the U.S. at very reasonable prices. I shipped gifts for Kathie to her home in Pittsburgh.

I returned to Tachikawa after dinner. I went back into Tokyo on the second day and remained on the base the third day. Transportation to Okinawa was available the next day.

CAMP KAWASAKI, OKINAWA

We landed at Kadena AFB; I reported to the TOQ. In my room was a sign on the dresser that read: "Okinawans steal—Beware! There are no locks on your room door!" This was the second warning! I placed my soft piece of luggage against the door and placed my .45 pistol, without a magazine inserted, on the table next to the bed. The sliding of the bolt action to insert a round into the firing chamber of a .45 caliber automatic pistol makes a distinct sound. If the bag moved and the intruder then heard the sound of .45 bolt action, he would think twice about entering the room.

The next day, I was introduced to the bird colonel who was in charge of relocating the division. His HQ was located in a Navy facility at Naha Harbor. I was informed that the 12th Marines would be occupying Camp Kawasaki, a former U.S. Army facility. The colonel introduced me to his staff, which included a captain who was the G-1 in charge of indigenous tradesmen and laborers and a major who was the G-4 who provided equipment, materials and supplies. Both officers provided me with requisition forms for making requests for materials and labor. I was informed that for heavy construction requirements, I was to rely on the advanced representative from the division's engineering battalion, which was also to be located at Camp Kawasaki. The proximity of the engineering battalion proved to be helpful.

I was advised that the U.S. Army, which had overall command of the island, would be inspecting and, if required, would be restoring the electrical, water and sewage systems of the camp. I was given a phone number to call for assistance.

I was provided with a map of Camp Kawasaki. All of the buildings to be occupied by the 12th Marines were highlighted on the map. The CO of the 12th Marines would also be the camp commander, so ancillary service buildings such as the theater and the hospital were highlighted for my attention, as was the security perimeter of the camp.

I was given the date the camp had to be ready for occupation by the 12th Marines. The division colonel expected me to deliver a restoration plan in two days.

I was introduced to a sergeant who would be assisting me. We grabbed as many notebooks, pencils, clipboards and tape measures as we could get our hands on.

I was issued a jeep for my use. The sergeant and I drove to Camp Kawasaki, 20 miles north of Naha.

The main gate was open and unattended. We began a survey of the camp. The barracks' heads had been stripped of washbasins and showerheads; toilets were still in place as the Okinawans did not use Western toilets. All of the seats in the theater had been removed. I could not imagine that the Army took the seats with them when they moved out. The mess hall kitchens were stripped of all equipment. The hospitals were stripped of all equipment, though I imagined that the Army would have taken the hospital equipment with them.

Most of the buildings were Quonset huts secured with several 3/4-inch steel cables anchored into 2x3x3-foot concrete blocks placed in the ground on both sides of each building to prevent the huts from being blown away in a typhoon.

The sergeant and I inspected the perimeter fence, which we discovered had been compromised in 10 locations. I made a note that no equipment was to be installed until we secured the perimeter fence and the main gate and could provide security both day and night.

I made contact with the engineering battalion representative and requested his people check the security cables on every Quonset hut and inspect, repair or replace sections of the perimeter fence to restore its integrity.

We had a PERT plan for each building ready in two days that indicated the timing for cleaning, painting, the restoration of doors and screens and then the installation of equipment in the heads.

I requested help in determining the equipment requirements for the kitchens and mess halls. I advised the colonel that we could have the hospital cleaned and painted, but the medical battalion would have to take responsibility for the selection and installation of the medical equipment, beds, etc.

I requested 25 Marine personnel to provide security once we began installing equipment. I needed four additional sergeants to supervise the work. I requested they be issued high-priority travel orders: "I want them here in fewer than four days."

It was my intention to have several buildings restored immediately to be able to house and feed my contingent of Marines. I went to Air Force supply at Kadena AFB, the closest military facility to Kawasaki, and requested the use of a field kitchen. The master sergeant I was dealing with didn't hesitate for a moment. The Air Force never went into the field, so they would have no need for a field kitchen. The sergeant told me he had four such vehicles.

I requested that the G-1 and G-4 at Naha assign me two cooks and all the equipment, utensils and furniture needed to feed about 40 people.

All of my personnel, staff NCOs, enlisted men and I slept and ate in the same two buildings.

I submitted my requests for laborers, painters, carpenters, electricians and plumbers. I made estimates of the time required to complete tasks. I had no idea of the competence of these tradesmen and, more importantly, no idea of their attitude about work and how proficient they would be. If they worked more slowly than my estimate, I could always request additional tradesmen. They had to be standing in line! I had a deadline to be ready for the arrival of the regiment.

I needed a truck to pick up equipment, so I went to the Air Force motor pool at Kadena. The warrant officer in charge of the motor pool was not as cooperative as the supply master sergeant, but he finally gave me one 6x6 truck. I requested a Marine driver from the G-1.

I had locks installed on all offices in HQ buildings and the rooms for field grade officers, junior officers and staff NCOs in the 12th Marines. It was not possible to lock a barracks. The installation of locks in the mess halls, the various clubs and the hospital would have to wait until the responsible parties arrived.

I reserved a room in the junior officer quarters for my buddy, Dave Ballash.

We were ready four days before the scheduled arrival date of the 12th Marines. The regiment was three days late in arriving because their ships could not get dock space in Naha Harbor to disembark. I had a staff NCO reporting to me who wanted to paint the Air Force truck we had requisitioned Marine Corps green. I discouraged the action: "Sergeant, we did not acquire the truck on a midnight requisition [meaning it had not been stolen]. I signed for the truck!"

The Malpractice of Leadership

I was reassigned to the 12th Marines and then assigned as a battery CO in a different battalion than I was associated with at North Camp. The battalion CO was the only negative leader I came across in my Marine Corps career. I do not intend to identify anyone whom I disparage in this book; it does not matter because I cannot remember his name. I will refer to him as Lt. Colonel Nil.

There was no welcome extended; he never outlined his expectations of officers under his command. He dwelled on the negatives, which he would not tolerate.

The most unpleasant encounter I had with him was on the OP during a live-fire exercise. I had resumed my teaching of young corporals and sergeants to perform as FOs to call in artillery fire. Their classroom training had been completed and on this day, I was coaching them to actually complete fire missions. As I had done in North Camp, I instructed them to requisition canvas stools, clipboards, paper and pencils.

Lt. Colonel Nil arrived on the OP. He came over to our training class and ordered me to get these people off the stools. He expounded: "They should be flat on their stomachs!" I responded that they were learning the fundamentals and once they learned the fundamentals the transition to combat conditions would be easy.

His response was to get rid of the stools. He had not called me aside to suggest the change; he reprimanded me in front of my students and many others who were on the OP that day.

That evening in the bar a mustang Captain who commanded one of the other batteries in the battalion and who had witnessed the incident encouraged me to continue the teaching my way and added, "For the next training session we will keep Nil off the hill!"

Lt. Colonel Nil was a negative person; he would be critical of your performance but never offered suggestions as to how to improve your performance.

TAKING CARE OF YOUR PEOPLE

My radio operator was a Black, buck sergeant who accompanied me in my jeep; when we were overnight in the field, we shared a pup tent.

He had served his time in grade at his present rating and was eligible for promotion to staff sergeant, which would be an important step in his career. He would have to pass a written exam to achieve the promotion. A manual existed which would prepare him for the examination. He claimed the language in the manual was designed to exclude Black men from being promoted to the ranks of NCO (Non- Commissioned Officers). I responded to him that I doubted that was the intention in creating the manual and I offered to teach him how to study. We worked together several afternoons each week and on the weekends.

I obtained a copy of the manual. I suggested we take three chapters at a time and that he study those chapters and highlight what he thought to be the essential points the manual was attempting to get across. I, too, would study the manual and identify the most essential points. We would meet and discuss our findings, then narrow down the essential points and agree upon those that would most likely appear on the exam. I coached him on how to recognize the essential elements in each chapter. Each week he elevated his understanding.

He passed the exam with flying colors and was promoted to staff sergeant! I was very happy for him and I now had to find a qualified, replacement radio operator.

The battery gunnery officer, "Gunny," became aware of my instruction and suggested that since privates and corporals must take a written exam to gain a stripe, I might teach them how to study. He recruited a group of 20 students from the three batteries in the battalion.

NON-COMMISSIONED OFFICERS TEACH AND MOTIVATE YOUNG LIEUTENANTS

It was during our first field fire and maneuver exercise with my new battery that I requested the gunny to accompany me in the advanced party to the new firing location. When we arrived at the new location I completed a reconnaissance with the gunny. I then formed up the section chiefs in a huddle; we were all on one knee and I began to draw my plan for the location of the guns and the FDC in the dust. It was just like the old days when I played sandlot football. Only now I was not designated to "...just block!" I was the quarterback calling the play!

An arm extended through the circle of section chiefs; the hand on the end of the arm erased my drawings and inserted new "Xs" for the placement of the guns and the FDC. Gunny had created the new plan.

One of the primary tenets of leadership is that you reprimand in private and praise in public. I delayed my discussion with Gunny until later that afternoon; we were alone and walking down a dirt road and I introduced the subject. I remember that my concluding statement was - "...after all, Gunny, I am the CO of the battery."

He stopped and turned to me. "Lieutenant." He was gesturing with his hands, pointing to me and then to himself throughout his response. "In our lifetimes, I have passed more lighthouses going to war than you have passed telephone poles!"

I got it immediately! From that point on I sought his advice and consulted with him frequently. We developed a strong bond!

EXPERIENCE MATTERS!

Fast forward to 1968. The United States was heavily involved in the Vietnam War. The Vietminh launched the Tet Offensive in January of 1968; it was a major escalation of the war by North Vietnam. U.S. troop strength reached its peak that year. I was an executive with Xerox; Kathie and I were taking our family to ski in Aspen over the Christmas holiday.

We were walking through the Denver airport to make our connection to Aspen when I saw Gunny, his wife and his family of three grown children approaching in the opposite direction. We stopped; he greeted me as "Lieutenant McLaughlin." I returned the greeting. He was now a master sergeant with another row of decorations. He informed me that he was on his way back to Vietnam for his second tour of duty! We introduced our families to each other; our children ranged from four to ten years of age.

Neither of us had time for a lengthy conversation. I came to attention and saluted him. He returned the salute. I said something like, "God be with you."

It was an emotional day for me. It had been 12 years since we had been together on Okinawa. Gunny was passing yet another lighthouse on his way to war. I would be enjoying a safe Christmas with my family in Aspen. Something was not right!

ADDITIONAL DUTIES

I was summoned to the regimental adjutant's office and advised that I was being appointed defense counsel in a summary courts-martial for a Marine who had been arrested by the U.S. Army military police and was being charged with being drunk and disorderly, participating in a brawl and destroying property in an Okinawan bar. The adjutant provided me with the name and rank of my client, a copy of the Manual for Courts-Martial and the date of the trial and advised me I could meet with my client in the regimental brig.

I was able to obtain a favorable verdict for my client. By favorable, I mean, no loss of stripes and no loss of pay other than the forfeiture of pay for the days he spent in the brig. It was a good outcome.

Three weeks later I was given a similar assignment and achieved a similar, successful outcome.

THE DIVISION LANDING EXERCISE ON IWO JIMA

The foremost training event of the year was the division amphibious landing exercise on Iwo Jima. The battle for Iwo Jima during WWII had been the bloodiest battle in the history of the Marine Corps, which suffered 26,900 casualties made up of 6,900 dead and 20,000 wounded. The Marines secured the island after 36 days of intense fighting. Twenty-seven Medals of Honor, America's highest military honor, were awarded to Marines and Navy corpsmen; that is the highest number of Medals of Honor to be awarded for one battle in U.S. military history!

Iwo Jima is sacred ground for the
United States Marine Corps.

It required a full day and into the night to load our trucks, guns and equipment aboard cargo ships. We cleared the port at Naha and rendezvoused with other ships in the convoy assembly area. When the convoy was assembled, we departed for Iwo Jima with Naval warships escorting the convoy. The voyage to Iwo Jima took three days.

Not all units in the 12th Marines participated in the landing exercise. For instance, my friend, David Ballash's battery did not participate. David participated in the exercise as an umpire and many of his men participated as members of the Red Team, the enemy force, that would play the role of defending the island.

I had inquired of David before his departure as to where the umpires were to be housed and fed. He mentioned there was a U.S. Air Force station on the island and the umpires would be fed in the O Club facility.

The Red Team and the umpires had departed Okinawa several days before the division convoy.

On 19FEB45 the Marine Corps put 70,000 Marines ashore in the invasion of Iwo Jima.

The beach on Iwo Jima is not a typical ocean beach. It is a steep dune composed of soft, black volcanic ash, which was difficult to get a footing in. Our trucks towing the howitzers had difficulty negotiating the entry avenues, created by the shore party's bulldozers, which led from the beach to higher, more stable ground.

Volcanic seams throughout the island vented sulfurous smoke which permeated the air. The island smelled like rotten eggs.

I remember digging in on the beach, waiting for our trucks and guns to arrive by LST—Landing Ship Tanks—and looking up at Mount Suribachi, towering 554 feet above the landing beach. It was a formidable defensive position, from which the Japanese defenders were streaming fire down on the Marines on the beach and thinking, "It must have been hell!"

We were in position and Ready to Fire before the No Later Time, NLT, assignment we had been given for the invasion day. We had responded to 16 simulated fire missions requested by the infantry battalion we were supporting when an umpire - umpires were identified by a white band circling the perimeter of their Gung Ho cap - entered our firing position and informed me that our personnel, guns and equipment had been destroyed by enemy artillery fire. My battery was to stand down and maintain radio silence for the remainder of the exercise - two more days.

At the regiment post-exercise critique, I introduced the thought that our battery could have returned to the beach area and played a role as though we were arriving on day two of the exercise and being assigned as a replacement unit at the disposal of the regimental commander.

It seemed to me that the exercise cost a lot of money to get us there and to just sit in the black, volcanic dust for two days doing nothing was a waste of time and money.

At twilight on that first day, I suggested to the gunny that he open a medical kit. I took out a roll of white adhesive tape, circled our Gung Ho caps with the tape and we became umpires.

We threw a large tarp in the rear of the jeep and headed off to find the Air Force O Club. Gunny was driving, and at each checkpoint, we were stopped and asked to identify ourselves. Gunny responded that we were lost and required directions to the Air Force O Club to have dinner. The personnel at each checkpoint were cooperative and provided directions to the next check point.

We eventually arrived at the O Club. Gunny stayed with the jeep; I entered the facility and went to the bar. The bar was being tended by an Air Force sergeant.

My friend David Ballash saw me, edged his way into the crowd at the bar next to me and in a quiet voice announced, "McLaughlin, you are not an umpire!"

I acknowledged his observation and suggested we change the subject.

The bartender approached and inquired, "What will you have Lieutenant?"

"I would like to have several cases of beer."

"How many?"

"Six."

"Where do you want them?"

"I have a jeep outside."

The sergeant went about extracting six cases of beer from a refrigeration unit and then made three trips delivering the cases to Gunny, who placed the tarp over the cargo in the rear of the jeep.

The sergeant returned and I inquired, "How much do I owe you?

He responded, "Nothing! Courtesy of the U.S. Air Force."

Ballash could not believe what was transpiring. I explained our situation and bid him farewell.

The trip back to our position was more difficult than our outbound adventure. It was now pitch black, dark. We did not have a story about looking for the mess hall. Gunny bullshitted his way through each check point and we arrived back at our firing position.

We rationed the beer to last for three nights. The next challenge was to keep the beer cold. Gunny, in his umpire's hat, was able to procure ice each day.

Care for your people!

The exercise concluded on day four and all units had free time. Gunny, several members of our battery and I climbed to the top of Suribachi. The fields of fire available to the Japanese in 1945 were daunting! Mount Suribachi had been neutralized in four days which denied the Japanese an excellent observation position of the entire island. The battle for the island continued for an additional 27 days after the neutralization of Mount Suribachi.

The iconic photograph taken by Joe Rosenthal, an American photographer, of the five Marines and a Navy corpsman raising the American flag over Mount Suribachi on 23FEB45, became the model for the statue of the Marine Corps War Memorial, which honors all Marines killed in action. The statue was dedicated in 1954 and is located near the Arlington National Cemetery in Washington, D.C.

We boarded our ships and returned to Okinawa.

Regiment Puts out a Call for Airborne Artillery Spotters

Regiment asked for volunteers to qualify as Airborne Artillery Spotters, which would result in the assignment of a secondary military occupation specialty (MOS) to our records. I jumped at the opportunity, thinking the assignment would be fun and break up the boredom of being on the island. The assignment qualified the recipient for flight pay, which is additional compensation paid to officers and enlisted personnel who perform military flight-related duties. In order to qualify for flight pay, a participant had to log a minimum number of hours each month performing these duties.

The observation squadron was attached to the 3rd Marine Division and was located at Kadena Air Force Base. The aircraft designation was an L-5, a single-engine, high-wing aircraft with a crew of two, the pilot and an observer. The nickname of the aircraft was "Grasshopper."

To arrange for flight time, I would call the squadron operations center and inquire if any pilots were flying on that day and if so, I requested to be placed in the back seat. On the day of my first flight, there were five pilots scheduled to fly. All of the pilots in the squadron were "hook tail" fighter jet pilots who were carrier-qualified. They were not happy being assigned to an observation squadron and flying grasshoppers.

Once we were airborne, I was informed by my pilot that the group intended to simulate dogfights to have some fun. This entailed diving, turning, climbing and diving, and simulating gunfire. "Charlie's dead," came over the radio!

The dogfights went on for two hours. I never got sick, but when we landed and I exited the aircraft, my knees almost buckled as I ventured across the tarmac to the ops shack.

When we had live-fire exercises, I would give command of my battery to the XO and organize aircraft from the observation squadron to participate in observing and calling in artillery fire. We were self-taught. There was not a senior experienced officer who would fly with us and provide coaching. We became more proficient with each live-fire exercise. Our most important function was the capability to call in fire on targets that were beyond the line of sight of spotters on the ground.

THE GREAT ORDER-CUTTING SNAFU!

I had been on Okinawa for seven months. It was a cultural desert. There was nothing to do. Bicycle riding was my favorite pastime. I worked out at the gym and attended a lot of movies; however, the time required to participate in those two activities relieved only three hours of boredom.

I was aware the Division Schools were still located in Yokosuka, Japan. I went to see the regimental operations officer and pleaded with him to assign me to a school, any school, just to get me off the island.

::::::::

Several weeks later I received orders to attend Airborne Terrain Appreciation School at the Division Schools. My report date was on a Tuesday, which I thought was odd. My travel orders were high priority; I obtained air transportation from Kadena AFB to Tachikawa AFB and reported in to the division school outside of Yokosuka on the appointed day.

I presented my orders to the first sergeant who looked them over and responded, "Lieutenant, your orders were cut improperly. The school started yesterday, and you should have arrived here on Sunday. I will arrange for a meeting with the colonel."

The meeting with the colonel took place at 0900 hours on Tuesday morning. Classwork for the course had been underway for nine hours since Monday.

The colonel advised me that he was ordering me to return to my unit on Okinawa. I protested, stating, "Sir, I do not know what you are teaching in this course, but I mastered calculus in college, I am a quick study and I believe I can catch up in short order for Airborne Terrain Appreciation!"

He responded, "Do not get smart with me, Lieutenant! Here are your orders. You are dismissed."

I spoke to the first sergeant explaining that I had been on that godforsaken island for seven months and was going out of my mind!

The first sergeant spoke. "Lieutenant, I am going to lose your orders in my bottom drawer..." at which time he opened his bottom drawer, dropped in my orders, closed it and continued "... for one week. Report in here next Monday; I will have recovered your orders by then. Now go into Tokyo and enjoy yourself."

FIRST SERGEANTS HAVE TREMENDOUS AUTHORITY!

I caught the next train to Tokyo and checked into the Imperial Hotel. I purchased yards of beautiful silks in the PX and sent them to Kathie, who created dresses from the material. I picked up my orders the following Monday and thanked the first sergeant for his kind gesture.

I reported to the TOQ at Yokosuka Naval Base and requested transportation to Okinawa. It took the normal eight days to complete the journey - three days in Yokosuka, the car and driver for transport to Tachikawa AFB took a day and then another four days to get a flight to Kadena AFB.

On my arrival at 12th Marine Regiment HQ, I presented my orders to the adjutant and explained the error in creating my original orders and being denied admission to the class.

The adjutant informed me that we had a new regimental CO and that he wanted to see me on my return.

I was expecting to be chewed out for taking 15 days to return to the regiment after being denied admission to the school.

The adjutant introduced me to the new CO, a bird Colonel and exited. The colonel explained to me that he had reviewed my personnel jacket and observed that I was a Purdue graduate; he informed me that he too was a Purdue graduate. BINGO!

He went on to say that he would like me to join the regimental staff reporting to Major Bill Siegler, the S-4 and to assume the role of the regimental embarkation officer. He continued that a ship transporting new 105 howitzers for the regiment was arriving at Naha the next day and I was to supervise the unloading.

I responded to the colonel that I knew nothing about embarkation and in the case of unloading the new 105s, I knew nothing about disembarkation of cargo either.

The colonel pushed a button on his telephone console and the adjutant reentered the room. The colonel inquired when the next Embarkation School would convene at the Division Schools. The adjutant departed and returned stating the school commenced the following Monday. The colonel commanded, "Get McLaughlin in it!"

I reported in to Major Siegler and informed him that the colonel had enrolled me in Embarkation School, which started at the Division Schools in four days. He was OK with that.

I returned to my battery and said good bye to Gunny, the first sergeant and others. Lt. Colonel Nil was not available.

I imagined he would write a negative fitness report on my performance.

I did check my orders and determined I was scheduled to arrive on a Sunday and report to the Division Schools on a Monday morning.

I walked into the division school's office on the appointed Monday and was greeted by the First Sergeant, "Lieutenant, what are you doing back here?" I informed him I was reporting in to attend Embarkation School.

The First Sergeant responded, "Lieutenant, embarkation school does not commence until next Monday!" Without hesitating, he stamped my orders, opened his bottom drawer and dropped in my orders.

"I'll see you next Monday. Enjoy Tokyo!"

I took the train to Tokyo, checked into the Imperial Hotel and realized I was going to be broke in a few days. I did not have my payroll file with me. I was going to have to cash a check using my bank account in the States. This took time, but I was able to accomplish the feat.

I completed the course on embarkation and was a significant contributor to the class. Several days before graduation I was called into the CO's office. He informed me that he had spoken with the CO of the 12th Marines and he had been granted permission to talk with me about becoming the lead instructor at the Division Schools. He went on to say that if I accepted the position, I would be required to extend my tour of duty in Japan for one year.

This was the same colonel who sent me back to Okinawa because I was one day late in arriving for Airborne Terrain Appreciation School.

I thanked the colonel for his confidence and for extending the offer. I politely declined the invitation. My focus was on completing my tour of duty, returning home, marrying Kathie and going to work.

ANCILLARY DUTIES

Major Siegler was a great officer to work for. He encouraged individual innovation; he never told me how to accomplish a desired state of affairs. An early assignment unfolded in the following manner: Major Siegler walked into my office, threw a file folder on my desk and said, "Unfuck this!" He turned and exited the office.

I had to scope the problem, determine the cause, obtain the resources to correct the problem, implement corrective action and write a standard operating procedure (SOP) to be followed so the problem would not occur in the future.

I returned the file folder to the major, placed it gently on his desk and informed him that the problem had been corrected and that an SOP had been created to avoid the problem occurring in the future. He reviewed the SOP, commented "Well done" and dismissed me.

It was a great learning experience!

I learned that Major Siegler was a graduate of Virginia Military Institute (VMI) and had played football for the university. I told him that my battery had supported Lt. Colonel Tom Mix's battalion in the 9th Marines and mentioned that he, too, was a graduate of VMI. Siegler acknowledged the colonel and informed me that Colonel Mix was his senior by several years and a legend at VMI.

Major Siegler assigned additional responsibilities to me for the operation of Camp Kawasaki; the operation of the camp was the responsibility of the 12th Marines. I was assigned as the typhoon control officer and the indigenous personnel officer for the camp.

During the summer of 1956, Okinawa was hit directly by three typhoons. The typhoon control officer was responsible for ensuring the camp was prepared to operate in severe, abnormal conditions.

Generators were provided to the hospital, mess halls and regimental HQ, which would be the typhoon control center. One of my responsibilities was to inspect the camp to determine that nothing had been abandoned which could become a missile in a high wind and cause personal injury or property damage.

It was during our preparation for the second typhoon of the season on my tour of the camp that I noticed the construction site for the new hospital was littered with materials and equipment which could become missiles in a high wind. The construction was being performed by an Okinawan construction company that had abandoned the site without cleaning it up. Kawasaki camp was divided into zones and individual units throughout the camp were responsible for policing areas of vacant land and construction sites within their zone of responsibility.

I returned to regimental HQ and searched the plot map of the camp to determine what unit had responsibility for the area in which the new hospital was located. The hospital was located in zone E6 which was the responsibility of my old battalion under the command of Lt. Colonel Nil.

I had a good relationship with the battalion's first sergeant. I called him and explained the situation with the construction of the new hospital and after reciting that the site was located in the battalion's zone of responsibility, asked if he would see to it that the area was policed and made secure. He acknowledged my request.

LT. COLONEL NIL GOES CRAZY!

A few minutes later my phone rang and it was Lt. Colonel Nil, who informed me that the construction site was not in his battalion's zone of responsibility and he would not be policing the area. I invited his attention to page 23 of the camp plot map. He ignored my invitation and stated emphatically that he was not assuming responsibility for the clean-up.

I was scanning the map to determine what unit was located nearby so I could request assistance in solving this problem when the Regimental XO, stepped into my office and inquired, "Lieutenant, is the camp secure?" I explained the situation of the hospital being in Zone E6 which according to the camp plot map was Lt. Colonel Nil's zone of responsibility - yet he refused to clean up the area. I informed him I was in the process of engaging another unit to perform the work.

The colonel was an Irishman; his face turned bright red. He was pissed. He said to me, "There is no need to find another unit to police the area." He turned and motioned to his driver, who was standing in the hall, that they were moving!

Carrying the plot map book, I followed the colonel out into the parking lot and inquired, "Sir, don't you want to take a look at the plot map?" He was seated in his jeep; he turned to inform me, "I do not need to see the plot map!"

My sergeant asked me how long I thought it would take before my phone would ring with Lt. Colonel Nil on the other end of the line. I responded, "Sergeant, if you can accurately estimate the duration of the ass-chewing the colonel is going to administer, I will provide you with the exact time of the phone call."

The phone rang. Lt. Colonel Nil was so angry, his voice was cracking. "McLaughlin... I will get you for this... I...I will get you!" He hung up.

The XO returned, stopped by my office, stuck his head in the door and stated, "Lieutenant, your camp will be secure in 20 minutes!"

I reported the incident to Major Siegler.

The remainder of this story was related to me by Major Siegler. I was not in the officer's mess that night for dinner. I was manning the control center in HQ as the leading edge of the typhoon was in close proximity to the island.

Major Siegler was eating dinner when Lt. Colonel Nil approached his table and spoke. "Siegler, I am going to get revenge on you and that lieutenant who works for you!"

Major Siegler did not acknowledge Nil. He rose and walked to the CO's table. The CO was aware of the incident concerning the construction site. Major Siegler informed the CO of his recent encounter with Lt. Colonel Nil and stated, "I have a lot of duties to perform, but I will not be able to perform them if I have to watch my back for attacks by Lt. Colonel Nil."

The CO interrupted his dinner, walked over to Nil's table and executed a royal ass-chewing observed by every officer in the mess.

I did not have a good opinion of Lt. Colonel Nil, and it was obvious that Nil must have had a history of poor relations with his superior officers.

DEFENSE OF ANOTHER MARINE

The regimental adjutant gave me another assignment as a defense counsel for a young Marine who was accused of breaking up a bar in Misato Village. It was an unusual case in that the Marine had not been arrested by the Army MPs for disorderly conduct; the claim for damages had been made by the bar owner through the Okinawan civil authorities.

The Marine was not confined to the brig; we had our meetings to plan his defense in my office. He confided in me that he had punched out several Okinawans in the bar but denied that he had destroyed the tables, chairs and glassware that were listed in the complaint by the bar owner.

I wanted to interview the bar owner. I procured a Polaroid instant camera from Regimental Supply, recruited an interpreter and obtained a jeep from the motor pool.

We needed the interpreter not only to translate but to provide directions to Misato Village, which was off the beaten path. We came over a very high hill and began the descent into Misato Village. Every male in the village was dressed in Marine Corps green fatigues! I learned from the interpreter that many of the villagers worked in Camp Kawasaki. They were stealing us blind!

As we entered the village proper, I noticed 50 to 60 people, all dressed in Marine Corps green, digging with picks and shovels on a hill and removing the dirt in baskets. I stopped the jeep and asked the interpreter to determine the purpose of their efforts. He returned and informed me that they were attempting to build a road through the hill and into the next village to improve commerce.

I visited with the bar owner. I asked her to identify the furniture that had been replaced. All of the furniture she pointed out looked like old furniture to me. I asked to see receipts for the purchases of the new furniture. None were available. I asked for a description of the incident that had caused the alleged damage, and she described it as a brawl with my client as a one-man wrecking crew. I came to the conclusion that my client was being set up.

When we returned to Camp Kawasaki, I asked the driver to take me to the engineering battalion office. I sought out the friend who had assisted me in restoring Camp Kawasaki months before. I knew he was always looking for opportunities to train his bulldozer and shovel operators, so I informed him of the road-building opportunity in Misato Village.

I prevailed in the trial of my client and had the case dismissed.

ASSIGNMENT TO A SPECIAL COURT-MARTIAL BOARD

The regiment then assigned me to be a member of a Special Court-Martial Board, an intermediate-level court chaired by a lieutenant colonel. The board included a major, a captain, a master sergeant and me. This was an honor; I felt I was being recognized for my good judgment.

THE INDIGENOUS PERSONNEL DRAGNET

The next morning, I positioned myself at the front gate and observed the indigenous workers entering the camp; the majority were empty-handed. I repeated the observation of the workers exiting the camp in the late afternoon. This time, everyone carried a cloth bundle! I asked the Officer of the Day (OD) at the gate if he knew what was in the bundles. His response was that he believed they were taking laundry to their homes to be washed and ironed. I responded that the laundry does not return.

I read up on the manuals governing the employment of indigenous personnel. Okinawan applicants had to be screened by the Indigenous Personnel Office and were to be issued a pass for entry into the base that had to be renewed every year. We examined the files. There were no applications on file and no records of entry passes being issued.

Far more important was that indigenous personnel being employed in the hospital and mess halls were required to have a medical exam. There were no records of medical exams on file for anyone employed in the hospital or mess halls.

How did these people obtain passes that permitted their entry onto the base? The regiment had been located at Kawasaki for eight months.

Three other officers and I employed a house girl who cleaned our rooms and washed and ironed our khakis and fatigues. I recalled that I was introduced to the house girl by a senior mama-san who was in charge of indigenous personnel employed in the barracks. They were organized.

I reviewed the situation with Major Siegler and informed him of my plan, which he approved.

I informed the OD that I wanted all passes checked, and any pass that was not issued by the 12th Marines was to be confiscated.

The 12th Marines HQ was located adjacent to the main gate. When I arrived at HQ at 0700, 150 Okinawans were sitting in the HQ parking lot. I found the OD on the main gate. He informed me that the guards had confiscated every pass of those seeking entry; none had been issued by the 12th Marines. All of the confiscated passes had been issued by the U.S. Army.

The workers who had been employed by the U.S. Army merely returned to work when the Marines reactivated the camp.

Many of the pass holders' names and photographs did not match the names and photographs on the passes. The passes had been transferred or sold to people who wanted to work at the camp.

I immediately inquired if there was an interpreter among the 150 personnel. There were four. We began by segregating the workers who claimed to work in the hospital and mess halls. We called their employers and had them come to HQ to claim their people and arrange for medical exams. Once we received the approved medical exam, we would issue a permanent pass. Many of the workers did not pass the medical exam and were denied a pass.

At about 0800, I was advised that the Regimental CO was on the phone and wanted to speak to me.

"McLaughlin, what is going on? Who are all those people sitting in our parking lot?"

I explained the situation beginning with the fact that the entire male population in Misato Village was dressed in Marine Corps green fatigues, and the people in the parking lot did not have legitimate passes to enter the camp. I explained my plan for correcting the situation. Major Siegler had obviously not briefed the colonel.

The colonel responded by commending my plan, but he was aware that his maid had been picked up in my dragnet and encouraged me to release her and allow her to report for work. I asked for her name and responded to the colonel's request.

It took about two weeks to bring the situation under control. I wrote a new standing order for the guards on the front gate, which the colonel approved. The standing order included the inspection of all bundles and the packages indigenous personnel were carrying on exiting the camp. If the contents were believed to be stolen property, the property was to be confiscated and the individual's pass revoked.

We installed facilities for washing uniforms and provided irons and ironing boards for the pressing of clothing for every enlisted barracks in the camp.

The stealing of fatigues stopped!

Several weeks later, I received a call from the sergeant of the guard on the main gate that the mayor of Misato Village and five councilmembers were at the gate and wanted to see me. I walked out to the gate and escorted the visitors to my office. They presented me with a letter of thanks written on fancy paper and framed. The letter was written in Japanese on the left side and in English on the right.

The letter stated:

> To Lt. Robert J. McLaughlin
> It is highly appreciated for the significance of American-Ryukyuan friendship that industrial road which was a long-pending hope of the villagers has been grandly opened out of your humanity and lofty mind of service.
>
> I, with villagers, shall be more assiduous to the development and growth of industry of the village and hereby express my heartfelt thanks to you and praise you forever and a day for your meritorious service awarded to the villagers of Misato Village.
>
> /s/ Kenei Tokeshi
> Mayor of Misato Village

The delegation also sent a Letter of Thanks to the lieutenant in the engineering battalion who had provided the equipment and operators to complete the work. I obtained two jeeps from the motor pool, and we drove to the engineering battalion HQ. In addition to the Letter of Thanks, the delegation presented a framed picture of the Marine operators and the Okinawan workers standing on and in front of a Marine bulldozer.

The American flag was prominently displayed, and everyone, Marines and Okinawans, was dressed in Marine fatigues!

TEMPORARY DUTY ASSIGNED TO A MAGTF

Whiskey, Tango, Foxtrot—we did not use that expression in 1956, though I remember using similar words in responding to the regimental adjutant when he informed me that I was being temporarily assigned to a Marine Air Ground Task Force (MAGTF) being assembled at South Camp, Gotemba, Japan, to create the OPSPLAN for the division landing exercise to be conducted in 1957. My assignment was to be in charge of 30 clerk typists who would type up the drafts and final documentation of the OPSPLAN.

I expressed to the adjutant that surely there was an officer in an HQ company somewhere in the 3rd MARDIV who was better qualified than me to manage a group of hard-charging clerk typists.

The adjutant responded, "Lieutenant, Division asked for our help in filling this assignment. The colonel thinks you are the best-qualified, junior officer to lead this group. Marine clerk typists are first and foremost Marine warriors, and you should be proud to be their leader!" WTF!

I took the normal transportation route—Kadena to Tachikawa to Yokosuka and then the train to Gotemba.

A one-star general, who was the XO of the 3rd Marine Air Wing (3rd MAW) was the CO of the MAGTF; a bird colonel from the 3rd MARDIV was the XO. Each staff position, i.e. G-1 Personnel, G-2 Intelligence, G-3 Operations and G-4 Logistics, were staffed with two field grade officers, one from the division and one from the wing. The senior ranking officer was the primary officer in each section.

Tom Mix, whose battalion in the 9th Marines my battery had supported, was now a bird colonel and the CO of the 9th Marines. He was the senior officer in the G-3 section. We renewed our acquaintanceship, and he welcomed me aboard. I informed him that I was now reporting to Major Siegler, the S-4 of the 12th Marines, who was also a VMI graduate, and asked if he knew Major Siegler. He responded that he did and that I could not be working for a finer officer.

I was introduced to the 30 clerk typists I was responsible for and was relieved to find a staff sergeant in the group who had organized the group and secured a large room and procured desks, typewriters and reams of paper. The staff sergeant informed me that we were ready to perform.

We were the guests of the U.S. Army at South Camp, and the Army provided us with offices, sleeping quarters, mess facilities and a bar complete with a bartender!

I had the opportunity to eat and drink with field-grade officers, which was an unusual experience. I listened and learned.

The officers from the 3rd MAW were very casual compared with the division officers. I mentally referred to them as "zoomies."

The clerk typists had very little work to perform in the morning. The officers spent mornings writing new operational orders for the exercise and modifying the operational orders for the 1956 Division Landing Exercise on Iwo Jima. The 1956 exercise did not include the involvement of the 3rd MAW, so there were mountains of paperwork to be created to support their participation. The objectives of the exercise were different from the Iwo Jima landing; the exercise was to be conducted on the island of Luzon in the Philippines, and new tactics adopted by the Marine Corps had to be introduced into the planning.

My involvement was a great learning experience!

I was able to sit in on the discussions of each of the sections and listen to officers create their plans and debate alternative strategies for accomplishing the objectives. I came to realize that one technique being employed by all sections faced with the huge problems associated with an effort of this magnitude was to segment the overall challenge into smaller problems to be solved.

The technique resembled the solution to a complex calculus problem. The Latin meaning of calculi is "small pebble." Solve a series of small problems, combine the solutions and you have the answer to a very complex problem.

I adopted the concept of what I referred to as *calculi segmentation*. I employed the concept throughout my business career. I had no fear of taking on substantial, complex business problems.

The assignment also involved a lot of fun! Each Friday during lunch, an officer from the MAW would stand on a chair in the mess holding a telephone; on the other end of the phone connection was the operations officer at Atsugi Marine Air Base.

The MAW officer would order silence in the mess and inquire, "How many would like to go into Tokyo for the weekend?" There would be a show of hands, which included mine.

The officer then spoke into the phone: "Send up two H-34s for a 1600 departure. Schedule a 1600 pickup in Tokyo for Sunday! Many thanks!"

The Sikorsky H-34 helicopter accommodated 12 to 16 fully equipped Marines; it was a very comfortable flight accommodating several field-grade officers and on occasion a lieutenant and one or two clerk typists.

The journey was far more efficient than taking three trains from Gotemba to Yokosuka and then transferring to a direct train into Tokyo.

The work of the 3rd MAGTF went on for one month; I did not go into Tokyo every Friday as it was just too expensive. I did arrange for the clerk typists to participate in the airlift and, each Friday a few would sign up for the journey.

When the assignment was completed, my return to Okinawa was the fastest on record. The MAW general had his own C-47, and he and some of the MAW officers were on their way to Hong Kong for R&R. The general dropped off the division officers in Okinawa. One day of travel versus eight days. Efficient!

BECOMING A SHORT-TIMER

It was late November when I returned from the 3rd MAGTF assignment. I was expecting to be rotated to CONUS (Contiguous United States) and discharged in late December or no later than the first week of January 1957. I did not know what to expect in regard to transportation for the return journey.

I had prepared my letters to the VPs of Personnel at Chevron and Kaiser Engineers and only had to insert the dates I expected to be in San Francisco for interviews.

The duty was rather routine. The typhoon season had passed; the indigenous people were under control. I served on two special court-martial boards, I was logging flight hours to qualify for flight pay and I was able to view a new movie every night. Time was flying by.

Major Siegler encouraged me to ship over, extend my tour of duty and apply to transfer my commission to the regular Marine Corps. I explained that my objective was to go into business. I did not want to make a commitment to a career in the Marine Corps.

Our paths would cross again in 13 years when I was in a position to offer employment to Colonel Siegler on his retirement from the Marine Corps. This is described elsewhere in the book.

It was mid-December when a corporal from the adjutant's office walked into my office, placed a manila envelope on my desk and informed me, "Lieutenant, you are going home; you will be home for Christmas! You leave in two days."

He went on to explain that the 3rd MAW was rotating six C-54s to the U.S. to be retired, and the division was sending 36 officers and NCOs—six men to each aircraft—to CONUS to be reassigned or discharged. The orders read that we could travel in fatigues.

There was no time to alert Chevron or Kaiser Engineers to arrange interviews as I would be in San Francisco before the letters would arrive. I also decided to delay contacting Kathie and my parents until I arrived in San Francisco.

I delivered my footlocker to regimental supply for shipment to my parents' home.

I said goodbye to a lot of good friends I had made during my tour. I expressed many thanks to Major Bill Siegler for the opportunities he provided to me and the excellent advice and training he rendered. I gave him a snappy salute, which he returned.

When we boarded the aircraft, we discovered why the passengers were limited to six. One-third of the cargo space contained large plastic bladders filled with aviation fuel. Our itinerary would be Okinawa to Wake Island to refuel, then into Barbers Point NAS in Hawaii and then into Moffett Field NAS in San Francisco.

The plane had the traditional bench seating along the bulkheads, and we were able to stretch out and sleep. Our aircraft lost an engine several hours out of Wake, and the aircraft gunnery sergeant enlisted our help in preparing the life rafts for ditching in the Pacific. The pilot was able to fly the plane into Wake. We spent two days on Wake while the engine was repaired. The only available transient quarters were tents— four officers to a tent.

We arrived at Barbers Point, threw our gear in our rooms at the TOQ and went to the O Club for a drink. The bartender informed us we would have to depart by 1630 as the squadron Christmas party was scheduled to begin at 1700, and the uniform was dress whites. We were in our fatigues. We exited the O Club promptly at 1630.

We flew into Moffett Field NAS the next day and were bused to Treasure Island in San Francisco Bay. I called Kathie; she was elated. I also called my parents; with the time difference, my call interrupted the poker club game they were hosting that evening. When my father announced to the group that I was in San Francisco, I heard a lot of "Hoorahs" erupt in the background!

The next day, a physical exam was administered. I received my discharge papers and the pay that was owed to me. I was presented with my reserve identification card. I was obligated to serve five years in the Marine Corps Reserve.

I telephoned Dave Ballash as we had been on the same set of orders, but his aircraft did not experience engine failure so he had arrived in San Francisco two days earlier. I thanked him for his friendship. Kathie and I would rendezvous with Shirley and Dave in five years when I became the West Coast manager for PPG Industries. I lost track of Dave after that visit.

I went out to SFO and caught the next nonstop flight to Washington, D.

Kathie and I spent a glorious few days together before I departed for Pittsburgh to be with my parents. Kathie followed a few days later for her Christmas vacation. We enjoyed our time together and made the plans for our wedding in June 1957, following her graduation from Georgetown University's School of Nursing.

I was now a civilian and ready to embark on a career in business.

Bearings

✦ *The world has an abundance of people who are capable of paddling a canoe in still water; what the world needs are people who can handle a canoe in whitewater. Whitewater moves fast; there are challenges at every turn in the river. It requires extraordinary skills and courage to navigate white water. Prepare yourself to handle whitewater!*

✦ *Join an elite organization, best in class! Join an organization that will demand excellent performance and provide extraordinary rewards for excellent results!*

✦ *Experience matters. Seek out high-growth organizations that need leadership and can provide greater opportunities for more experience and advancement.*

✦ *Always be prepared to carry out your mission. Ensure your equipment is in operating order. If your next encounter is a meeting, ensure your data is up-to-date and accurate. Ensure that those in your organization are well-trained and ready to perform their mission.*

✦ *Always have a plan. Plan for your week. Plan for the year. Set your goals. Raise the performance bar. Provide skill training for those in your organization to clear the raised bar.*

PPG INDUSTRIES

I had been a member of an elite military organization for two years and three months if you count the three months of involvement in the Platoon Leaders Course during the summers of my sophomore and junior years at Purdue. I had been trained and rewarded to ACT; taking action was my default state of being. It was an attribute I would retain for the remainder of my life.

I had been exposed to outstanding leadership during my tour of duty with the Marine Corps. I was also able to quickly recognize the malpractice of leadership.

My self-confidence was extremely high. I'd had so many successful experiences in the Marine Corps that I felt there was no challenge that I could not overcome. I was entering civilian life with an attitude that success would be inevitable.

My job as a financial analyst at PPG Industries was available to me, but my career objectives had changed. I was not interested in a career recording what had happened; my orientation was to make things happen and be rewarded for it. I wanted to be employed where the action was taking place. I realized I had to be careful in expressing this to Stan Williams, my original boss, and to Bob Fay, my mentor, both of whom were career financial executives.

I had arranged for a meeting with Stan Williams on the first business day of 1957; his administrative assistant escorted me into what I remember was Mr. Fay's office. Stan Williams welcomed me back, thanked me for my service and informed me that Mr. Fay was now the president of the paint division, one of the largest divisions of PPG Industries.

Stan Williams had succeeded Mr. Fay as CFO. Stan went on to say that Mr. Fay would like to talk with me and then escorted me to Fay's office.

Bob Fay explained to me that the paint division was losing money, and he had been given the assignment to return it to prosperous operations. He said he wanted me to join him in his quest. I was surprised and very pleased.

I explained my desire to make things happen rather than to report on what had happened. Fay responded that he needed good people to make good things happen and asked what field I wanted to participate in. I said I was thinking of marketing or manufacturing. Fay arranged for interviews with his vice presidents of marketing and manufacturing.

The vice president of manufacturing did not put forward any investment plans to reduce manufacturing costs. He was not an advocate for change.

The vice president of marketing did not propose any plans to change the division's product mix to emphasize products with higher profit margins that would lead to improved profits. There was no mention of plans to improve the skill level of the existing sales force.

Neither of the vice presidents spoke of raising the performance bar. They did not seem to share Mr. Fay's goal of improving the division's profitability.

I chose to go into marketing. The division had an attractive commission plan that would be rewarding. I informed Mr. Fay of my decision, and he asked me where I wanted to work. I responded that the economies of the Southeastern and Southwestern United States were the fastest growing and therefore would provide the best opportunities for growth. Mr. Fay informed me that the division had plants and sales offices in Atlanta and Houston.

I chose Atlanta; it was closer to Georgetown University and Kathie.

MY TERRITORY, A SOLE PROPRIETORSHIP SUPPORTED BY A STRONG FORTUNE 500 TECHNICAL ORGANIZATION

I reported to the Atlanta industrial sales manager; I soon recognized that he was not a good leader. As it turned out, I would not need his leadership. It would be my territory, my business, and I would create the plan to accomplish my objectives.

My training involved four months of working in the technical department of the Atlanta plant. The technical manager was a highly competent technician; he was aggressive and had assembled a group of talented technical people in his department.

Industrial coatings are customized products designed to meet the customer's specifications for performance and method of application.

I was introduced to each field request from the field for a new product. I would work with the technician to develop and test the product so it met the customer's specifications. We could test all methods of application in our laboratory. I accompanied the technician to the field and observed the test run at the customer's location.

An industrial coating has three components: 1) solvent, which provides fluidity for ease of application and evaporates during the application and curing process; 2) resin, a non-volatile substance that provides a protective coating to the surface and 3) pigment, which is ground into the resin during the manufacturing process and provides color.

The paramount technical knowledge I learned in my training was that the most important measurement of an industrial coating's economic benefit was the percentage of solids (%solids) in the "can." The %solids is the ideal amount of material that would remain on the surface of the customer's product after application.

Each method of application has different efficiencies. Spray painting was the least efficient because a large percentage of the coating did not reach the product, but the application was fast, so the production line could move quickly.

The most efficient application was high-speed roller-coating for the application of coatings on coils of aluminum and galvanized steel, which after curing could be formed into a variety of products.

I created charts for identifying the cost per square inch of coverage for each known method of application at various film thicknesses and various %solids. My objective was to illustrate to a purchasing agent or factory superintendent how to reduce their costs. If I could assist these two people in becoming company heroes, I was going to get the business. The fundamentals of this technique were taught to me by the technical department, not by my sales manager. I created the illustrations for distribution to potential customers to educate them as to how to reduce their costs. My passion for teaching motivated the creation of these illustrations.

My territory was to be the state of North Carolina. The sales manager showed me the customer list and the current and past years' sales. The annual sales were close to zero. The salesman I was replacing had been in the territory for three years. He was not terminated for poor performance; he was transferred to the Milwaukee office to work on a service desk.

I was paid a salary for the first nine months in the territory. After that, I would be compensated at a reduced salary but with an attractive commission plan. For each industrial coating, the company assigned a minimum selling price, which paid a four-percent commission. I had the freedom to set the selling price higher; the maximum commission I could earn was six percent. I intended to sell my products at a price that would generate a six-percent commission.

I set a goal of earning $40,000 in commissions above my base salary. This was a lot of money in 1957. To earn six percent in commissions, I would have to generate $700,000 in annual sales to receive $40,000 in commissions.

I felt it would be reasonable to secure a minimum of eight customers in my first year. Therefore, the annual purchases by a potential customer had to be $90,000 or greater!

My sales manager did not provide me with an annual budget target I was expected to achieve. He did not identify potential customers on whom I should focus my efforts. No direction was provided. In the two years that I was in the territory, he visited with me once, and that was to play golf with the purchasing agent of a customer I had acquired. He provided no coaching and no motivation during the two years I reported to him.

I acquired an Industrial Classification Manual (ICM) for the state of North Carolina. An ICM classifies every business in the state—industrial, retail and service—with a four-digit code. I focused my attention on the four-digit code for metalworking industries whose products would be used outside and required protection from sunlight and rain.

The ICM did not identify the annual revenues generated by the companies, which would have given an indication of the size of the company, but the manual did provide the number of people employed by the company.

I identified 20 companies in the metalworking category with 300 employees or more. These became my target accounts to qualify for further efforts during my first month in the territory.

My objectives were to introduce myself and the resources of PPG Industries, which could assist them in reducing their costs, determine the customers' annual purchases of industrial coatings and determine if their purchases would meet my minimum account target of $90,000 in annual sales.

I also wanted to determine their specifications, which we would use in developing a product for their use.

I explained the value of measuring the concept of %solids in a gallon of paint and discussed reducing their coverage cost. I would then ask for a quart sample of their current product. It was interesting that some purchasing agents would not provide a sample of their current product. This was not a problem; I was able to return at a later date and relate a success story with another customer in reducing their costs. Eventually, I was able to collect samples from every targeted customer.

NOTABLE SUCCESSES

Wix Corporation of Gastonia, North Carolina, a manufacturer of oil filters, became my first customer. We were able to reduce their coating costs significantly.

Homelite Corporation, a manufacturer of chainsaws and portable generators, was building a new factory in Gastonia. I introduced myself to the plant manager, who was on-site supervising the new construction. He immediately bought into the concept of %solids and lower coverage cost. He arranged to ship quart samples of three products they were using in their plant in Massachusetts directly to our lab in Atlanta. When the plant opened, PPG Industries was the paint supplier.

Thomas Brothers of High Point, North Carolina, assembled school buses. "School-bus yellow" was the big volume item. I had learned in my training that the highest-cost step in the manufacturing process was milling the pigment into the resin and that the ideal batch size was the equivalent of the material needed to generate 275 gallons of a coating—five 55-gallon barrels. I established a five-barrel minimum order size for my customers. PPG Industries had no such criteria.

However, if a parish in Louisiana purchased two school buses to be painted purple, we made an exception and produced 20 gallons for Thomas Brothers to satisfy their customer.

General Electric of Hendersonville, North Carolina, produced electric transformers that were mounted on utility poles. After achieving a reduced coverage cost for the customer, the plant manager suggested I introduce the concept of %solids and lower coverage cost to their sister plant in Lynchburg, Virginia, which manufactured large transformers for placement on the ground outside of manufacturing facilities. He provided me with the name and phone number of the plant manager.

On meeting the plant manager, my first question to him was, "Has a representative of PPG Industries ever solicited your business?" The answer was no.

All requests for technical support and product development were submitted to the sales service desk in Atlanta, recorded and then transferred to the technical department for fulfillment.

I received a call from my sales manager informing me that the General Electric plant in Lynchburg was located outside of my territory, so the lead and request for product development would have to be turned over to the Newark, New Jersey office.

I responded, "No, we are not going to turn the lead over to Newark; they have never called on the account. I have an introduction from the plant manager in Hendersonville, and I believe we can successfully reduce their costs. The best plan is to first obtain the business and then discuss the terms and conditions under which we would turn the customer over to Newark."

We were able to win the business, and I never heard about turning the account over to Newark again.

I also ventured into Tennessee, a Milwaukee sales territory, and obtained the business of a hardwood flooring manufacturer. It was the first wood finishing account for the Atlanta office.

I was on a roll and achieving my financial objectives.

Mr. Fay, my mentor, suffered a heart attack and died in December 1958. I telephoned Stan Williams and asked if he could obtain Alice Fay's mailing address for me as I wanted to send her a letter of condolence and express my thanks for the great opportunity her father had provided for me.

I was driving by textile plants in the state every day and noticed that they had railroad tank cars staged on the rail sidings. Some mills had as many as eight tank cars parked on the rail siding next to the mill. I was curious about the contents of the railroad tank cars.

My business objective had been to identify potential customers that would purchase a minimum of 6,000 gallons of industrial coatings annually.

A railroad tank car in 1959 could carry 13,000 gallons of material. Eight cars would contain some 100,000 gallons of material. I needed to know what the textile mills were purchasing.

Once when I was returning home on a Friday afternoon from Gastonia, my route took me through Rock Hill, South Carolina, which was outside my territory. Rock Hill was the home of a huge textile mill. I stopped by, introduced myself to the receptionist and asked if I could talk with a chemist.

I introduced myself to the chemist and inquired about what was in the tank cars on the rail siding. His response: resins! I inquired further as to what types of resins and who were the suppliers. The suppliers were the same chemical companies from which PPG Industries purchased resins for the manufacturing of industrial coatings.

I asked what properties he was looking for in the resins they were applying on the textiles. The first requirement was that the resin had to provide flexibility so that the textile would return to its natural state after being crushed. The second was "color-fastness" so that the pigment would not fade when exposed to sunlight.

I explained that PPG Industries had developed and patented a thermosetting acrylic resin that was very flexible; it was used in the coatings applied to aluminum and galvanized steel and then roll-formed into residential and industrial siding. The roll-forming process required that the coating be flexible and not crack when being formed. The resin was also impervious to sunlight. The chemist asked to receive a quart sample to test.

I asked the chemist where I could find data on the use of resins in the textile industry. He responded that the best source of information would be the Textile School at North Carolina State University in Raleigh.

I spent an entire day at North Carolina State researching the type and amount of resins being consumed by the textile industry in the Southeast. I created an estimate for the market potential of PPG's thermosetting acrylic resin in the textile industry.

The chemist completed his test of the quart sample, asked me to stop by and told me that he was impressed with the test results. He outlined some modifications he wanted to have introduced to the product.

I sent his request to the Atlanta Technical department along with my report on the market potential for thermosetting acrylic resins in the production of textiles.

Atlanta Technical explained that the modification of the resin was beyond their capability and referred the task to R&D in Pittsburgh. They included my report on the market potential.

I had purposefully sent the market potential report to Atlanta Technical because I was sure my sales manager would not know what to do with it.

R&D made the modifications and provided a quart sample. The chemist at Rock Hill tested it and then requested 15 gallons of the resin for a pilot production run.

I received a call from Dr. Elmer C. Larsen of PPG, who introduced himself as the vice president of commercial development in the Paint division. Dr. Larsen further informed me that he had been hired by Mr. Fay two months before his death. My report on the market potential for resins in the textile industry had been forwarded to him by R&D, and he expressed an interest in observing the pilot production run.

Dr. Larsen, two chemists from R&D and a technician from Atlanta attended the pilot production run. It was a success; PPG Industries was in a new business!

Dr. Larsen spent the next two days with me visiting other textile plants in the state and then visiting with the dean of the North Carolina State Textile School.

The dean introduced us to a new product being developed by the school referred to as a "non-woven fabric." It consisted of fibers held together by resin and was so inexpensive to manufacture that it could be used as a disposable product. We were introduced to another potential market.

I had the opportunity to inform Dr. Larsen about my business philosophies, the objectives I had set for the developing business in my territory and the selling techniques I had employed in convincing potential customers that PPG Industries could reduce their costs. He was impressed.

One week later, I received a call from Dr. Larsen asking me to come to Pittsburgh; he wanted to talk with me about joining his staff.

I learned during my meeting with Dr. Larsen that he had been hired by Mr. Fay to identify new markets and new products that would contribute to increased revenues and profits for the division. Mr. Fay had also granted Larsen a "hunting license" to scrutinize the operation of each of the divisions' businesses and to make recommendations that would lead to growth and improved profitability. Mr. Fay had intended to have Dr. Larsen be the division's agent for change.

Mr. Fay's successor as president of the division had been the vice president of the division's retail operation, which sold paint to consumers through its Pittsburgh Paints retail outlets.

Dr. Larsen assured me that Fay's successor had endorsed the role that Fay intended for him to play and had validated his "hunting license" to improve the profitability of each of the division's businesses. Dr. Larsen asked me to join his staff as an analyst to assist him in improving the profitability of the division's businesses.

There were two other analysts in the organization, both of whom were chemical engineers who were engaged with the division's R&D organization. They focused on developing new products that could be patentable and therefore generate high profit margins, modifying existing raw materials to achieve lower costs to improve profits and developing new market opportunities.

Dr. Larsen was a superior leader and a great teacher. He set the performance bar very high. He taught me how to analyze business; he identified the key operating ratios to measure and how to determine the key operating ratios of competitors and their manufacturing costs by examining their annual reports. He taught me how to determine competitors' market share using industry reports.

In scrutinizing the division's businesses, he emphasized that the free cash flow generated by a business was the key performance measurement. He taught me to identify investment opportunities for the division's businesses that would improve profitability and how to measure the return on these investments through the use of discounted cash flow analysis (DCF) and internal rates of return (IRR).

The two years I spent with Dr. Larsen provided a far better education than I could have had attending an MBA program because I was applying the analysis and performance measurement techniques in real business situations. I was not analyzing passive case studies.

Several Notable Scrutinization Studies

Pittsburgh Brush Department: The first business scrutinization I was involved in at PPG was a study of the department that manufactured paintbrushes sold at Pittsburgh Paint retail outlets.

The brushes were being manufactured in three very old manufacturing plants. The cost of manufacturing was high, and the profitability of the three plants was marginal. The attitude of the manufacturing management was, "The real profit can be made in the retail store!" We did an analysis of the profitability of the brush business from the factory to the consumer at the store, and the profitability was not attractive.

We determined the investment required to build a new factory, but the return on the investment in a slow-growth market was not attractive.

The most attractive alternative was to sell PPG's business to a competitor whose costs were lower and then enter into an attractive purchase agreement with the buyer and sell Pittsburgh private-label brushes through the Pittsburgh Paints retail outlets.

The plan was approved and implemented with great success. Fay's replacement was so impressed, he asked that the next business scrutinization be conducted on his former department, the Pittsburgh Paints retail outlets.

Pittsburgh Paints: The retail paint market was dominated by Sherwin-Williams, which had a 1.5 market share over its closest rival. Four companies controlled 80 percent of the retail market, and Pittsburgh Paints had the lowest market share of the four. Revenues had grown a mere 3.5 percent over the past five years. The profitability of the stores was marginal.

We recommended permanently closing 10 stores, relocating 26 stores to better economic locations within their markets and an expansion to 30 new stores in high-growth markets. We recommended the department consider increasing its advertising budget to increase revenues; we offered no suggestions for the actual expenditures as advertising was beyond our area of expertise.

Our report noted that the West Coast operations of Pittsburgh Paints was the poorest performing area in the nation with the lowest market share and the lowest profitability of any region. The president suggested that the West Coast operations should be scrutinized further. I will address this opportunity later in this section.

Automotive Finishes: PPG Industries was the second-largest supplier of automotive finishes to the nation's auto manufacturers behind DuPont.

I accompanied Dr. Larsen on visits to each of the Paint division's seven manufacturing plants. Dr. Larsen conducted interviews with the manufacturing managers in each location, and one of the critical questions he asked was, "What investment in equipment would result in improved efficiency and improved profitability for your operation?"

The most knowledgeable of the managers all responded that the automotive industry typically ordered their primary colors in 40-barrel quantities, but the largest milling equipment they had to grind the pigment into the resin could only produce a sufficient quantity of material to produce 10 barrels of the finished material. It would take four batches of milling preparation to satisfy a 40-barrel order of an automotive finish.

A larger milling capacity would result in improved efficiency and lower costs.

Why had the vice president of manufacturing not asked this question?

My takeaway was that you cannot learn how to improve your operations standing at the base of the flagpole at headquarters. You have to be on the factory floor talking to the people who perform the work. That is how you can determine how you can assist in lowering costs.

Dr. Larsen asked each of the contributing managers what the utilization of the larger grinding mill would be: "What is the frequency of the 40-barrel automotive orders?"

The conclusion was that if we invested in the larger milling equipment in each of the plants, the equipment would be underutilized. Dr. Larsen then came up with the concept of centralizing the production of automotive finishes in one plant, which could achieve 100-percent utilization of the larger milling and blending equipment. The plant could be sized to a scale that would permit 24/7 operation to satisfy the market demand.

My assignment, under the direction and coaching of Dr. Larsen, was to complete the financial analysis to justify the concept and then, working with marketing, manufacturing and finance, to prepare the investment package that would be submitted to Corporate Finance and then to the board of directors for approval. The investment was approved.

Our report included the observation that Industrial Marketing would have to expand its market share for non-automotive coatings to replace the automotive volume that was going to be transferred to the central plant to maintain the plant's utilization and profitability. We included recommendations for hiring additional sales personnel and improved sales training for the existing sales force. Marketing had 15 months to achieve this goal before the new central plant came on stream.

It was a great learning experience to be working with Manufacturing Engineering on the design of the plant and determining the required investment. The next step was to work with Manufacturing and Finance to calculate the manufacturing costs of the finished products in the efficient plant.

I completed a great deal of research on five-year forecasts for automobile production in the United States and generated forecasts for our automotive finishes based on PPG Industries 1) maintaining its market share and 2) improving its market share. It was difficult to get a commitment from Marketing to improve its market share.

Dr. Larsen encouraged me to write a report identifying how to improve the skills of the existing automotive sales force to convince automotive customers we could lower their costs and thereby increase our market share. I included the recommendation to hire engineers who possessed good persuasive skills to become the automotive sales managers. They could engage with the senior management of the three automotive companies and convince them that we could reduce their costs.

Manufacturing Engineering needed to know the location of the plant in order to determine the construction cost. The task of the location study was given to me. The location of the plant would be determined by calculating the combined lowest freight cost for the delivery of raw materials to the plant and the lowest cost for the delivery of the finished product to the customer.

I worked closely with purchasing and our Transportation department to determine the inbound costs of raw materials and worked closely with Marketing to determine the expected volumes to be shipped to each customer location. I visited the customers' headquarters with Sales management to determine if new manufacturing facilities were under consideration in the next three years. Two of the customers were reluctant to share this information, but one thing became clear in the discussions: Any new facilities would be in the Western U.S. After discussions with Dr. Larsen, I included three additional phantom plants in our transportation cost model: Denver, Seattle and San Francisco.

I completed all of my calculations with my slide rule and determined the ideal location for the plant was Circleville, Ohio. Eleven years later, as the vice president of field engineering of Xerox Corporation, I initiated a study for the location of a national school for the training of our service personnel. In 1972, computers did all of the calculations. The ideal location of the school was identified as 50 miles southwest of Circleville, Ohio.

In the development of the DCF and IRR calculations, we included an estimate of the increased costs the seven plants that were transferring volume to the central plant would incur in the event Marketing could not replace the volume. The IRR exceeded a 40-percent return on the investment.

The board of directors approved the investment, and the automotive finishes plant in Circleville became a reality!

PPG INDUSTRIES CULTURE

PPG Industries did not have a work ethos similar to the Marine Corps' military ethos. In 1962, it could not be considered an elite industrial corporation. The performance standards of a corporation are set by the top management. In the four years I had been with PPG Industries, I had not heard one inspiring motivational statement emanating from the president of the company!

I was impressed with Mr. Fay's replacement's initiatives to improve the performance of the Paint division. As I pointed out earlier, Dr. Larsen was his agent for change.

Dr. Larsen's leadership skills were far superior to the other vice presidents in the division, yet he was not supercilious in his behavior. He never embarrassed his colleagues. He gathered more data about their operations than they had ever thought about obtaining and compared their performance with their best-in-class competitors. He left it to the president of the division to raise the bar and demand improved performance.

I had interviewed with the vice presidents of Marketing and Manufacturing when I returned to the company following my military service and was not impressed. After working with them for 18 months, I was convinced they were ill-suited for leadership roles.

PPG Industries tolerated poor performance.

Skill Training and an Awareness Event

PPG Industries employed a professional consulting firm to improve the communication skills of the senior management and selected employees. I have forgotten the name of the consulting company; I will refer to it as The Benefit Company (TBC). The Paint division was given allocations for placement in the school; I was one of several people from the division to be assigned.

The training focussed on the development of communication skills to persuade a person to accept your idea, which would lead to improved performance.

The techniques employed could be used in oral or written communications. It was an excellent program; I adopted the techniques for writing my report recommendations. I also recognized that the skills could be used to develop superior selling methods to persuade customers to use our products.

I incorporated the TBC techniques in my sales training classes when I became the Western regional sales manager the following year.

Seven years later, I retained TBC to develop a customized sales training program for the Information Systems Division of Xerox when I became the director of marketing.

I attended an American Coatings Association trade conference. The primary purposes of the conference were for the presentation of technical papers and the identification of changes that were taking place in national and international markets. In addition, there were breakout sessions conducted by vendors desiring to sell their services to members of the association.

In the introduction of the session presented by RHR International, it was stated that the firm assisted management in accelerating change in performance. The introduction aroused my interest as I was an agent for change in training.

The session was very enlightening. The speaker first outlined the attributes of managers who were capable of bringing about change and then outlined how they went about assessing if potential hires and existing management possessed these attributes. The firm provided additional services to management for the continuing development of executives.

The company provided handout materials that included a series of questions the firm employed in the interview process to evaluate if a candidate possessed the attributes to bring about change.

::::::::

This introduction to RHR International and their evaluation techniques to identify managers capable of bringing about change would prove to be extremely beneficial to me in two years.

SCRUTINIZATION OF THE PACIFIC COAST OPERATIONS (PCO)

In the summer of 1962, we launched the scrutinization of PCO. The company treated the operation like it was a foreign subsidiary. The operations were far away—3,000 miles from the HQ in Pittsburgh. PCO had its own president and a vice president of operations. The attitude at HQ seemed to be: Do not bother them. They will do their best.

Dr. Larsen and I toured the operations, starting with a visit with the president and the vice president of operations at their offices in Berkeley, California. We had compiled a significant amount of PCO operating data as well as the operating data of competitors who were engaged in the market.

California had the highest growth rate of gross domestic product over the previous five years of any state in the nation. The revenue growth of CPO was modest during the five-year period. CPO was dead last for market share for both retail and industrial sales. The return on assets employed was totally inadequate.

The president and vice president were clueless as to the causes of the poor performance. Dr. Larsen asked if they had developed plans to improve the performance. They responded, "No." We inquired if they intended to plan for improved revenue and profit growth in the development of their 1963 operating plan. They responded that they had not addressed the 1963 op plan at that time.

We visited the paint plant in Torrence, California, the newest paint manufacturing facility in the company. Located in the fastest-growing economy in the nation, it was operating at only 50 percent of capacity. Retail sales generated 90 percent of the volume; industrial sales generated the remaining10 percent.

The president and vice president of PCO were incompetent. The performance of PCO and the fact that it was tolerated for so many years was a prime example of the malpractice of corporate management.

Our report was very critical of the operation. Dr. Larsen had provided a copy of the report to the president of PCO two weeks before the scheduled review meeting, which would be held in Pittsburgh. I learned that the president had not been in Pittsburgh in five years.

I attended the review meeting. It was obvious the two PCO officers had not given much thought as to how they were going to improve performance. The division president used the strongest language I had heard him use to date demanding a plan to improve performance, and it was to be delivered to Dr. Larsen in two weeks.

It was now obvious to me that the president was certifying Dr. Larsen as his chief operating officer of the division.

I had the opportunity to review and comment on the PCO plan when it arrived. The plan was inadequate in purpose and thrust. It was not aggressive; it was doomed to failure.

I was not invited to attend the meeting in which Dr. Larsen critiqued the plan with the president and the other senior division officers.

It was a week later that Dr. Larsen asked me to join him in a meeting with the president.

The president spoke first. "Robert, we are going to take several steps to shake up the management of PCO. I have been informed about your performance in North Carolina; we admire your aggressive thinking. We would like you to assume the responsibilities of the industrial sales manager for PCO."

We exchanged some pleasantries, and I thanked the president and Dr. Larsen for the confidence they had in me.

The president went on to say that I would be reporting to the vice president of operations. My reaction was there was no way I would work for that man.

I had to think fast as to how to respond. I expressed that I would be making dramatic changes in the management of the organization and it was most likely that I would have to replace possibly half of the sales force if they did not respond to my guidance and training. I would be raising the performance bar and installing new policies regarding the solicitation of potential customers. I suspected the vice president would object to many of my ideas and therefore obstruct my progress. I stated that I wanted a free hand to implement my philosophies.

I then took a high risk, a long shot, and continued, "You will eventually have to eliminate the present PCO management structure and install a structure similar to the existing one employed in the rest of the country. Start now! My suggestion would be for me to report to the vice president of industrial marketing here at HQ."

My unspoken thoughts were: 1) I did not think highly of the vice president of industrial marketing, but he was a far more capable manager than the PCO vice president, 2) he did not have a stake in the recruiting of the existing sales force, and I would be free to make changes and 3) he would be 3,000 miles away and would not bother me frequently.

The president asked Howard Mather, the vice president of industrial marketing, to join the meeting. The president related the essence of our conversation, and Mather agreed.

In January 1962, Howard Mather installed me as the western regional industrial sales manager. I was 30 years old.

 *Bearings*

♦ *Mentor was a friend of Odysseus and an advisor to his son Telemachus in Homer's Odyssey. Mentor was a trusted guide. A trusted guide can be invaluable to you in your development and your ascent to greater responsibility. You do not find mentors; you do not recruit a mentor as you would hire a tutor. Mentors, the trusted guides, find you.*

♦ *If you excel, you will be noticed by superiors who appreciate your value system and talents. They will adopt you, coach you and promote you.*

♦ *Lt. Colonel Don Beck, Robert Fay and Dr. Elmer Larsen were mentors to me.*

♦ *If you join an organization that does not set high performance standards, set your own high standards. Create a hill to take! Assume the leadership role to identify the objectives to be achieved and the development of the plans to achieve your objectives. Set the performance bar high; excel in your performance and you will be recognized.*

◆ *Never turn down an opportunity to work in the headquarters of your organization. You will have a significant advantage for promotion over contemporaries located in the field. Your performance and your attitudes will be observed by senior management. You will be the first to be considered for assignments of greater responsibility.*

◆ *My presence at the 12th Marine Regiment HQ provided me with numerous assignments in which I gained invaluable experience. My experience with Dr. Larsen at PPG Industries HQ was not only a great learning experience; in addition, my talents were recognized by the senior management who endorsed my promotion.*

◆ *Associate with an organization that provides superior training either internally or through professional external training. Ask the question when interviewing for the job: "What training and continuing education will you provide to improve my skills during my career?"*

◆ *Knowledge is power; segment the performance variables of any endeavor you are involved in and measure the performance. If you do not measure it, you cannot improve it. Compare the performance with best-in-class performance. Raise the performance bar!*

My First Management Assignment

I accompanied Howard Mather to Los Angeles; he had arranged a dinner to introduce me to members of the Sales organization. He invited the technical manager, the plant manager and the controller of the Torrance factory to attend. To my surprise, he also invited the president and vice president of PCO.

I delivered the first "fire in the hole" speech of my career, warning that an explosion in a confined place was imminent.

I would be blowing up the existing performance standards and replacing them with higher standards; the performance bar was about to be raised. Both Mather and the president of PCO were uncomfortable with the speech. The vice president of operations was furious; he sat through the speech with his arms folded across his chest.

In the first week, I met with the plant controller, the technical manager and the plant manager.

I asked the controller to generate a profit and loss statement for industrial sales. When Dr. Larsen and I conducted the scrutinization of the PCO, there was no P&L for industrial sales; we had to create a pro forma P&L. The controller informed me that he did not generate a P&L for industrial sales. I responded that I wanted to have one created. I also requested that once he developed the format and methods of calculating the input for the statement, he needed to send the information to the Finance division in Pittsburgh, request a review and obtain their agreement that the P&L format would be valid.

I also requested the generation of a monthly and YTD report for each salesperson. I would provide a monthly budget for each salesperson and wanted the report to show actual sales and variances to the plan.

I also informed him of my intent to introduce the sales commission plan, which was used in all other regions in the U.S., and requested that he be prepared to implement the plan no later than April.

I asked the technical manager to help me prepare an introduction to the %solids concept to determine the cost of coverage for introduction to the sales force at a meeting the following week.

I had talks with the plant manager about my intent to establish a five-barrel minimum order for all new customers. He applauded the concept.

I purchased a California Industrial Classification Manual and used the same criteria of 300 employees to determine the primary candidates for solicitation that I had used in North Carolina. California was a target-rich environment for potential customers.

The sales force consisted of four salesmen in Los Angeles and two in San Francisco. There were no annual revenue budgets. There were no designated territories. Theoretically, a salesman was able to solicit business anywhere in the state.

I created territories, allocating 20 of the highest-potential customers from my analysis of the California Industrial Classification Manual to each territory. I met with each salesperson, explaining what I was attempting to accomplish and why I was assigning the potential customers to him. If the salesman was working with a high-potential customer outside of the territory I was proposing, I included that customer in his territory.

I created identical annual revenue budgets for each territory. I set the performance bar for each salesperson to obtain five new customers who would generate $700,000 in annual revenues. The monthly revenue goal increased each month.

I conducted a sales meeting in Los Angeles in week two. The theme of the meeting was:

We are not selling paint! We are selling industrial coatings coverage cost-reduction concepts!

The first day was devoted to introducing the %solids coverage concept for various film thicknesses and methods of application. I had reprints of the illustrations I'd used as handouts for customers in North Carolina.

I introduced methods for using our Technical department's resources in developing superior products to meet the customers' specifications.

I introduced the concept of obtaining a quart sample of the customer's current industrial coating. I established the goal for each salesperson to obtain samples from 20 high- potential customers over the next two months, which the Technical department could use in developing competitive products. We would measure this goal weekly.

The second day was devoted to training on how to introduce the %solids concept. I introduced the techniques I learned at The Benefits Company seminar for effectively communicating the concept. I introduced role-play into the training; I played the role of the customer. I asked the salesmen to critique the performance of their peers and suggested improvements in their performance. Training would be a critical element in achieving our goals.

I requested that each salesperson provide a schedule of his daily call plan by customer for the following week to be on my desk by Friday of the preceding week.

My routine would be to make customer calls with each of the four Los Angeles salesmen for one day each week.

The second week, I worked with each of the San Francisco salesmen for two days.

We set our objectives for the sales call before arriving at the customer's location. I left the solicitation of the customer to the salesperson, interjecting myself into the discussion only if the salesperson failed to introduce a significant benefit to the customer.

After the call, I would conduct what I called "curbside coaching," pointing out opportunities for improvement in the salesman's presentation. Training was important!

I conducted monthly sales meetings to reinforce The Benefit Company's techniques to strengthen our presentation of the benefits of the %solids concept. I had individual salesmen present success stories of how they were able to open a new, high-potential account. We continued the role playing to improve the salesmen's skills.

We were increasing our revenues each month. The investment in training was paying off! I had only one salesman in Los Angeles who was not responding to the training. After four months, I terminated him. He had been employed for four years and had failed to generate any significant revenue.

I wrote up our success stories and sent them to Howard Mather. I never saw a communication from Mather to the other four regional managers outlining our successes and how we accomplished them. Mather never communicated a success story to me from other regional managers to assist in increasing my regional sales.

By August 1962, our operation broke even, and we generated profits in September and October. I had been sending monthly copies of our P&L to Dr. Larsen for his eyes only. Howard Mather came to visit me in early November.

I reviewed with him how we had been able to accomplish the results and informed him of my plans for 1963 when I intended to replace the Los Angeles representative I had terminated and open new territories in San Diego/Phoenix and Seattle/Portland.

I asked what my reward would be for these accomplishments, and he responded that a $75-a-month salary increase might be in order, and if approved, would be effective the first of the year.

I was disappointed and expressed my feelings to Mather. I had expected a bigger increase in salary and a bonus. My most ambitious expectation was to become the national operations manager reporting to Mather and duplicate the success in all of the regions nationally. Mather did not think this way. Raising the performance bar for his entire organization was beyond his orientation.

I updated my resume.

I subscribed to *Sales Management magazine.* I was reading the November 1962 issue, which included an article on the Haloid Xerox Corporation, a small photographic paper manufacturer located in Rochester, New York.

I joined Xerox in November 1962.

THE SUTTER GROUP

While performing as the interim CEO of AWD, I was introduced to Tom Lumsden, the Price Waterhouse manager of advisory services for financially distressed companies. Tom suggested we form an alliance to provide the management services to turn around the performance of US Leisure, which had recently filed for bankruptcy. Tom would assume the role of trustee for the company; I would serve as the COO and manage the operations.

I observed the management of a company operating in bankruptcy to be a high-risk business and decided to create a corporation to protect my personal net worth.

I contacted my friend John Larson at Brobeck, Phleger & Harrison. He put me in touch with his partner, who would assist me in creating the corporation and developing a contract that would protect TSG in performing services for companies that were in a state of financial distress.

The language to protect TSG was incorporated into a single paragraph stating that TSG made no promises to return the company to prosperous operations in exchange for the fees paid by the client. TSG's commitment to the client was limited to providing its best efforts to return the enterprise to prosperous operations.

I intended to minimize the size of the payroll. I chose not to employ analytical talent. When required, I would purchase analytical services from Lumsden's organization.

I created the name for the corporation. Remembering that an employee of John Sutter had discovered gold in California in 1849, I thought I might be able to discover gold in California a second time.

Tom and I won the "beauty contest" among the competing bidders who were soliciting the assignment. Our contracts were approved by the bankruptcy court.

US LEISURE

Pat Murphy, the founder of Murphy, Weir & Butler, was considered to be one of the top five bankruptcy lawyers in the United States. He was the attorney representing the debtor. Working with him was a great learning experience!

US Leisure had four operating divisions. The largest revenue division, which manufactured redwood outdoor furniture, was located in Willits, California, in the heart of the California redwood timberlands.

A second division manufactured lightweight, stackable plastic chairs by injecting thermoplastic polypropylene into molds under high heat and pressure. The plant was located in Indiana.

A third division manufactured outdoor furniture cushions in two plants located in Indiana and Georgia.

The fourth division manufactured above-ground swimming pools in a plant located in Wilkes-Barre, Pennsylvania. It operated as a subsidiary of US Leisure and was the only division that was making money. The subsidiary had its own line of credit with a local bank, so the creditors chose to form their own committee rather than be associated with the three divisions that were not making money.

The committee was represented by Jim Lopes, a highly competent bankruptcy attorney.

Pat Murphy had secured a line of credit for the company referred to as debtor-in-possession (DIP) financing, which was senior to all other debt and would be the first to be repaid under a plan of reorganization. The company had sufficient liquidity to continue to operate.

It was on a Wednesday afternoon that Pat Murphy scheduled a US Leisure board of directors meeting. The CEO also performed as the chairman of the board. There were three independent directors, all well-known San Francisco businessmen. I knew one of the board members as I had served with him on the San Francisco Chamber of Commerce board.

Pat Murphy possessed an ability to distill very complex legal decisions and events into very simple, understandable terms.

He informed the board that Janet Reno, the United States attorney general, was now the chairwoman of the board, and Tom Lumsden would be her representative. On Monday of the following week, Tom, with the support of the two creditor committees, would seek the approval of the bankruptcy court to remove the CEO and chairman. Tom Lumsden would assume the role of chairman, and he intended to appoint me to be the COO of US Leisure.

The CEO mounted a vigorous protest, claiming he was the largest shareholder of the company's stock and possessed the best knowledge of the company's markets and operations of the various businesses. He contended that he was therefore the best-qualified individual to manage the reorganization of the company.

He had the audacity to suggest that he should interview me to determine if I had the skills and experience to implement the reorganization. Murphy dissuaded the board from even considering that notion; it was not going to happen.

It was late on Friday afternoon of that week that Pat Murphy scheduled a conference call with Lumsden and me to inform us that the CEO had committed suicide.

It was hard to believe that someone would be compelled to commit such an act. His suicide was a portent of the financial catastrophe we would uncover once we took control of the company.

I felt so sorry for his family; it was a tragic event. It was an onerous start for TSG's first assignment!

The redwood furniture business was the largest revenue-generating entity in the company, yet it was hemorrhaging cash. We immediately focused our attention on this entity.

Redwood is a species of timber that absorbs large quantities of water from the soil. Lumber formed from redwood timber has a high moisture content and must be dried before it can be fabricated. There are two market designations for redwood lumber. "Green redwood" has a high moisture content; after the product has been dried, it commands a higher selling price as "dried redwood." The drying process can be accelerated by first drying the lumber in heated kilns and then air-drying it. The total drying cycle can take months to complete.

What we discovered was that the board of directors had approved the purchase of "dried redwood" from a company owned by the CEO.

The CEO's company was purchasing "green redwood," delivering the lumber to the company plant in Willits, using company labor to load the lumber into the company kilns, using company energy to fire the kilns, and after weeks of drying (using company labor to remove the lumber from the kilns and stack the lumber), placing half-inch pieces of wood between each row of redwood lumber to promote air circulation. The ends of each piece of redwood had to be painted with a sealer to prevent the board from splitting. It was a labor-intensive process.

After weeks of air-drying, the CEO's company sold the "dried redwood" to US Leisure at a significant profit. The value added to the "green redwood," including energy and labor, had been provided by US Leisure.

The more "dried redwood" the CEO could sell to the company, the more profitable his own company became. As the CEO of the redwood furniture division, he maximized the production of furniture without orders and placed the finished products in inventory.

We discovered the company had rented warehouses in numerous locations throughout the U.S. They were filled with finished goods inventory.

The banks contributed to this fraud by providing customary finished goods inventory (FGI) financing for up to 65 percent of the market value of the inventory. However, they did not place an absolute dollar limit on the amount of financing they would provide. US Leisure had an unlimited source of cash to produce redwood furniture.

The US Leisure balance sheet reflected its ballooning inventory of finished goods, yet no director blew the whistle.

I reported the situation to Lumsden, Murphy and the creditor committee lawyers. I recommended that we shut down the factory and terminate the CFO and the vice president of marketing, whom I thought were implicitly involved in the fraud.

I recruited an experienced CFO, who became my first partner and had his contract providing services to US Leisure approved by the bankruptcy court.

Lumsden's organization provided forensic accountants who examined the company's financial statements to identify fraudulent conveyances of money to the CEO's company during the 90 days prior to the company's filing for bankruptcy.

Lumsden and Murphy were able to "claw back" (recover) a large number of fraudulent conveyances from the former CEO's company and his estate.

I asked Murphy why the three independent directors chose to remain on the board. He responded that he had advised each director to retain legal counsel because each of them could be found to be derelict in his duties as a director and personally liable for the collapse of the company. Each director had hired legal counsel and their attorneys had advised them to remain as directors so they would know what was being discovered by the trustee. It was better to be on the inside knowing what was going on than to be on the outside looking in.

I ordered management to initiate parking-lot sales of redwood furniture in each of the cities in which we had warehouses. The initial pricing was to be 50 cents on the dollar, and the pricing was to be reduced by five percent each week until the inventory was liquidated.

It was necessary to conduct similar parking-lot sales in the plastic chair and outdoor cushion divisions. For the above-ground swimming pool division, we authorized newspaper and TV advertising in major Southeastern cities, selling the pools for cents on the dollar. We authorized the payment of shipping from Wilkes-Barre, Pennsylvania.

All four of the US Leisure divisions had common customers. The largest customer was Sears Roebuck & Company; the company sold products to both its retail stores and its catalog sales unit. Other big-box retailers included Walmart, Home Depot, Lowe's, Costco and Sam's Club.

I visited with the purchasing department of each of these retailers in the first month. There was an environmental movement underway in the Western U.S. to stop the harvesting of redwood trees. The buyers for each of the retailers informed me that their companies intended to phase out the marketing of redwood furniture.

I advised all of the interested parties that the redwood furniture division was not a viable business, the plant would not be reopened and we would liquidate the assets. Pat Murphy introduced me to a highly competent industrial auctioneer from

Houston who did an excellent job selling the plant, land and machinery. I would use his services many times in the future.

We did not find any fraudulent activities in the three other divisions, but each division was poorly managed. The former CEO was not an effective manager.

The outdoor furniture cushion division was a seasonal business. The factories continuously produced product until the end of the season without having purchase orders. The bank provided FGI financing without absolute dollar limits. Products became obsolete due to buyers' color or design preferences. I walked through every warehouse and observed that much of the inventory had accumulated inches of dust. The inventory had been there for years.

It became standard operating procedure for future TSG assignments on day one of our assignment to visit inventory locations with management and conduct what became known as the "dust test" in which I would run my hand across the top of a box, show the amount of dust on my hand to the local management and provide them an estimate of how many years the item had been in inventory.

This would be followed up with a lecture on the real cost of carrying inventory, which was 25 percent annually. It was an effective visual technique to introduce the need for strict control of inventories.

We could not come up with a viable business plan for the cushion division, and my advice to the interested parties was to liquidate the business. The plan was accepted; the Houston auction firm conducted the auctions.

The objective of the creditors was to recover their losses. They had no interest in a reorganization plan that resulted in their being equity holders in companies that produced above-ground swimming pools and plastic chairs. They wanted cash!

In addition, both divisions were involved in seasonal businesses. It would be very difficult to achieve a satisfactory return on assets employed in businesses that operated only six months of the year. Therefore, our objective was to improve the profitability of the two divisions and find buyers for the businesses at prices that generated large amounts of cash. This was an activity that I had repeatedly performed at Fibreboard for three years.

My CFO partner and I visited the above-ground pool factory in June, though the factory was closed. The plant manager knew about our closure of the redwood furniture and cushion manufacturing plants and was confrontational. His attitude was that he knew everything about manufacturing, and there was nothing new that we could introduce that would bring about improvements in his operation.

We visited the warehouse area and observed large quantities of FGI that had been produced but not sold the previous season. I commented that I had given instructions to sell FGI inventory at cents on the dollar. He explained that he had not been able to get around to it. I ordered him to implement a plan by the next day.

There was an area in the warehouse in which returned product was stowed. It resembled a trash heap. It contained boxes that looked like a customer's forklift had pierced the box and damaged the pool. There were damaged pools that were not in a box. I inquired how a freight company could deliver such an item. I identified boxes of competitive products and inquired as to how we would accept the return of a competitive product.

I inquired whether these returns had been accounted for and whether refunds had been issued to the customers. The answer was no. I asked the plant manager when he intended to complete the work. His response was that it would be completed in October when the accounting personnel returned to work.

I pointed out that we really did not know whether we had made money or lost money during the past season.

The CFO ordered him to have the controller and accounting personnel in the office the next day to complete the transactions or we would have Lumsden's organization provide personnel next week to complete the transactions and close the books. Poor management! We recognized we had a problem.

The plant manager informed us that the company manufactured five types of pools of different diameters and depths. I asked that he walk us through the quiet factory and identify each step of the manufacturing process to complete the production of each of the five products.

I sketched out the process for each of the products. We would refine the process mapping, but I wanted a rough idea of how each product flowed through the factory.

As we moved through the factory, we observed areas filled with junk, raw materials, partially-completed components and unused packing materials. I instructed the plant manager to sell anything that could be recycled, and everything else was to be taken to the dump.

We visited the workers' locker rooms and bathrooms. The facilities were deplorable. I ordered that the facilities be pressure-washed and painted, and that any pieces of equipment, lockers or bathroom fixtures in poor condition were to be replaced.

We returned to the factory floor, and I instructed the plant manager to clean up the entire factory and replace the lighting.

We were going to provide good working conditions.

We examined the wage rates we were paying for various positions and compared our rates with the published average rates for similar positions in the county. We were paying below the median county rates.

We reviewed the hiring practices the plant manager employed when he recalled the workforce to start up the plant in October and determined we could attract workers with higher skills, which would lead to improved productivity if we offered higher wages.

We had the cash available to make the improvements in the workplace and to pay higher wages because of the availability of the DIP financing.

Tom Lumsden and I were able to convince the two creditor committee lawyers and Pat Murphy that these expenditures would result in lower unit costs of production.

We then instructed the plant manager to recall key management, staff personnel and skilled veteran workers to form PIP (Profit Improvement Program) teams that would streamline the production workflow to reduce the time and labor involved in the production process. The PIP teams were to be supported by engineers, cost accountants and members of Tom Lumsden's organization who were familiar with Toyota's TPS.

The team would be encouraged to make recommendations for investment in new equipment to lower our costs.

We set a date for the completion of the team's work in two weeks. Then we would convene a meeting with the PIP team and additional personnel from sales order entry, production scheduling and procurement. Senior marketing personnel were included, as was a lawyer from Murphy's firm, who would draft a new standard sales contract.

The group was to develop a coordinated marketing/ production plan for the coming season.

The key objectives of the plan were to eliminate the creation of FGI and to develop a sales contract that prohibited the return of product at the completion of the season.

The PIP team's first recommendation was to eliminate two product lines of shallow, small-diameter pools. Lumsden's people supported the recommendation with analysis showing that the two product lines contributed very little revenue and profitability to the enterprise and complicated the staffing of the production lines due to the infrequency and small size of the orders.

The second observation the PIP team introduced was that if we wanted to achieve the uninterrupted flow of production,

Marketing had to eliminate emergency orders that product had to be produced immediately. These orders were being introduced late in the production season and disrupted the production flow.

The plant operating plan embraced by former management was to begin production in October to satisfy a product mix that marketing was forecasting for the coming season. The production was placed in FGI. Beginning in November, customer orders would begin to arrive, and the production scheduling could be refined.

The major customers, big-box retailers, typically wanted product in their retail stores located in the Southeast and Southwest in March. Stores in the mid-Atlantic and Midwest expected delivery in April, and stores in the Northeast expected delivery in May.

Purchase orders were accepted without delivery dates. Purchasing agents would advise the company of the delivery dates and location at some point in the future.

The company was basically producing product for inventory that was going to cost two percent per month to carry.

Tom Lumsden's analysts created production models using different product mixes and delivery dates and determined that optimum profitability could be achieved by maximizing production from January through April. The modeling showed that a second shift employing new, untrained employees was expensive and was to be avoided. The modeling showed that it would be more profitable to stop production late in the season on the least profitable product line and employ those employees on a second shift to produce a more profitable product line.

Their analysis also showed we could extend the shifts from eight hours to ten hours in April, the last month of production, to generate more volume and profits. Employing this procedure early in the production cycle would lead to employee burnout.

The role of marketing was going to change from that of soliciting orders to that of selling production time for various products. The plan would require the customer to commit to a delivery schedule at the time of purchase. We established minimum order sizes for February through April.

The company had a few customers with one to three pool equipment outlets who placed small orders. We informed those customers that they had to commit to their orders in December. The product would be produced in January, and if the customer chose to have his order held in inventory, the selling price would be two-percent higher for each month the product was held in inventory.

The big-box retailers were encouraged to purchase production time early because if we were sold out of April production products for May delivery, their purchase would have to be produced in March for May delivery and the selling price would be two-percent higher to cover the cost of holding their product in inventory for an extra month.

Customers could obtain a lower selling price by taking delivery when the product was produced and storing it in their warehouse.

Our lawyers created the terms and conditions of our sale contract, which had to be executed by the customer before we would accept an order. The terms included a no-return policy.

The young salesman who I promoted to vice president of sales when I terminated the incumbent responded positively to the raising of the performance bar. We taught him the skills to convince customers that our new method of doing business was in their best interest.

I accompanied him on the customer visits; there were only six big-box retailers where we could introduce our new terms and conditions of sale. We met with immediate rejection from the purchasing agents, particularly from Walmart, whose attitude was: You will sell to Walmart under the terms and conditions Walmart chooses, or you can take the first bus departing Bentonville, Arkansas.

We had two things going for us. First, the company had a reputation for building a high-quality product free of defects. And yes, we would accept products for return that were defective.

Secondly, Tom Lumsden completed research that revealed one of the highest gross-margin SKUs generated by big-box retailers was the margin achieved on the sale of above-ground swimming pools.

It required several meetings with purchasing officials before we gained their acceptance of our sales policies. In the case of Walmart, our negotiations ascended to a meeting with the vice president of purchasing. I knew that when we reached this level of authority that they wanted to do business with us. The VP was blunt in telling us what a unique privilege it was to be a supplier to Walmart. If we wanted to do business with Walmart, we would have to surrender our no-return policy.

I decided to be equally blunt and informed him that we would accept returns if a product was defective, but if Walmart overestimated their unit sales for the season, we were not going to accept the return of pools in good condition and end up holding the inventory for nine months. I reminded him that Walmart enjoyed a lucrative profit margin on the sale of above-ground swimming pools. I suggested that if Walmart had unsold inventory at the end of the selling season, they could discount the price and still enjoy a satisfactory profit. If that did not work, I suggested, "You could ship the product to a store in Bolivia and sell it for the full price plus freight." I was risking the loss of the Walmart business, but in the end, we prevailed!

We created an office in the factory with no walls that was well-lit and air-conditioned. We moved sales order entry, production scheduling and procurement from their individual offices into the office with no walls. We included a desk for Marketing.

One of the primary roles of this group was production scheduling: identifying voids in the production schedule and advising Marketing to obtain orders for a specific number of units of a product for production in a specific week to fill the void.

Another primary objective of this group was to establish alliances with our suppliers and to schedule deliveries JIT (just in time) for production. We found that all of our suppliers produced for inventory, so we were able to provide them with monthly forecasts of our requirements and firm weekly and daily shipping requirements.

We delayed the opening of the plant from October to December. We had zero investment in raw material inventory and reduced our FGI over the previous year by 60 percent. We were earning two percent per month on the FGI we held for customers.

For the 1978 season, the above-ground swimming pool division generated three times the absolute dollars of before-tax income that it had achieved during the previous season on 80 percent of the unit volume.

In addition, we had thousands of square feet of manufacturing space that had been committed to inventory storage in the past that was now vacant and available for production.

In the plastic chair division, we organized PIP teams to determine how to improve the process flow and reduce our manufacturing costs. Injection molding of plastic chairs is a simple four-step process; there was little opportunity to improve the process flow.

The polypropylene powder is heated and, when melted, introduced into the mold, which is placed under high heat and pressure. The cooling step requires time. When the mold is opened, four chairs are ejected.

The operator charges the mold with polypropylene for the next production cycle. While the cycle is being completed, the operator removes any burrs on the previous batch of chairs with an electric disk sander. The units are placed on a trolley and moved to the Shipping department.

The customers were the same big-box retailers the above-ground pool manufacturer division sold to, but the plastic chair business enjoyed a full-year market. It was not a seasonal market, but spring and summer were the times of highest demand for the product.

We adopted the practice of selling production time to enable the factory to operate more efficiently.

We had excess capacity and needed more unit sales. The market was very competitive. We examined the opportunity to capitalize on our improved unit manufacturing cost (UMC) to lower our selling prices and still maintain our profit margin. Increased volume would absorb our fixed manufacturing costs and reduce our UMC.

We became aggressive in obtaining increased volume by lowering our selling prices. We initiated the practice of charging the customers for inventorying their product.

The simple manufacturing process enabled us to add shifts to our production schedule, bringing additional capacity online to coincide with customers' delivery requirements.

We dramatically improved the profitability of the division.

We then embarked on the sale of the businesses.

The above-ground pool manufacturers held an annual trade show in Miami. US Leisure participated in the event with a large display booth. I attended the show and, while walking the floor, came across a display of what I would refer to as a large, inflatable industrial barge made by Zodiac, the French manufacturer of inflatable boats. I asked a Zodiac salesperson if they classified this barge as a swimming pool. The response was that the barge was sold in Europe as a wading pool.

I arranged to meet the senior officer of the company who was attending the show and was introduced to Jean-Marc Dailance, the president of the Zodiac division and a young Harvard Business School graduate. I inquired if he was interested in entering the U.S. market. If so, we had a manufacturing plant with excess capacity available for sale.

Jean-Marc expressed interest in the idea, and we arranged to meet the following week in Wilkes-Barre. We entered into negotiation for the sale of the business. Jean-Marc was very smart and very detail-oriented. It was the most difficult business negotiation I had experienced in my career.

We obtained Zodiac's public financial statements and determined their profit margins for inflatable boats, which we assumed they would manufacture in the Wilkes-Barre facility for distribution in the U.S. market. We modeled the profitability of the plant operating 12 months of the year producing inflatable boats and above-ground swimming pools in order to determine a selling price for the business that would return an attractive IRR for Zodiac.

We prevailed in obtaining our asking price. On the morning of the closing, I arrived at Zodiac's lawyer's office at nine o'clock. Each document that was required to be signed by both parties was positioned around the conference room table. I moved around the table and executed each document. Jean-Marc arrived at 9:30 and was to begin signing the documents.

He pulled up a chair next to mine and said that he felt the carve-out for uncollectible accounts receivables to be accounted for in 90 days after the close was inadequate. He wanted a larger carve-out.

I paused and then said to him that I would like to speak with his lawyer in private. I followed his lawyer to his office and said, "I want you to deliver this message to your client. If I were to deliver it, I may lose my temper. The negotiations involving this deal were concluded at 4:30 yesterday afternoon. I have executed the documents. If your client would like to close the deal, he merely has to sign the documents. You are aware that we have arranged for a closing lunch at Giambelli's on 50th Street at noon. Your client is welcome to attend the lunch even if he chooses not to close the deal. The negotiations are over, and we are out of here!"

I went back into the conference room, opened my briefcase, packed up my papers and gestured to my associates to pack up.

I said goodbye to Jean-Marc and told him that his lawyer would explain our position.

We pushed the down button for the elevator, and before the elevator arrived, Jean-Marc's lawyer appeared. "We will sign the documents and be at Giambelli's at noon!" he said. The deal closed.

Jean-Marc advanced in the Zodiac organization and retained TSG to improve the profitability of two companies Zodiac acquired in the United States. These were the only advisory engagements TSG would be involved in. Jean-Marc nominated me to be Zodiac's director of a joint venture they formed in southern California. We enjoyed a good relationship for many years, and whenever Kathie and I were in Paris, we would have dinner with Jean-Marc and his wife.

The European plastic furniture manufacturers conducted an annual trade show in Dusseldorf, Germany. Our vice president of marketing suggested that we visit the show "just to see what's going on in that market." The sale of plastic furniture was far greater in Europe than it was in the United States.

Two fortuitous events occurred during our visit.

We introduced ourselves to the officers of a Belgian company that produced furniture of a superior design. We inquired if they would consider making US Leisure their exclusive distributor in the United States. We negotiated an agreement that provided the Belgian company with a higher royalty until their investment in the molds they would provide to us was recovered; then the royalty would be reduced. We were able to penetrate a new market with a superior product with a higher gross profit margin. We improved the utilization of the factory.

We introduced ourselves to the owner of an Israeli company who was displaying products and inquired if he had an interest in entering the United States market. He expressed interest, and we informed him of the capability of our factory and our market share. He was particularly interested in the unit sales to Home Depot.

Two weeks went by before I received a call from the president stating that he would like to visit our plant. During that visit, we learned that he was a good friend of Arthur Blank and Bernard Marcus, two of the original five founders of Home Depot.

We modeled the profitability of the plant, assuming that the new owner could double the unit volume sold to Home Depot. We used the increased volume of the Belgian product, which had a superior design, at the lower royalty, to be paid after the cost of the molds had been amortized. That established a selling price the Israeli company could afford and could achieve a satisfactory IRR. We closed the sale

After the sales of the two divisions closed, US Leisure had a large amount of cash on its balance sheet. Pat Murphy and Tom Lumsden began to negotiate the plan of reorganization with the two creditor committees.

Murphy and Lumsden offered the above-ground swimming pool creditor committee 100 cents on the dollar. The committee demanded the payment of interest on the funds they were denied use of during the bankruptcy. They reached an agreement to return 108 cents on the dollars owed to the creditors. All of the creditors, including the division's bank, were paid in full. The remaining balance of cash was available for US Leisure obligations.

The bank that provided the DIP financing was repaid in full. Interest payments had been paid each quarter.

The remaining cash balance represented 80 cents on the dollar available to the creditors of US Leisure's redwood furniture and cushion businesses, which they accepted.

The plan of reorganization was supported by the creditors and approved by Tom Lumsden, the trustee and the bankruptcy court. US Leisure exited bankruptcy and was dissolved.

All of the stakeholders were extremely pleased with the outcome.

Tom Lumsden and I enjoyed a working relationship that would go on for 25 years. I would employ his analytical teams, and he would recommend TSG for executive officer turnaround assignments.

Jim Lopes, the lawyer for the above-ground pool division creditors, would recommend TSG for turnaround assignments until his retirement.

Pat Murphy wrote a letter of recommendation to the chief investment officer of Prudential Life Insurance. I had a copy of the letter framed and hung it in my office. I referred to it as a "two-million-dollar letter"—the sum of the fees we would earn representing Prudential in the following 18 months.

The US Leisure assignment was a successful beginning for The Sutter Group.

 Bearings

- ✦ *It is possible to assume responsibility for a financial catastrophe and return it to a state of prosperity. Never accept the status quo; seek to improve the operation of any enterprise for which you are given responsibility.*

- ✦ *Never hesitate to take on the responsibility of managing a business that you know nothing about. Learning the fundamentals of how that business works and initiating new management practices that lead to improved profitability will build your self-confidence.*

◆ *I will repeat the adage that you cannot learn how to improve the performance of your business standing at the base of the flagpole at your HQ. Visit your offices and plants, visit your customers, visit your vendors, visit your competitors and participate in trade shows. You will learn how to improve the performance of your business!*

◆ *Know your customers' finances. If you are selling to a retailer, visit their stores to determine their selling price for your product and the profit margin they are making on your product.*

◆ *When you are selling a business, model the profitability of the enterprise as the buyer will be operating the assets. Then calculate the selling price the buyer can pay for the assets while generating a satisfactory IRR.*

Prudential Life Insurance

Two weeks had gone by since Pat Murphy had written the letter of recommendation to the chief investment officer of Prudential Life when he called me and informed me he was going to be in San Francisco. He invited me to lunch.

He explained to me that Spreckels Sugar had defaulted on the payment of interest on bonds underwritten by Prudential. The covenants associated with the bonds provided that on default, Prudential could convert their bonds into equity. As a result of that conversion, Prudential now held a controlling interest in the equity of Spreckels Sugar. He was looking for a CEO to turn the company around.

Spreckels operated six beet sugar refineries in California. Over the years, the company had sold off the farmland once used to grow and supply sugar beets to the refineries to residential and commercial real estate developers.

The growing season for sugar beets in California was six months and therefore allowed for only one harvest each year. The operation of the refineries was limited to six months, so the return on invested capital was modest.

The U.S. Department of Agriculture (USDOA) controls the production and pricing of sugar in the United States by guaranteeing a selling price to the growers of sugar beets and sugarcane, limiting the production of sugar and limiting imports.

Beet sugar refiners in California paid even higher prices than the USDOA guaranteed price to farmers in order to persuade the farmers to plant sugar beets because the farmers had alternative crops to grow that could generate higher profits. California beet sugar refiners were the high-cost producers of refined sugar.

Once you started up a refinery, you did not shut it down; a sugar refinery operates 24/7. Spreckels did not produce for orders; it produced product for inventory that was stored in silos. Spreckels shipped product to retail and commercial customers from inventory during the off-season; the company hoped they would finish the season with little or no inventory. Spreckels was a high-cost producer of sugar.

Spreckels had not used its full USDOA production allocation for the past two years. They needed more customers to maximize the utilization of their refineries; if they could succeed in obtaining new customers, they would have to motivate more farmers to plant sugar beets.

I called for a marketing meeting and asked the management to identify the 10 largest Californian purchasers of sugar by volume with whom we did not do business. Once the potential customers were identified, I asked why we did not do business with these accounts. I was told that each of the 10 companies used a common quality assurance consultant to evaluate our manufacturing facilities and processes and assess our ability to produce a quality product. Spreckels refineries had failed the quality control (QC) inspections the previous two years.

The cause of the company's failure to pass the test was that the windows in the receiving sheds of the refineries were not screened so birds were flying through, creating a threat to our quality assurance.

The receiving area for the beets contained two expensive devices to turn railcars and truck trailers upside down and dump out sugar beets, rocks and dirt from the harvest fields. Birds flying through unscreened windows of the receiving sheds were not going to contribute to the contamination of the final processed product, which was packaged in clean rooms in which the workers wore white uniforms without pockets and hair, beard and mustache nets.

We did not have a marketing problem; we had a manufacturing problem. I called for a meeting of the refinery managers to address how we could install screens on the windows. Five refinery managers offered multiple reasons why screens could not be installed. The sixth refinery manager was silent, and when I asked him why, he responded that he did not have this problem as his receiving shed had no walls and therefore no windows and no need for screens. He added that birds flew freely through his shed. His refinery had always passed the customers' QC audit.

I asked that an engineer be invited to the meeting and requested a design and cost estimate for the removal of the walls of the five refineries' receiving sheds with walls.

We passed the next audits and were able to obtain orders from new customers. Management had been aware of this problem for two years but never initiated any action to correct it

We modeled the six refineries operating at 90-percent utilization for six months each year, using 100 percent of our USDOA production allocation and paying a premium to the farmers to grow sugar beets. The return on assets employed was not attractive.

My recommendation to Prudential was to sell the company.

The largest producers of refined sugar in the United States were the grower associations in Minnesota, North Dakota and Idaho that farmed sugar beets and owned their refineries. The ambient temperature in the location of these operations allowed them to store sugar beets in open sheds year-round, so they were able to operate their refineries year-round.

I asked Spreckels' management what the alternative crops were for the farmers in those northern latitudes, and the agriculture manager responded, "Weeds!"

The northern states' grower associations were the low-cost producers of refined sugar in the United States.

The largest producer of cane sugar in the United States was the US Sugar Corporation, a privately owned company located in Florida that had been formed in 1956 by sugarcane land owners who fled Cuba after Fidel Castro, the communist revolutionary, had overthrown the government and confiscated their land and refineries.

Savannah Sugar operated one sugarcane refinery in Savannah, Georgia.

Imperial Sugar operated two sugarcane refineries, located in Sugarland, Texas, and New Orleans.

The California market for refined sugar was fiercely competitive.

Holly Sugar, headquartered in Colorado Springs, Colorado, operated five sugar beet refineries in California and multiple refineries in Colorado, Idaho and upstate Michigan.

C&H Sugar operated a cane refinery in Crockett, California, which was supplied with sugarcane shipped from Hawaii in bulk ship carriers. C&H dominated the California retail market as a result of an effective advertising campaign that convinced consumers that cane sugar was a healthier alternative to beet sugar.

The liquidation strategy that would maximize the absolute dollars for the sale of Spreckels' refineries was to sell individual refineries to the various growers' associations located in the northern United States, who would then close the refineries and transfer Spreckels' USDOA production allocation to their existing refineries. With the help of Tom Lumsden's analysts, we created operating models of the expanded growers' associations' refineries and determined the selling prices they could pay and make a satisfactory IRR on their investment. This sale option would require time as six individual purchase agreements needed to be perfected.

Imperial Sugar was a private, family-owned company formed by John Kempner in 1843. James Kempner, a descendent, was now the CEO and had publicly announced that Imperial Sugar intended to dominate the United States sugar market. The board of directors of Imperial Sugar was composed of Kempner family members. There was one outside director, an investment banker.

I suggested to Prudential that we establish the asking price for the entire company equal to the sum of sale prices for the individual refineries to the northern growers and reach out to

Imperial Sugar to determine if they had an interest in purchasing Spreckels Sugar.

I arranged a meeting with James Kempner. I found him to be condescending. I listened and did not have to do much selling regarding the price. He knew everything about the production and marketing of sugar. He did not ask for permission to talk with the president of our growers' association, so I assumed that he conducted limited due diligence regarding the competitive nature of procuring sugar beets in the California market. He agreed to our asking price.

Prudential recovered 135 percent of the face value of the bonds they had converted to equity. The chief investment officer would continue to engage The Sutter Group for turnaround assignments until his retirement.

The most salient takeaway for me regarding the assignment was the knowledge that when insurance companies underwrote bond offerings, the indenture usually contained covenants that in the event of a default the debt could be converted to equity or the bondholder would have the right to several seats on the board of directors or the right to name a new CEO.

I was compelled to reestablish my relationship with Bob Schwartz, the chief investment officer of MetLife who supported my management of Fibreboard and introduce The Sutter Group.

MetLife

To my surprise, Robert Schwartz was now the CEO of MetLife. I arranged to meet him in New York and informed him of the formation of The Sutter Group and our successes with the US Leisure bankruptcy and the sale of Spreckels Sugar for Prudential. He informed me that Dan Clarke, the MetLife account manager for Fibreboard, was now the chief investment officer for MetLife. He contacted Dan by phone and arranged for a meeting with him and his staff the next day.

Dan Clarke introduced me to Jackie Jenkins, a tough-minded businesswoman in charge of the distressed assets department whose mission was to recover MetLife's bond investments in companies that had defaulted on their obligations.

Jackie and I shared a common value orientation. It was a good meeting.

She called me within three weeks and invited me to come to New York to be introduced to an assignment. She suggested that I be prepared to stay on the East Coast for a week. If we were interested in the assignment, she wanted to move fast as the financial situation of the company was deteriorating rapidly and MetLife wanted to install new management promptly.

My CFO and I arrived the next day and were introduced to Coatings Technologies International (CTI), headquartered in Columbia, South Carolina. The company was composed of three divisions. The pressure-sensitive tape division manufactured duct tape, masking tape and other products, including postage stamps for the USPS in factories located in Columbia, South Carolina, and Cleveland, Ohio.

The second division manufactured cloth bookbindings in a plant located in Holston, Tennessee. The third division manufactured paper bookbindings; the plant was located in upstate New York.

We signed a contract for the employment of myself and my CFO and flew to Columbia that afternoon. Jackie Jenkins installed us as the new officers of the company.

During our introduction, three gentlemen sat in the last row of seating in the conference room; their arms were folded across their chests in defiance of the changes that were being introduced. I asked them to identify themselves and learned they were the vice presidents of manufacturing, personnel and finance. I asked them to unfold their arms, relax and become a part of the new management as we were going to need their skills and experience to return the company to prosperous operations.

The vice president of finance responded positively, adapted and became a contributor to the successful turnaround. The vice presidents of manufacturing and personnel were not responsive and had to be terminated.

The tour of the plant that day was difficult; the aisles in the plant were clogged with WIP, jumbo rolls of duct tape and masking tape that had been removed from the production line in order to make way for the production of emergency orders.

We realized that in order to introduce TPS, we had to train the foreman to play the role of coach rather than supervisor. We were fortunate to discover a local consulting company familiar with TPS that trained supervisory personnel to make the transition from foreman to coach. TSG would employ their services for the CTI assignment and for each future turnaround assignment in which we were engaged.

A majority of the hourly workers could not perform basic arithmetic functions: adding, subtracting, multiplying and dividing. We would not be able to institute a quality assurance program if the workers did not possess these basic skills. We hired a local high school math teacher to teach arithmetic every afternoon at four p.m. for an hour and a half until the entire workforce was competent. We compensated the workers for the time they spent in class.

When we were prepared to introduce TPS, we conducted meetings with the plant workers on each shift. I was introducing the concept that no worker would have to search for a tool to perform his or her assignment. The tools and measurement devices to complete their work would be positioned on a board at their workstation.

A woman rose to her feet and exclaimed that she did not have a complete set of slitter knives for her slitting machine and therefore was always searching for knives. A man rose to his feet, interrupted her and stated, "She is not searching; she is stealing! I have the only complete set of slitting knives in the factory!" It became obvious that we were experiencing a lot of lost productivity as workers searched for tools.

I asked for a show of hands as to the number of slitter operators who did not have a complete set of knives. Ten hands were raised. I turned to the plant manager and told him to begin recording the numbers and types of tools that had to be replaced.

The operator of a coating line informed me that the thermostats on the curing ovens had not functioned properly for two years. It took him multiple trips on his bicycle between the end of the coating line, where he tested the product, and the thermostat to control the heat before the quality was correct. We were creating a lot of waste.

At the end of the day, the plant manager had compiled a list of replacement tools and measurement devices that filled two 8 1/2 x 11 pages. The estimated cost of replacement totaled $37,000.

We completed this exercise in the other three plants in the ensuing weeks. Productivity improved. Waste was reduced.

We employed an executive recruiting firm to find a vice president of manufacturing with the specification that the candidate be experienced in the TPS. We were able to attract a highly qualified individual who introduced significant changes to our production methods, which led to the reduction of our costs.

All of the plants employed the "push" theory for production similar to what we had found at US Leisure. We initiated the concept of the "pull" theory—only producing a product if we had an order.

We organized sales order entry, production scheduling and procurement into one large bullpen with no walls at each of the plants.

We established alliances with our vendors. The best alliance we developed in the manufacture of pressure-sensitive materials was with Shell Chemical. We had 26 vendors of chemicals. Four of those vendors produced specialty chemicals that no other company produced.

The procurement team determined the number of chemical companies that produced each of the remaining 22 chemicals we purchased. The companies with multiple factories near our plants would enable them to provide an uninterrupted supply in case of a disaster at one of their plants.

We engaged with Shell Chemical, which agreed to provide a 10-percent discount on all products if we gave them 100 percent of our chemical requirements. In addition, they offered the free services of their R&D department to assist us in developing new products. It was a big win!

We had a large warehouse area devoted to the inventory of barrels full of unused or infrequently used cores of various widths and diameters, which were used for winding tape onto smaller, retail-size cores.

I remembered from my Fibreboard experience that there was a paper company located in Columbia that produced only one product—paper cores. I made contact, and they agreed to purchase our core-making equipment and hire our employees. They established a plant within our plant to make cores on demand. We provided them with our monthly and weekly production requirements; they provided the labor and material requirements to produce our cores JIT. We eliminated inventory.

We developed an alliance with one textile manufacturer to supply fabric for the manufacturer of cloth book covers in the Tennessee facility. We developed an alliance with one paper manufacturer to supply paper on demand to the Columbia and Ohio plants that produced pressure-sensitive materials and to the paper book cover manufacturer in upstate New York.

Tom Lumsden's organization had created standard cost metrics for various production processes and the full-time equivalency (FTE) of personnel required to perform administration functions, e.g. the number of FTEs per $100,000 of accounts receivable. These metrics enabled us to reduce our administrative costs.

The SEC was demanding more segmentation of public financial statements, so it was becoming easier to obtain competitors' cost information and determine where we had cost reduction opportunities.

At one time, we had 30 profit improvement program (PIP) teams operating in the company. Each one was supported by an engineer, a cost accountant and one of Lumsden's analysts.

The most notable success was achieved by a PIP team in the Columbia plant. A process-mapping effort revealed that it required on average 72 hours to manufacture an order of duct tape. A PIP team was formed to develop a plan to reduce the time. The process mapping study showed that there were many interruptions and delays in the process, which contributed to the long production cycle.

The finished jumbo rolls of product were transported to the slitting department in another building. Transporting a product to another department or another building was a major violation of the TPS.

We had eliminated the need to carry inventories and had freed up thousands of square feet of space that could be used for manufacturing. The PIP recommended that the slitting machines be relocated in the building to where the jumbo rolls of tape were produced. Production of duct tape, the responsibility of the duct-tape team, would be continuous. The investment to remove walls within the plant and install an overhead crane to move the jumbo rolls cost $475,000.

The time to produce an order of duct tape was reduced from 72 hours to four hours, and we could produce and ship orders on demand! I had the PIP team present the request for approval of the $475,000 investment to the board of directors.

We were able to realign the production equipment for various types of products into a continuous process flow in each of the four plants.

In nine months, the hourly associates had transformed the various manufacturing processes into prosperous, cash-generating operations. We posted production statistics and financial performance prominently throughout each plant. We even installed a profit-sharing plan for the associates! The production teams became elite teams; they were proud of their status and their association with the company.

The CTI PIP teams were very successful. Several team members emerged as outstanding contributors to the teams. We created a job classification for a PIP team leader, and those individuals who had distinguished themselves became permanent team leaders who were assigned to new opportunities as they were identified.

During the course of negotiating alliances with our vendors, we introduced the TPS concept and the role of our PIP teams. We offered to make a PIP team available to the vendor to identify cost-reduction opportunities for the product we were purchasing.

In return for this service, we asked the vendor to pass on their savings to CTI in the form of a reduced selling price.

The vendor was able to improve its profitability by maintaining the selling price for the product to other customers.

On my first visit to the paper bookbinding manufacturing plant in upstate New York, I asked the general manager what his biggest challenge was in operating his business. He replied that his customers were informing him that his competitor was able to ship a custom order in four days. I asked him, "How many days does it take you to ship a custom product?" He could not answer the question. He did not know the answer.

Whenever he had learned of the threat, he had taken no action to determine the time required for his organization to produce a custom order and, if required, take corrective action.

I asked that he bring an engineer into the meeting. I explained the rudimentary principles of process mapping to the engineer and requested he map the steps to be taken from sales order entry through shipping and then note the time of entry and time of departure in each step in the process.

I instructed him not to stand and watch the process flow but to ask the responsible person at each step to inform him by telephone when the paperwork arrived and departed. I suggested he follow four or five orders to get an average time estimate. I informed the GM and the engineer that I would be back in two weeks and would like to review what they had discovered and the actions they had taken to improve the flow.

On my return, the engineer began to walk me through the mapping that he had completed. He explained that a sales order spent a day in sales order entry and then moved to the credit department where, on average, the order spent three days before being transferred to production planning.

I interrupted the presentation at this point and exclaimed, "Our competitor shipped on day four, but our customer's order is no further than our credit department! Why?"

The general manager did not know; he'd had the results of the mapping process for several days before my arrival and had not pursued a solution to the problem! Passive management; he was not oriented to taking action.

I suggested we visit the credit manager's office and inquire about the amount of time that an order sits in her office.

The credit manager informed us that she had to approve every order and was overwhelmed by the number of orders. I asked for a clarification: "Are you required to approve orders for long-time, creditworthy customers?" The reply was yes.

I suggested that she publish a weekly report of creditworthy customers for the order entry department. If a customer was on that list, the order could bypass credit and go directly to production planning.

The only orders to be sent to credit were orders from new customers whose credit had to be approved or existing customers with whom we were experiencing collection problems.

I made the judgment that the general manager was incompetent and incapable of making the operation profitable. I appointed my partner, the CFO, as general manager and assigned the general manager to be sales manager of the division.

Our CFO was able to streamline the production processes and return the company to prosperous operations.

It was in the tenth month of the assignment that I informed MetLife that we could begin selling the businesses. We had optimized the profitability of each of the businesses. We had also paid down the working capital bank loan by $30 million as we had little need to finance raw material inventory and operated with no FGI.

I recommended that we begin by selling the cloth bookbinding business as it was going to be the most difficult asset to sell. The other businesses were generating significant cash flow, so there was no need to sell them quickly.

Holliston Mills produced bookbinding cloth. The binding of books in heavy cloth covers was a dying industry in the 1980s.

Legal reference books that had filled the bookshelves of law firms' conference rooms were now being provided on electronic disks. Cloth book covers were expensive, and publishers were using paper bookbindings to lower their costs. The demand for bookbinding cloth had been declining for several years.

Holliston Mills had been founded in 1893. The company had one competitor, with a factory in Chicago; the competitive company was owned by a New York City private equity firm.

I had introduced myself to the principals of the private equity firm early in our assignment; I assumed the private equity firm would be the sole potential buyer for Holliston Mills once we were ready to sell the business and wanted to know with whom I would be dealing. They had made their investment in the Chicago company in the past five years. I believed it had been a mistake for them to have invested in a dying business.

I visited the competitive factory in Chicago with our vice president of manufacturing and a talented engineer. The building was three stories in height—an inefficient manufacturing facility.

We paced off the street side of the building and estimated the depth. We observed the location of the receiving and shipping docks and estimated the space devoted to warehousing raw materials and finished goods. We estimated the amount of office space in the building and did some guesswork on the number and location of industrial elevators located in the building. We sketched out what we thought would be the process map for the production functions on each floor.

We employed a Chicago commercial real estate appraisal firm to provide us with the market value of the office/industrial building, which would be vacant and in broom-clean condition. We instructed the firm not to contact the building owner nor to enter the building. Their appraisal was to be conducted from the street using recent sale prices of similar properties in the area.

We engaged the executive recruiting firm we employed for executive searches to identify recently retired or terminated managers who would be willing to consult with us.

We would not be asking for any proprietary information regarding the manufacturing processes; our objective was to identify the types and operating speeds of the equipment being employed in the manufacturing process and then to complete an accurate process map.

The recruiting firm identified three former employees who were willing to work with us. We paid them handsomely for eight hours of their time and had them sign a confidentiality agreement concerning our relationship and our discussions.

We were able to model the competitive factory and determine that their UMC was 25 percent higher than our UMC at the single-story factory at Holston where we had achieved a continuous manufacturing flow and a lower UMC.

We modeled the production of the combined volumes in the Holliston factory. We had ample vacant space to accommodate the production equipment to be transferred from Chicago to Holston because we had eliminated the warehousing space required for RMI and FGI.

The additional volume absorbed more of the factory's fixed cost and reduced the overall UMC of the combined volume. The gross profit margin of the combined production increased dramatically. In creating the profit and loss statement for the combined companies, we estimated a reduction in the absolute dollars spent on marketing and administration. The pretax profit for the combined companies became attractive.

There was another issue to contend with. Holliston Mills had created a major pollution problem by burying toxic production waste in 55-gallon drums on the factory site. The drums had rusted and the toxic materials were leaking into the Holliston River.

The Tennessee Department of Environment and Conservation (TDE&C) had cited the company for violation of federal and state regulations, and the company was under enforcement proceedings to provide a plan to remediate the site.

I retained AWD, my former employer, to scope out the extent of the pollution and develop an estimate of the cost to remediate the site. The cost of remediation was a big number, and the time required to complete it was estimated to be 12 months. We wanted to sell the business promptly. We had to act.

I contacted the Brown to Green Environmental Remediation Company (BTGC). We modeled an investment plan for BTGC to purchase the factory site and enter into a lease for the factory to the Chicago company with an option to purchase the factory site after the remediation was completed and approved by the TDE&C. Our modeling showed that BTGC could receive a very attractive return on their investment, and the Chicago company would pay a reasonable market price for a guaranteed green site.

I asked MetLife to retain an environmental law firm to first review the sale, cleanup and resale processes. If the concepts were feasible, the law firm would determine how to structure the various legal documents to shield MetLife from future liability.

We made our presentation to the New York private equity firm.

We first showed them our estimate of their UMC at their Chicago factory. We knew from the looks the partners displayed to each other that we were right on target with our estimates.

We then showed them the model of the combined businesses in Holliston, the lower UMC that could be achieved and the attractive P&L statement of the business.

We advised them of the asking price for the business excluding the factory and land and introduced the concept of their leasing the plant from BTGC with an option to purchase the factory and land.

We then showed the operational cash flow estimates for each year and included the investment required to purchase the Holliston business, the source and timing of the cash from the proceeds of the sale of their Chicago factory and the timing of the purchase of the Holliston factory and land from BTGC. The IRR was attractive!

It took months to negotiate and complete the numerous legal documents to perfect the transactions. CTI was able to get rid of a dying business, dispose of a polluted manufacturing site and generate an extraordinary amount of cash.

The New York private equity firm was able to salvage what was originally a bad investment. However, the cloth bookbinding business was a dying business, and the combined business would file for bankruptcy in three years.

Pajco, the CTI subsidiary that was engaged in the paper bookbinding business, was operating at 100 percent of capacity and was very profitable. Their sole competitor was owned by Rexham Corporation, a specialty paper manufacturer headquartered in Charlotte, North Carolina, which was the obvious buyer for the Pajco business. We set the selling price at an attractive multiple of EBITDA and promptly closed the transaction.

The pressure-sensitive tape business was the crown jewel of CTI. It was the second-largest producer of duct tape and masking tape in the United States behind 3M Manufacturing Company.

We approached 3M to inquire if they would be interested in purchasing the company. They declined. We were successful in identifying a private equity investor who bought the company for an attractive EBITDA multiple.

MetLife recovered 175 percent of its original underwriting and was a very happy client! The assignment had taken 18 months to complete and was a very profitable assignment for TSG.

The CTI vice presidents of Finance and Manufacturing declined to work for the private equity firm that purchased the pressure-sensitive tape business and asked to become partners in TSG. They were talented managers, and I welcomed them aboard. We now had the human resources to take on multiple assignments.

We celebrated a victory lunch at Giambelli's on 50th Street, only a few blocks from the MetLife headquarters building. After lunch, Jackie Jenkins walked us to the offices of Northwestern Mutual Life, where we were introduced to the distressed asset manager. Northwestern had cosponsored a bond offering with MetLife to a company that had defaulted on the interest. We went immediately into our next assignment.

Over the next 25 years, Prudential, MetLife and Northwestern provided the majority of TSG's assignments. The insurance companies were our best clients.

Commercial banks did not have covenants in their loan agreements that provided for the removal of the chief executive if the borrower defaulted on the terms of their loan. Commercial banks were reluctant to insist the boards of directors of defaulting borrowers replace the CEO. The banks would recommend consultants who provided advisory services to defaulting companies on how to restructure the company. TSG did not provide advisory services. Our specialty was to provide executive management to turn around financially distressed companies and restore prosperous operations.

We completed assignments for Citibank, JPMorgan Chase and GE Capital in which they gained control of the debtors under some unusual circumstances.

The insurance companies engaged TSG for the turnaround of a $1 billion-revenue aircraft parts manufacturer, a $2 billion-revenue international automobile parts manufacturer and several companies involved in telephone communications.

TSG was actively engaged most of the time; we experienced very few months of downtime. One of the advantages of working for insurance companies with whom we negotiated performance bonus compensation was that the insurance companies could purchase annuities that were to be paid out over three to five years. The annuity payments enabled us to differ income, reduce taxes and provide a continuous flow of revenue when we experienced downtime. The insurance companies were good clients.

Bearings

+ *Creative Destruction involves the introduction of new objectives and new standards of performance for a business organization and destroys whatever objectives and standards existed previously.*

+ *The destruction of the old criteria for performance is essential for a successful transition from failure to prosperity.*

Create a vision of the state of affairs you want to achieve. Create models to illustrate the financial performance that can be achieved.

✦ Think in multiple dimensions—think outside the box! Do not restrict your thinking within the confines of your assets. Explore opportunities beyond the walls of your assets.

✦ Employ synthesis thinking. Which assets can be acquired, which businesses could be combined and which third-party organizations can provide skills and resources that your organization does not possess that will create a greater value for your enterprise?

✦ The model-building associated with the sale of Holliston Mills' assets is an excellent example of thinking in multiple dimensions and synthesis thinking. It included the use and liquidation of another company's assets and the employment of a third party to purchase and then resell assets and provided a service that was beyond the capabilities of CTI.

✦ When you are selling a business, always create a model of the business' operation under the new ownership to show the buyer the benefits of combining the two businesses. Never assume the buyer is capable of identifying and developing the advantages of combining the two businesses. We used this type of modeling for the sale of timber mills at Fibreboard to competitors located within our working circle and to determine the value of Spreckels Sugar's production quotas to the owners of beet sugar refineries in the northern states—the sum of which established the minimum selling price for the sale of the entire company to Imperial Sugar.

✦ The modeling we completed for the sale of Holliston Mills to the New York private equity firm was one of our most creative modeling exercises. It was beyond the capabilities of the partners of the New York private equity firm. We developed the concept of a multiple-step transaction, completed the financial analysis and maximized the selling price for Holliston.

✦ There is a defeatist's proverb that states, "You can't make a silk purse out of a sow's ear." We blew that proverb out of the water in the values we were able to return to the creditors of US Leisure, which was a hopeless financial disaster, and the value we obtained for the sale of Holliston Mills, a company engaged in a dying business.

BOARDS OF DIRECTORS ASSIGNMENTS

After the sale of Spreckels Sugar, the Prudential chief investment officer (CIO) appointed me as a director of Grubb & Ellis (GBE), a San Francisco-based commercial real estate brokerage firm. GBE had defaulted on the interest payment of a bond offering underwritten by Prudential, which under the terms of the underwriting converted their bond investment into equity, and were granted two board seats in case of a default. Prudential was not the controlling stockholder. The GBE stock price on the NYSE was $1.35.

After attending several meetings, I recommended to Prudential that the CEO be removed; he did not have the skills to return the company to profitable operations. We were able to convince the other board members to terminate the CEO. The board conducted a search for a new CEO; I was named as a member of the selection committee.

The new CEO did a splendid job in turning the company around in 18 months, and the stock price increased to $15. Prudential recovered 130 percent of their original investment; they sold their equity position to Warburg Pincus, a New York City private equity investment firm. I remained on the board as a director.

Warburg intended to turn GBE into one of the premier commercial real estate investment firms in the United States, on par with Jones Lang LaSalle, CBRE and Cushman & Wakefield.

Warburg was successful in convincing Goldman Sachs and Michael Kojaian, a successful real estate developer, to each invest $10 million in the company to finance the transition.

Warburg's plan was, in my analogy, to transform GBE from a Chevrolet franchise into a Cadillac franchise. The plan was to recruit experienced, finance-oriented agents who were capable of closing large commercial transactions, which would generate extraordinary revenues and profits.

All of the board members agreed that the CEO had done an excellent job in returning the company to a prosperous operation, but he was not the manager to upgrade the enterprise to the new Cadillac level of performance. We provided the CEO with a generous severance package.

I was again asked to serve on the selection committee. Warburg was intent on hiring a candidate to whom I strongly objected. The candidate was a consultant; he had never managed an organization of any size in his career. He talked a good game, but in my opinion, we were in the people business, and the candidate had never been in a situation where he was required to attract, direct and motivate highly talented people.

Warburg insisted on hiring him. I felt I had provided my best advice and was being ignored. I resigned. Two years later, the company was operating in the vicinity of bankruptcy.

Michael Kojaian bought out Warburg for cents on the dollar. Michael called me several months later and asked if I would consider coming back on the board. I rejoined the GBE board.

MetLife appointed me as a director in two private firms in which they had equity investments.

Northwestern Life appointed me as a director of a private company in which they had an equity investment.

With each of the board assignments, I was asked to be the chairman of the audit committee because of my financial acumen.

I attended a three-day Harvard Business School executive session entitled "Making Your Audit Committee More Effective" to sharpen my saw. I learned new skills that I was able to employ on the several audit committees on which I served.

I served on the GBE board of directors the second time for four years. Michael Kojaian kept alive the vision of converting GBE into a Cadillac franchise.

We went through two CEOs and two CFOs in our attempt to transform the franchise. None of these officers had the self-confidence to destroy the existing culture in the core brokerage business, which was losing money and whose return to profitability was essential to make the transition to a Cadillac franchise.

We embarked on a strategy to add the services to achieve the transformation and financed the growth with an offering of preferred shares and increased bank debt.

However, management was not initiating action to make the core brokerage business profitable. We should have been closing offices in small markets in which we had a minor market share to stop the hemorrhaging of cash.

We should have replaced managers in major markets who did not have the capability to attract, motivate and direct highly talented professionals.

During my first engagement as a GBE director, the board agreed to relocate the company headquarters to Chicago. The GBE headquarters and the Chicago brokerage office were located in prime office space in downtown Chicago. Rent was the second-largest expense item behind payroll costs.

Successful service providers were making the transition to a concept known as *hoteling*, which eliminated the need for renting large areas of office space filled with private offices.

When a principal required a private office for a client meeting, they called the office administrator and made a reservation for a corner office. The administrator retrieved the principal's framed license, hung it on the wall and placed the photograph of the principal's spouse and their children on the credenza. The office was personalized.

The CEOs and the branch managers balked at implementing the concept, stating that they could not recruit talented brokers unless they could offer them a permanent corner office. Not true. We should have insisted the concept be initiated!

We also should have insisted that the headquarters administrative staff, i.e. Accounting and Payroll, be relocated to lower-rent locations in Wisconsin.

The competition was fierce; competitors were hiring away our best brokers as fast as we could recruit new talent.

I described our financial situation in aerodynamic terms: To get a plane off the ground, sufficient thrust is required to move the aircraft down the runway, which creates airflow over the wings and in turn creates lift, which is required to overcome the drag created by the weight of the aircraft. If the *lift* overcomes the *drag*, the aircraft becomes airborne.

The core business of GBE was not profitable and created excess drag on the enterprise. We were running out of cash, our runway, and were not able to create *lift*. We were going to hit the wall.

I had adopted the position that a director of a corporation should be a significant stakeholder. I remembered that Steven Roman, when he was seeking a board seat on the Fibreboard board of directors, observed that collectively the then-current directors owned less than one percent of the outstanding shares of the company.

The GBE stock price began to decline rapidly. I had taken a large position in GBE stock. I informed Michael that I was compelled to sell my shares and felt I should not remain as a director without having an equity position in the company. He understood. I resigned as a director.

It was a year later that GBE reorganized under a prepackaged plan of reorganization, and the equity was transferred to a new owner. It was a tragic ending for GBE.

Michael Kajoian was one of the most astute businessmen I worked with in my career and an exemplary person. We have remained friends over the years.

Imperial Sugar

I am going to fast-forward 19 years.

I received a call from Jackie Jenkins, who was now a senior officer in the MetLife Investment department, who asked if she was correct that I had turned around a sugar company some years ago. I replied that the company was Spreckels Sugar and that I had sold the company to Imperial Sugar.

She informed me that Imperial Sugar had defaulted on the interest payments for a $250 million bond obligation that MetLife had underwritten. The bondholders were about to agree to a prepackaged bankruptcy reorganization plan that would exchange the bonds for 100 percent of the common equity of Imperial Sugar. She asked me to come to New York to discuss becoming chairman of the board of Imperial Sugar.

I learned that James Kempner, the CEO of Imperial, had continued to acquire sugar companies after his acquisition of Spreckels. He acquired Holly Sugar, the beet refiner head-quartered in Colorado Springs, and then acquired Savannah Sugar, the cane sugar refiner in Savannah, Georgia. He financed these acquisitions using debt. Imperial's balance sheet was highly leveraged, and the cash flow was not sufficient to cover the cost of the debt.

When Prudential sold Spreckels to Imperial in 1981, Imperial was a private, family-owned company. I learned the company had been issuing Imperial stock to its employees as incentive compensation because they did not have sufficient cash flow to provide cash incentives.

The Securities Exchange Commission (SEC) forced Imperial to conduct an Initial Public Offering (IPO) when the number of stockholders exceeded 500, the highest number of share-holders permitted for a private company. If the Kempner family intended to retain private ownership and control of the company, the issuing of stock rather than cash as incentive compensation was a major mistake on the part of the board and the company's financial advisor.

MetLife had retained $100 million of the original $250 million Imperial bond offering. The value of that investment prior to the reorganization was $15 million.

MetLife converted a 15-cent bond for a share of Imperial stock, which was selling for 75 cents on the New York Stock Exchange and experienced a 400-percent increase in the value of their investment on the date of the conversion. The value of MetLife's investment was now $60 million.

Lehman Brothers' vulture capital department had been accumulating Imperial bonds for cents on the dollar, anticipating bankruptcy and the opportunity to exchange the bonds for equity and the subsequent appreciation of the equity. Lehman Brothers would be the second-largest equity holder in Imperial after the prepackaged bankruptcy.

MetLife introduced me to the managing partners of Lehman's vulture capital group, and it was agreed they would install me as chairman of the board. James Kempner was to remain as CEO.

The prepackaged bankruptcy was completed within a month. The company's business continued uninterrupted. The only change made to the company's balance sheet was the elimination of the $250 million bond liability.

At the first board meeting, I directed the board's attention to the fact that the balance sheet contained a $775 million bank credit obligation. The ratio of EBITDA to the credit obligation was 8.0. The company would not be able to support this level of debt. I predicted that we could find ourselves in Chapter 12 (a second Chapter 11 proceedings) within a year unless we took actions to reduce debt and improve the earnings of the company.

The board agreed with my recommendations. At the conclusion of the regular board meeting, I called for an executive session of the board that excluded the CEO.

I submitted to the board that James Kempner was not financially motivated to improve the company's performance as he and his family had lost all of their equity in the reorganization. Most important was the fact that he would not enthusiastically pursue the dismantling and selling of the assets he had assembled over the past 20 years.

The board and Kempner worked out a plan for his resignation. I was appointed as the CEO and was asked by the board to initiate a search for a permanent CEO. I made it clear to the board that I would not be a passive interim CEO. I would be introducing change.

I made what would be my last Fire in the Hole speech to the management the next day.

I recovered the financial analysis I had made to Prudential 21 years ago concerning the flawed business strategy of operating beet refineries six months a year.

I informed them about the constraints to profitability imposed by the USDOA and government regulations. No board member had been aware of these regulations!

I illustrated the selling prices and subsequent cash generation that could be achieved by selling the beet refineries to grower associations in the northern latitudes who would close the refineries and transfer the production allocations to their refineries in the North.

The board approved the sale of the sugar beet refineries, and we embarked on the mission.

The alliance between Lumsden's organization and TSG over the years had enabled us to achieve extraordinary reductions in costs and improved profitability in each of the assignments we undertook. I was confident in advising clients that whatever the fees we paid to Lumsden's firm, we could expect to achieve cost reductions of eight times the fees paid.

In the case of our combined efforts at Imperial, the fees paid to Lumsden's firm amounted to $400,000; we attributed more than $3 million in cost reductions to the expenditure.

Lumsden and his analysts would identify substandard performance, determine the root causes for the poor performance and assist the profit improvement program (PIP) teams in developing actions to improve the performance.

At the peak of the restructuring, we had 44 PIP teams at work in Imperial. These teams of associates were implementing kaizen—continuously making small improvements in operations.

One of the procedures I had adopted over the years was to visit the accounts payable department early in an assignment and ask for a printout of every county in which the company was paying property taxes on land or a facility. I then reviewed the locations with Manufacturing and Distribution to determine if we were still utilizing each property.

In the case of Imperial Sugar, we identified properties in which the company had ceased to operate but had not sold the properties and was continuing to pay property taxes. The sale of these abandoned properties generated $35 million in proceeds. Passive management!

On my tours of the refineries, I made it a priority to walk the premises. What I noticed on each tour was the number of company-owned tractors and trailers that were parked on the grounds.

I spoke to the vice president of manufacturing: "The asset classification of this equipment is rolling stock. The classification implies movement. Why are these assets parked and not moving?"

We were able to sell our entire fleet of tractors and trailers to an equipment leasing firm. We established an alliance with the firm and our distribution department in each refinery and were able to schedule effective pickups and deliveries for our customers. The alliance enabled us to generate cash and improve our productivity.

We were not able to recruit a talented CEO with sugar manufacturing experience. After discussions with the board, we advised the executive search firm to focus the search on an

312 / ROBERT MCLAUGHLIN

executive with retail sales experience because our largest customers were retail grocers, big-box retailers and manufacturers such as Nabisco, Hershey and Kellogg's, which sold their products to grocers and big-box retailers.

We then turned our attention to the cane refineries in Sugarland, New Orleans and Savannah.

Each refinery was operating at 60 percent of capacity. We could not increase our production due to the USDOA production restrictions. In creating an index model of our cane operations, the company could not produce more than 180 units of production in the three refineries.

The Sugarland refinery was the oldest of the three refineries. Sugarland's production was dependent on imported sugarcane that was unloaded in the port of Galveston, Texas, and then transported to Sugarland by rail. The Sugarland refinery was Imperial's highest-cost producer of refined sugar.

We determined that by closing the Sugarland refinery and transferring the production to New Orleans and Savannah, those refineries would be operating at 90 percent of capacity, greatly improving their profitability. We would not be exceeding the USDOA production limit.

The stock price of Imperial increased to $15. Jackie Jenkins asked me if I thought the price could go higher. I thought we had optimized the profitability of the company. I could not advise her to hold MetLife's position. MetLife sold its position in the market over the next six months; it achieved sales proceeds of $120 million. MetLife was again a happy client. Jackie resigned as an Imperial director.

Lehman Brothers was now the controlling shareholder of Imperial Sugar and would retain its position until the Great Financial Crisis of 2008 when Lehman Brothers declared bankruptcy. The U.S. trustee forced the sale of Lehman's position in Imperial Sugar and subsequently the entire company to the Louis Dreyfus Company, a Swiss commodities firm.

Lehman preferred to have its own chairman of the board, and I was not reelected at the next annual meeting. I remained on the board as a director.

We closed and demolished the Sugarland refinery and sold the polluted refinery site to BTGC.

Because Sugarland was an affluent Houston suburb, the refinery land was very valuable. We were able to sell the land to BTGC at an attractive price, and they in turn were able to sell the land after the remediation at an attractive profit.

In total, we paid down $775 million in bank debt! We negotiated a revolving line of credit of $40 million with one bank, which was available to finance 100 percent of the cane cargos required to support the Savanah refinery plus the occasional purchase of cargo to support the New Orleans refinery.

The two refineries were operating at 90 percent of capacity, 24/7. We had doubled the turnover of the assets employed! The company was a cash-generating machine.

The value of the Imperial stock increased to $30 per share. When I retired from the board due to my age exceeding the age limit imposed by the bylaws, I sold my stock at a significant profit.

I never understood why Lehman Brothers retained their position in Imperial. They had a significant profit on their investment and could have liquidated the investment and put it back to work within the corporation. They held the investment until they were in bankruptcy and the U.S. Trustee forced the sale.

TWILITE OF THE SUTTER GROUP

The Sutter Group remained active until 2005 at which time I turned out the lights! It had been a great run. I gained a great deal of satisfaction from owning and operating my own company. I had the privilege of working with some very talented partners and associating with talented advisors and third-party service providers.

Our clients had one overriding objective: They wanted to recover their investment! TSG had a reputation for making three blades of grass grow where only one had grown before our arrival.

Our clients trusted us; they provided the resources of money and time to complete our assigned mission. They were patient, confident that in the end, we would be able to deliver an extraordinary outcome for them.

We promised our clients nothing but our best efforts to recover their investment. We served them well!

Epilogue

My intention in writing this memoir was to assist the reader in sharpening his or her saw, which will enhance their management skills and lead to advancement and promotion.

Outlined below is a review of the bearings I believe will assist you in enhancing your career.

Bearings Review

- **Trust.** *This is the primary attribute of a leader. Your trustworthiness will be your most precious asset. Never compromise.*

- **Seek out leadership roles.** *Start out early in life. The Boy Scouts or Girl Scouts and similar organizations for young people offer leadership opportunities. Accept roles for difficult tasks; the experience will be rewarding.*

- **Passion.** *You must have a strong desire to be out in front of an organization. To be on the point is a dangerous position; you must be courageous!*

- **Be Aggressive.** *Taking action has to be your default state of being.*

✦ *Show Resilience.* You will inevitably fail at some point. Be courageous, pick yourself up, determine the cause of your failure, take corrective action and get back in the game.

✦ *Associate with elite, high-growth organizations.* The performance bar will be high, you will receive excellent training and the growth environment will abet opportunities for new experiences and advancement.

✦ *Think!* Never be satisfied with the status quo. Create visions and models of the state of affairs you desire to create. Be creative; think outside the box. Aim high.

✦ *Do not allow big challenges to overwhelm you.* Employ calculi segmentation. Think of kaizen— make small improvements continuously.

✦ *Employ employee involvement* (EI). Involve your people; let them make performance improvements. Support them with resources; they will take owner-ship, pride will flourish and productivity will improve.

✦ *Embrace a passion for teaching.* You will be raising the performance bar, so you have an obligation to teach your associates the new skills required to clear the raised bar. Early in your career, you will be leading small units and will have to personally provide the instruction. As you advance and take on greater responsibility, the unit size will increase, and you will need to create departments within your organization to instruct or employ outside advisors to conduct the education.

✦ *Finance!* Cash flow is the lifeblood of any entity. It is essential to your career to gain an understanding *of both operational and corporate finance. I had the opportunity to learn operational finance in actual operational assignments under the direction of an outstanding teacher, Dr. Elmer C. Larsen of PPG Industries. My indoctrination to corporate finance was provided by Xerox through the executive education provided by Harvard Business School and Professor Colyer Crum, an outstanding instructor and motivator.*

If you gain your understanding of finance in an academic environment, you cannot just listen, take notes and pass the exam. You must adopt the principles of sound finance with a passion. Those principles must become a part of your business creed.

✦ *Sharpen your saw! Continuously improve your skills.*

✦ *Develop your communication skills. You will be introducing significant changes in your organization. It will be critical to your success to be able to communicate your objectives—first, to your superiors, who will be providing the resources you will require to achieve the objectives, and second, to your associates, who you must motivate to achieve the objectives.*

✦ *Risk! Taking actions to improve performance implies risk. Obtain intelligence about the existing conditions in the area you wish to improve before introducing change that will reduce the chances of failure. Do not bet the farm. Segment the challenge; employ kaizen— make small improvements continuously. Think, create your objective, measure the risk and then execute.*

I wish you good fortune on your journey!

Acknowledgments

 The most enjoyable endeavor in writing a memoir is the opportunity to recognize the people who helped you along the journey.

My Family

My parents, who instilled in me the attribute of honesty and who provided me with a good education, which I almost bungled but salvaged after my first summer session in the Marine Corps PLC program

Kathie, my wife of 65 years, to whom I have dedicated this book

My Aunt Florence, who showed me what the good life was like and instilled in me a keen sense of ambition

My Uncle Clint, who taught me how to work

Mentors, Sponsors and Advisors

Lt. Colonel Don Beck, USMC, retired

Colonel William Siegler, USMC, retired

Several Marine gunnery sergeants whose names I have forgotten, who contributed significantly to the formation of my leadership skills

Robert Fay, PPG Industries

Dr. Elmer C. Larsen, PPG Industries

Colonel Roy La Hue, USMC, retired; Xerox Corporation

Ray Hay, Xerox Corporation
Robert Potter, Xerox Corporation and a close friend
Colyer Crum, Professor of Finance, Harvard Business School
John Larson, Brobeck, Phleger & Harrison and a close friend
Doug Moorhouse, CEO of Woodward-Clyde Consultants
   and a close friend
Dick Elkus, CEO of AMPEX and a close friend
Tom Lumsden, Advisor, Alliance Partner and a close friend
Pat Murphy, Managing Partner, Murphy, Weir & Butler
Jackie Jenkins, Investment Officer, MetLife
Michael Kajoian, President, Kajoian Real Estate and
   a close friend

Friends who supported me during my time in the wilderness

Mason Flemming, Gary Scales and Stu Spence.

I am grateful to all of you!

CREATIVE DESTRUCTION

The author's successes, chronicled here, in turning failed companies into prosperous operations are complex and enlightening. Readers will learn unique approaches for selling products and services, expanding market share, reducing costs, justifying investments, improving financial performance, achieving extraordinary returns on the sale of assets and generating extraordinary returns for shareholders.

Whether you are young and aspire to be a leader, a seasoned manager seeking to be a CEO or somewhere in between, this essential read will accelerate your advancement.

Creative Destruction—the rejection of existing cultures and standards—is required to make the transition from subpar performance to prosperous performance.

Creative Destruction is more than a memoir. It is a critique of how inferior management practices impaired the performance of numerous companies and how the introduction of astute, aggressive management practices enabled the transformation of those businesses into valuable, cash-generating enterprises.

The purchase of *Creative Destruction* will be your best investment of the year!

Made in USA - North Chelmsford, MA
1356674_9781737450245
01.31.2023 1613